PIETY AND PYTHAGORAS IN RENAISSANCE FLORENCE
THE *SYMBOLUM NESIANUM*

STUDIES IN THE HISTORY
OF
CHRISTIAN THOUGHT

FOUNDED BY HEIKO A. OBERMAN †

EDITED BY

ROBERT J. BAST, Knoxville, Tennessee

IN COOPERATION WITH

HENRY CHADWICK, Cambridge
SCOTT H. HENDRIX, Princeton, New Jersey
BRIAN TIERNEY, Ithaca, New York
ARJO VANDERJAGT, Groningen
JOHN VAN ENGEN, Notre Dame, Indiana

VOLUME CI

CHRISTOPHER S. CELENZA

PIETY AND PYTHAGORAS IN RENAISSANCE FLORENCE
THE *SYMBOLUM NESIANUM*

PIETY AND PYTHAGORAS IN RENAISSANCE FLORENCE THE *SYMBOLUM NESIANUM*

BY

CHRISTOPHER S. CELENZA

BRILL
LEIDEN · BOSTON · KÖLN
2001

This book is printed on acid-free paper.

Die Deutsche Bibliothek - CIP-Einheitsaufnahme

Celenza, Christopher S. :
Piety and Pythagoras in Renaissance Florence : the symbolum Nesianum / by
Christopher S. Celenza. – Leiden ; Boston ; Köln : Brill, 2001
   (Studies in the history of Christian thought ; Vol. 101)
   ISBN 90–04–12211–7

Library of Congress Cataloging-in-Publication Data

Library of Congress Cataloging-in-Publication Data is also available

ISSN   0081-8607
ISBN   90 04 12211 7

PRINTED IN THE NETHERLANDS

For Professors Dieter Harlfinger and Walther Ludwig

CONTENTS

ACKNOWLEDGEMENTS

This work was originally submitted as a doctoral dissertation for a Dr. phil. at the University of Hamburg, as part of the "Graduierten-kolleg 'Textüberlieferung,'" second cycle, and was defended on 10 December, 1999. I would like to thank the Deutsche Forschungs-gemeinschaft along with the Freie und Hansestadt Hamburg for the financial support which made my participation in that interdisciplinary program possible. The financial support was complemented by an incomparable intellectual environment, centered in the University's Institut für Griechische und Lateinische Philologie. I thank all my fellow former students, and am especially indebted to Anna Mastrogianni, Marwan Rashed, and Burkhard Reis, whose knowledge in their respective fields and willingness to share it with me helped to shape this study and, more generally, was a source of personal growth and intellectual enrichment. I dedicate the work to Professors Dieter Harlfinger and Walther Ludwig, with whom I was privileged to study from 1994–1996. Uncompromising models of professional dedication, they have read and critiqued this work, and have saved it and me, here and elsewhere, from errors too numerous to count. I would also like to thank Prof. Klaus Alpers, whose wit and boundless intellectual curiosity was a constant inspiration.

Since 1996, this project has benefited from the financial support and generous working conditions of Michigan State University, to which I am grateful for a Small Projects Completion Grant in 1998 and an Intramural Research Grant in 1999-2000. In the same year I received a fellowship from Villa I Tatti, the Harvard University Center for Italian Renaissance Studies, under whose aegis I completed final revisions to the work. I thank I Tatti and its director, Walter Kaiser, for that memorable and fruitful year. A number of people have been kind enough to read all or part of this book and/or to offer helpful suggestions. Among them, I thank Concetta Bianca, Gregory Bucher, John Buckler, Salvatore Camporeale, Georgia Clarke, Craig Gibson, John Monfasani, Ronald G. Witt, Heiko A. Oberman, and an anonymous reader for this series of monographs. I would also like to thank Professor Oberman for being so generous as to

accept this book into the *Studies in the History of Christian Thought.*
Finally, I thank my wife, Anna, for her constant and unwavering
support, love, and companionship.

Christopher S. Celenza
East Lansing, Michigan
December, 2000

Postscript: The important study of Florence Vuilleumier Laurens reached
me too late to be included meaningfully in this study. It treats "symbolic"
discourse of all sorts, including the Pythagorean *symbola*. See *La raison des
figures symboliques. Fondements philosophiques, théologiques et rhétoriques de l'image à
la Renaissance et à l'Âge classique* (Geneva: Droz, 2000).

ABBREVIATIONS

ASD	*Opera Omnia Desiderii Erasmi Roterodami*, chair of editorial board, H. Trapman (Amsterdam and the Hague, 1969–).
Burkert	Burkert, W., *Lore and Science in Ancient Pythagoreanism*, trans. E. Minar, Jr. Cambridge, Mass., 1972 (a revised and translated version of Burkert's *Weisheit und Wissenschaft: Studien zu Pythagoras, Philolaos und Platon.* Nürnberg, 1962).
CAG	*Commentaria in Aristotelem graeca* (Berlin, 1882–1909).
CCSL	*Corpus Christianorum, Series Latina* (Turnholt, 1954–).
CM	*Corpus Christianorum, Series Latina, Continuatio Medievalis* (Turnholt, 1971–).
CSEL	*Corpus Scriptorum Ecclesiasticorum Latinorum* (Vienna, 1866–).
CTC	*Catalogus translationum et commentariorum* (Washington, DC, 1960–).
CWE	*Collected Works of Erasmus*, chair of editorial board, J. McConica (Toronto, 1974–).
DBI	*Dizionario biografico degli Italiani* (Rome, 1960–).
Della Torre	Della Torre, A., *Storia dell' Accademia platonica di Firenze* (Florence, 1902).
DK	Diels, H. and W. Kranz, *Die Fragmente der Vorsokratiker*, 6th ed. (Berlin 1951–52).
Ficino, *Op.*	Marsilio Ficino, *Opera Omnia*, 2 vols. (Basel, 1576; repr. Turin, 1959).
Giraldi, *Aenigmata/Symbola*	*Lelii Gregorii Gyraldi ferrariensis libelli duo, in quorum altero aenigmata pleraque antiquorum, in altero Pythagorae symbola, non paulo quam hactenus ab aliis, clarius faciliusque sunt explicata, nunquam antea in lucem editi. Accesserunt eiusdem Lilii, et alii duo libelli, Adversus ingratos,*

	et Quomodo quis ingrati nomen et crimen effugere possit. Cum Caesaris Maiestatis gratia et privilegio ad quinquennium. Basileae per Johannem Oporinum. [Colophon]: Basileae per Ioannem Oporinum, Anno Salutis humanae M.D.LI. Mense Ianuario.
GW	*Gesamtkatalog der Wiegendrucke*, eds. E. Von Rath et al., 8 vols. to date (Leipzig and Berlin, 1925–).
Hier., *Ep. Ruf.*	Jerome, "Epistola adversus Rufinum," in *S. Hieronymi Presbyteri opera*, 3.1, *CCSL*, 79, ed. P. Lardet (Turnholt, 1982) 73–116.
Kristeller, *Iter*	Kristeller, P.O., *Iter Italicum: A Finding List of Uncatalogued or Incompletely Catalogued Humanistic Manuscripts of the Renaissance in Italian and Other Libraries*, 6 vols. (Leiden and London, 1963–1995).
Lardet, *Comm.*	Lardet, P., *L'Apologie de Jérôme contre Rufin: Un commentaire*, Supplements to Vigiliae Christianae, 15 (Leiden, 1993).
Migne, *PG*	*Patrologiae cursus completus, Series graeca*, 161 vols. (Paris, 1857–1866).
Migne, *PL*	Migne, J.P., ed., *Patrologiae cursus completus, Series latina*, 221 vols. (Paris, 1844–1864).
Nesi, ed. Vasoli	Vasoli, C., "Giovanni Nesi tra Donato Acciaiuoli e Girolamo Savonarola: testi editi e inedti," *Memorie Dominicane*, n.s., 4 (1973) 103–179.
Nesi, *ONS*	Iohannis Nesii Florentini *Oraculum de novo saeculo* (Florence, 1497).
Poliziano, *Lamia*	Angelo Poliziano, *Lamia: Praelectio in priora Aristotelis analytica*, Studies in Medieval and Reformation Thought, 38, ed. A. Wesseling (Leiden, 1986).
Polizzotto, *Elect Nation*	Polizzotto, L., *The Elect Nation: The Savonarolan Movement in Florence, 1494–1545* (Oxford, 1994).
Savonarola, *OpNaz*	*Edizione Nazionale delle opere di Girolamo Savonarola* (Rome, 1956–).
Suppl.	Kristeller, P.O., ed., *Supplementum ficinianum*, 2 vols. (Florence, 1937).

Swogger   Swogger, J.H., "Antonio degli Agli's 'Explanatio
                     symbolorum Pythagorae:' An Edition and a Study
                     of its Place in the Circle of Marsilio Ficino." Un-
                     published Ph.D. diss., University of London, 1975.
TLL   *Thesaurus linguae latinae* (Munich, 1900–).
Verde, *Lo studio*   Verde, A., *Lo studio fiorentino, 1473–1503: Ricerche e
                     documenti* (Florence, 1973–).
Walther, *Verz.*   Walther, H., ed., *Alphabetisches Verzeichnis der Vers-
                     anfänge mittellateinischer Dichtungen,* 2nd ed. (Göttingen,
                     1969).
Walther, *M*   Walther, H., ed., *Lateinische Sprichwörter und Sentenzen
                     des Mittelalters in alphabetischer Anordnung,* 5 vols.
                     (Göttingen, 1963–7).
Walther, *FN*   Walther, H., ed., *Lateinische Sprichwörter und Sentenzen
                     des Mittelalters und der frühen Neuzeit in alphabetischer
                     Anordnung,* 3 vols. (Göttingen, 1982–6).
Verde, *Lo studio*   Verde, A., *Lo studio fiorentino, 1473–1503: Ricerche e
                     documenti* (Florence, 1973–).

Abbreviations of classical texts are self-explanatory or as found in
S. Hornblower and A. Spawforth, eds. *The Oxford Classical Dictionary*,
3rd edition (Oxford, 1996) xxix–liv. Editions used, unless noted otherwise, are the most recent from either the Oxford Classical Text series
or the Teubner series. References to scripture refer, unless noted
otherwise, to the texts established in the *Biblia sacra iuxta vulgatam versionem*, eds. Robert Weber, Roger Gryson, et al. (Stuttgart: Deutsche
Bibelgesellschaft, ⁴1994). Abbreviations of specific books are those
found at p. XLIII of same. References to the *corpus iuris canonici* refer
to the edition of E.L. Richter, with revisions by E. Friedberg (Leipzig,
1879; repr. Graz, 1959). In the commentary, when referring to canon
law, I use the "modern" citation system, as recommended in J. Brundage, *Medieval Canon Law* (London and New York, 1995) 190–205,
always giving in addition, in parentheses, the page numbers in Richter
where the references can be found.

INTRODUCTION

The transitions in Florentine intellectual life in the waning years of the fifteenth century have not ceased to evoke historians' attentions.[1] In the last two decades of the fifteenth century Florentine intellectuals and elites underwent what has seemed to some a wrenching intellectual and moral crisis. The humanist movement had matured and evolved into what was becoming a Europe-wide educational and intellectual ideal.[2] In the city of Florence, the movement had grown increasingly more technical. If, early in the century, it had had an ideologically civic orientation, by the end of the century the movement had become more outwardly neutral ideologically, as Poliziano expanded exponentially the range of technical humanist philological expertise, and as intellectuals under the gradual Medici ascendancy ceased preoccupying themselves so efficaciously with the *vita activa*.[3] For the last three decades of the century a major part of Florentine intellectual life was the Neoplatonic revival, for which the foundations had been laid in the late 1450s, but to which the name of Marsilio Ficino (1433–99) has become intimately and intextricably linked.[4]

---

[1] See A. Della Torre, *Storia dell' Accademia platonica di Firenze* (Florence, 1902); P.O. Kristeller, *Studies in Renaissance Thought and Letters* (Rome, 1956) esp. 99–122 and 221–247; E. Garin, *La cultura filosofica del Rinascimento italiano* (Florence, 1961); *idem*, *L'età nuova* (Naples, 1969); G.C. Garfagnini, ed., *Marsilio Ficino e il ritorno di Platone: Studi e documenti*, 2 vols. (Florence, 1986); A. Field, *The Origins of the Platonic Academy of Florence* (Princeton, 1988); J. Hankins, *Plato in the Italian Renaissance*, 2 vols. (Leiden, New York, etc., 1990); *idem*, "Cosimo de' Medici and the 'Platonic Academy.'" *Journal of the Warburg and Courtauld Institutes* 53 (1990) 144–162; *idem*, "The Myth of the Platonic Academy of Florence." *Renaissance Quarterly* 44 (1991) 429–75.

[2] For the latest literature on the evolution of humanism (as well as a challenging interpretation) see the survey of R. Black, "Humanism," in ed. C. Allmand, *The New Cambridge Medieval History* (Cambridge, 1998) 243–277 and 906–915; and for a recent broad, Europe wide overview, see A. Rabil, ed., *Renaissance Humanism: Foundations, Forms, and Legacy*, 3 vols. (Philadelphia, 1988).

[3] On Poliziano, his context, and his influence, see V. Branca, *Poliziano e l'umanesimo della parola* (Turin, 1983); P. Godman, *From Poliziano to Machiavelli: Florentine Humanism in the High Renaissance* (Princeton, 1998); and A. Grafton, *Joseph Scaliger: A Study in the History of Classical Scholarship*, 2 vols. (Oxford, 1983–93) 1.9–100.

[4] For surveys of the literature see T. Katinis, "Bibliografia Ficiniana," *Accademia* 2 (2000); and P.O. Kristeller, *Marsilio Ficino and his Work After Five Hundred Years*, Quaderni di Rinascimento, no. 7 (Florence, 1987), reprinted from Garfagnini (as in n.1). In general see the recent contributions of M.J.B. Allen, *Icastes: Marsilio Ficino's*

   This Ficinian Neoplatonism always had within it a touch of the
the apocalyptic, and it was never monolithic.[5] As a sense of crisis
deepened among Florentine intellectuals, many members of the vital
coterie which comprised Ficino's followers became *piagnoni*—followers of the reform-minded Dominican apocalypticist Girolamo
Savonarola, whose spiritual and political ascendency in the republic
from 1494 onward ended in his being hung and then burned in
1498.[6] The *Symbolum nesianum*, attributed to the *piagnone* Giovanni
Nesi, is a prime witness to these transitions.[7] Sandwiched in the mas-
sive *Eptathicum* of Paolo Orlandini, the *Symbolum* presents an interpretation of the Pythagorean sayings (*akousmata* or *symbola*) which
oscillates between Ficinian Neoplatonism and Savonarolan apoca-

---

Interpretation of Plato's Sophist (Berkeley, Los Angeles, and London, 1989); *idem, Nuptial Arithmetic: Marsilio Ficino's Commentary on the Fatal Number in Book VIII of Plato's* Republic (Berkeley, Los Angeles, and London, 1994); *idem, Plato's Third Eye: Studies in Marsilio Ficino's Metaphysics and its Sources.* (Hampshire and Brookfield, Vermont, 1995); and *idem, Synoptic Art: Marsilio Ficino on the History of Platonic Interpretation* (Florence, 1998).

[5] Apocalypticism: I accept the use of the term "apocalypticism," embedding as it does notions of revelation and prophecy, endorsed by C.V. Bostick in his *The Antichrist and the Lollards: Apocalypticism in Late Medieval and Reformation England*, Studies in Medieval and Reformation Thought, LXX (Leiden, Boston, Cologne, 1998) 1–18; see there for a survey of the literature and clarification regarding terminology. See also E.R. Daniel, "The Spread of Apocalypticism, 1100–1500. Why Calvin Could Not Reject It," *Calvin Studies* 5 (1990) 61–71, at 61 (cit. Bostick, 7), who argues that apocalypticism is well "understood as the expectation of an imminent, final crisis, which will bring to an end the present, corrupt era and inaugurate a new one, whether within history or outside it." Never monolithic: in addition to Hankins, "Cosimo de' Medici" and *idem*, "The Myth," see also his "Lorenzo de' Medici as a Patron of Philosophy," *Rinascimento*, 2nd series, 34 (1994) 15–53; R. Fubini, "Ficino e i Medici all'avvento di Lorenzo il Magnifico," *Rinascimento*, 2nd series, 24 (1984) 3–52; *idem*, "Ancora su Ficino e i Medici," ibid., 27 (1987) 275–91 (both studies now in R. Fubini, *Quattrocento fiorentino: Politica diplomazia cultura* [Pisa, 1996] 235–301); and C.S. Celenza, "Pythagoras in the Renaissance: The Case of Marsilio Ficino," *Renaissance Quarterly* 52 (1999) 667–711.

[6] On these "piagnoni" and on the fate of the Savonarolan party see the fundamental study of Polizzotto. On Savonarola in general see D. Weinstein, *Savonarola and Florence: Prophecy and Patriotism in the Renaissance* (Princeton, 1970); R. Ridolfi, *Vita di Girolamo Savonarola*, 2 vols. (Rome, 1952); J. Schnitzer, *Savonarola*, 2 vols. (Milan, 1931).

[7] On Nesi see Polizzotto, 100–08; Weinstein, D., *Savonarola and Florence: Prophecy and Patriotism in the Renaissance* (Princeton, 1970) 192–205; Vasoli, C., "Giovanni Nesi tra Donato Acciauoli e Girolamo Savonarola: testi editi e inediti," *Memorie Dominicane* n.s. 4 (1973) 103–179; *idem, Filosofia e religione nella cultura del Rinascimento* (Napoli: Guida Editori, 1988) 139, 140 n.3, 223; *idem, Tra 'Maestri' umanisti e teologi: studi quat-trocenteschi* (Firenze: Casa Editrice Le Lettere, 1991) 212–248, 212, 217; and on the *Symbolum nesianum* specficially, *idem*, "Pitagora in monastero," *Interpres* 1 (1978) 256–272. For the political positions held by Nesi, see D. Fachard, ed., *Consulte e pratiche della repubblica fiorentina, 1498–1505* (Geneva, 1992) *ad indicem*. For Nesi and Florentine confraternities see K. Eisenbichler, *The Boys of the Archangel Raphael: A Youth Confraternity in Florence, 1411–1785* (Toronto, Buffalo and London, 1998) 180–2 with notes.

lypticism. The text is a parallel vision born of the Italian Renaissance, an updating of an ancient, pagan communal society for the modern age, albeit in a very restricted context, that of monastic living. The author functions under the assumption that the precepts of a sect, the Pythagoreans, whose believers nourished thoughts of reincarnation, can and should enter the everyday lives of monks, accompanied by an interiority fully consonant with the ideals of monastic life. The author's notion of a *latens energia*, a "hidden energy," possessed by the symbols is perhaps the most powerful kind of expression of what a true believer in the *prisca theologia* tradition had in mind: a set of linguistic units which could have life breathed into them at any time by the right hermeneutical approach.[8]

This study will proceed in the following fashion. In the introduction's first section, I offer a brief history of the Pythagorean symbols from antiquity to the mid-fifteenth century. In the second, there is an examination of the different interpretive styles that Florentine thinkers brought to the symbols in the latter part of the fifteenth century. The focus narrows in the third part, as I turn to Giovanni Nesi himself and the context of the original redaction of *Symbolum Nesianum*. Finally, I turn to the wider European context, in order to see how other thinkers, writing later, treated the symbols (specifically Filippo Beroaldo the Elder, Erasmus, Johann Reuchlin, and Lilio Gregorio Giraldi). After some concluding comments to the introductory study, there follows a critical edition of the *Symbolum Nesianum* (the text's *editio princeps*) along with an English translation. The edition and translation are followed by a source commentary and three appendices.

At the outset it is necessary to note that J.H. Swogger in his 1975 doctoral dissertation offered a critical edition and English translation of the *Explanatio symbolorum Pythagore* of Antonio degli Agli, a prelate and mentor of Ficino.[9] In a lengthy introduction Swogger provided a study of the reception history of the symbols from antiquity to the Renaissance. Although I have occasionally disagreed with and supplemented Swogger's account below, on the whole his survey of the

---

"Attributed to Nesi:" the question of authorship of the treatise is complicated and is addressed below.

[8] *Latens energia*: see the *Symbolum nesianum*, Introductio.6.

[9] J.H. Swogger, "Antonio degli Agli's 'Explanatio symbolorum Pythagorae:' An Edition and a Study of its Place in the Circle of Marsilio Ficino," Ph.D. diss., University of London, 1975. Agli offered a discussion of over forty-five symbols. The work is present in MS Naples BN VIII F 9, fols. 1–47. Cf. Kristeller, *Iter* 1: 426. I have examined this manuscript in person and address Agli below.

late ancient, medieval, and Renaissance transmission of the symbols is thorough enough that repeating the enterprise would be superfluous.[10] While I do address in a skeletal fashion the transmission of the symbols, my concern here is with a different side of *Überlieferungsgeschichte*. I seek to examine the manner in which the social context of intellectuals in late fifteenth-century Florence was conducive to appreciating the Pythagorean symbols. I maintain that for a short time the spiritual and philosophical needs of certain leading Florentine intellectuals meshed well (if certainly not exclusively) with the late ancient appreciation of Pythagoras in particular and of philosophy and its place in general. Marsilio Ficino's views embodied this Florentine predilection, and, in a limited respect, he can be seen as contributing to a Florentine prophetic sensibility.[11] Since Ficino's Platonic orientation was heavily influenced by the late ancient Neopythagorean presentation of the Pythagorico-Platonic tradition, it is unsurprising that the Pythagorean symbols came to the attention of a *piagnone* like Giovanni Nesi in the mid-1490s.[12] Moreover, Nesi's treatment was well enough regarded that, almost twenty years later, Paolo Orlandini included it in the manuscript on which the text in this edition is based, perhaps redacting and modifying it himself. I begin by addressing Pythagoras and the Pythagorean tradition.

Pythagoras, Pythagoreanism, and the Pythagorean Symbols: Antiquity Through Mid-Fifteenth-century Florence

From the earliest reports in Plato, there have always been two dimensions reported about the Pythagorean tradition: the religious and the scientific. The trouble for later interpreters has come in reconciling

---

[10] Moreover I am informed that John C. Thom, author of *The Pythagorean Golden Verses with Introduction and Commentary* (Leiden, New York, Cologne, 1995)—to which reference will be made below—is now engaged in a comprehensive study of the symbols.

[11] See Celenza, "Pythagoras in the Renaissance".

[12] For Ficino and late ancient Neopythagoreanism, see Celenza, "Temi neo-pitagorici nel pensiero di Marsilio Ficino," in ed. S. Toussaint, *Actes du XLIIe Colloque International d'Etudes Humanistes "Marsile Ficin 1499–1999,"* Cahiers de l'Humanisme, Les Belles Lettres, forthcoming (Paris, 2001); *idem*, "L'antiquité tardive et le Platonisme Florentin: Ficin et la tradition post-Plotinienne," forthcoming in Fosca Mariani Zini, ed., *Philosophie et Philologie au Quattrocento* (Lille: Presses Universitaires du Septentrion, 2001); and *idem*, "Late Antiquity and Florentine Platonism: The 'Post-Plotinian' Ficino," forthcoming in M.J.B. Allen and V.R. Rees, eds., *Marsilio Ficino: His Sources, His Circle, His Legacy* (Brill, 2001).

these different sides. The principal source in reconstructing Pythagorean teachings is Aristotle, who was especially concerned to separate Pythagoreanism from what he perceived to be its Platonized version.[13] The reports in his *Metaphysics*, his *Physics*, and his *De coelo* are crucial, as is his lost monograph on Pythagoreanism, some of which has been reconstructed.[14] Other important sources for the Pythagorean tradition include lives of Pythagoras by Diogenes Laertius, Porphyry, and Iamblichus.[15] Especially significant as well are the late ancient commentators on Aristotle, especially Themistius and Simplicius.[16]

Walter Burkert has argued that the history of modern scholarship on the sources of the Pythagorean tradition shows a tendency to allow "the material . . . to fall into the pattern each inquirer is looking for."[17] Burkert's own work pointed toward the necessity of connecting the religious facets of Pythagoreanism with the various "rational" ones, in order to gain a more complete view of ancient Pythagoreanism in its social, ritual context, and he has been followed in this tendency—sometimes disputatiously—by more recent scholars.[18]

There are always facets of the religious serving as counterweights to the "purely rational." On the rational side one learns that Pythagoras

---

[13] Cf. G.S. Kirk, J.E. Raven, and M. Schofield, *The Presocratic Philosophers*, second edition (Cambridge, 1983) 215.

[14] See ed. W.D. Ross, *Aristotelis fragmenta selecta* (Oxford, 1955); this includes a reprinting of the fragments of Aristotle's book on the Pythagoreans which were first published in V. Rose, *Aristotelis fragmenta* (Leipzig, 1886); but see the criticisms in Burkert, 166 n. 4.

[15] Diogenes Laertius, *Lives of Eminent Philosophers*, 2 vols., ed. and trans. R.D. Hicks (Cambridge, Mass., and London, 1938), book 8.1 (2: 320–367); *La vie de Pythagore de Diogène Laërce*, ed. A. DeLatte, (Brussels, 1932); Porphyry, *Vita Pythagorae*, in *Opuscula selecta*, ed. A. Nauck (Leipzig, 2nd ed., 1886) 17–52; Iamblichus, *De vita pythagorica*, ed. L. Deubner (Stuttgart, 1937); and see *idem, On the Pythagorean Life*, tr. G. Clark (Liverpool, 1989).

[16] Themistius, *In Aristotelis Physica paraphrasis, CAG* 5.2, ed. H. Schenkel (Berlin, 1900); Simplicius, *In Aristotelis de caelo commentaria, CAG* 7, ed. J.L. Heiberg (Berlin, 1894); *idem, In Aristotelis Physica commentaria, CAG* 9 and 10, ed. H. Diels (Berlin, 1882–95).

[17] Burkert, 9, after a summary of modern scholarship from Zeller to Rohde, DeLatte, and others. He goes on (ibid.): "The historian of science rediscovers Pythagoras the scientist; the religiously minded show us Pythagoras the mystic; he who believes in a synthesis above rational analysis tries to show that in Pythagoras the *coincidentia oppositorum* is comprehended in a Basic Idea; the anthropologist finds 'shamanism;' and the philological scholar may play off against one another the contradictions of the tradition, so that critical virtuosity may sparkle over a bog of uncertainty. Pythagoreanism is thus reduced to an impalpable will-o-the-wisp, which existed everywhere and nowhere."

[18] Cf. Burkert, *passim*. More recent scholars: P. Kingsley, *Ancient Philosophy, Mystery, and Magic: Empedocles and the Pythagorean Tradition* (Oxford, 1995) and to an extent C.A. Huffman, *Philolaus of Croton: Pythagorean and Presocratic* (Cambridge, 1993).

was the first to use the term "philosophia"—the love of wisdom; counterbalancing this, however, one must consider just what this "wisdom" was for Pythagoras and his followers. One can connect this with the notion of Pythagoras as a "wise man," with shamanic resonances.[19] The rationalist tradition marks Pythagoras as the first to introduce into Greek philosophical (as opposed to mythographic) speculation the notion that the soul is immortal; but connected with this is the notion of metempsychosis (the transmigration of souls), a metaphysical theory of eternal recurrence, and the position, emphasized by Burkert, that many Pythagorean theories, including metempsychosis, might be much closer to Orphism, especially from a ritual perspective, than previously assumed.[20]

Pythagoras and the Pythagoreans considered number to be the first and most important principle of the universe. But they were not in the tradition of the material monists, like Thales; rather (and closer to Orphic tradition) their number theory was not ontological but cosmogonic, an almost embryological reflection of the birthing of the universe.[21] We learn that Pythagoras discovered the harmonic ratios; but far from being "purely scientific," this discovery was part and parcel of a larger appreciation of *harmonia* in a broad sense, part of a world view stressing balance and moderation. It is in the context of a cultural environment where there is a self-conscious and inseparable mixture of "rationalistic" thought with "religious" ritual, that the symbols are best understood and are most apt to come to life.

The symbols consist of a series of brief, enigmatic sayings. For the sake of clarity it should be mentioned that the symbols are distinct from the Pythagorean *Aurea carmina*. The symbols (*symbola* or *akousmata*), that is, consist of a very loose configuration of apophthegmata, which changes with every author who cites them or comments on them. It is impossible to speak of a corpus at all. It is otherwise, however, with the Pythagorean *Aurea carmina*—the *Golden Verses* known in Greek as the Χρυσᾶ ἔπη, Χρυσᾶ παραγγέλματα, or Ἱερὸς λόγος. This was a doctrinal poem which in a recent study has been dated to 350–300 B.C.[22] It may have served an institutional function, having been designed as an introduction to the teachings of a group of Pythagoreans, and is structured in a twofold manner: first, there is

---

[19] Cf. Burkert, 120–65.
[20] See Burkert, 162–5 and the literature cited there.
[21] Cf. Celenza, "Pythagoras in the Renaissance."
[22] See Thom, *The Pythagorean Golden Verses*, 35–58.

a list of imperatives; second, the poem sets forth what one who follows these imperatives can expect.[23] It is a coherent though gnomic work that deals thematically with matters of moral and metaphysical insight, and its overriding purpose is religious.[24] Certain of its sayings and maxims appear in different lists of symbols, but the *Aurea carmina* is distinct from the symbols and, in its coherence, unlike them. Each listing of the symbols, on the other hand, is *sui generis* and is as much a reflection of its compiler as it is of Pythagoreanism.

The symbols themselves present a perfect example of the above-mentioned complexities attendant upon understanding Pythagoreanism. For in the ancient Pythagorean communities to which they owed their origin, the symbols functioned as cultic taboo-precepts, which had to be followed at the time of festivals, when they served a purgative, purificatory function. For the symbols to make sense they must appear in an environment where there is a hierophant-like figure leading the cult, such as was Pythagoras; through his suprahuman wisdom he commands in a vatic fashion what is prohibited and what is allowed. Thus the symbols are not to be "understood" by believers in a demonstrative, apodeictic manner; instead, they are to be obeyed. In this sense the precepts bind the community together, creating insiders (those who know the requisite practices of purification and, under the guidance of the vatic figure, follow them) and outsiders (those who stand apart from the community's prescribed ritual unity).[25]

The vatic figure, however, is the key to understanding the symbols in the integrity of their ritual social context. Without such a figure the precepts' ontological status changes. Ungrounded by the lens of an inspired person's interpretations they seem meaningless proscriptions and can easily be subject to misunderstanding, if not outright ridicule.[26] After Pythagoras' ascendency, it would seem that the symbols functioned only to mark off Pythagoreanism as something separate and apart. To later exegetes (ancient, medieval, early modern, and modern), the symbols appeared perforce in need of explication: stripped of their ritual context, in order to make any sense at all, they had to be interpreted.

---

[23] Thom, 59–64.
[24] Ibid., 66–8.
[25] Burkert, 178.
[26] It is exactly this type of treatment to which Ficino's and Nesi's contemporary Angelo Poliziano subjected the symbols in his *Lamia*, addressed below.

We can state with relative certainty, then, that this "interpretive"
approach does not reflect the original or primary importance of the
symbols as ritual markers in early Pythagorean communities. There
is no philosophical doctrine lurking behind them as coherent as in
Aristotle's works, or as intertextual as in Plato's. Nevertheless, the
nature of the symbols makes commentaries on them all the more
useful for the modern interpreter. Since the symbols, that is, are
gnomic and enigmatic, they possess a certain malleability. Given this,
a commentary on them (such as the *Symbolum Nesianum*) will reflect
the assumptions and goals of the commentator in a less veiled fashion than occurs, say, in the case of medieval or Renaissance commentaries on Aristotle. Those who comment on the symbols must
per force invest them with meaning, and this meaning will vary dra-
matically according to the interpreter. The history of their transmission demonstrates this.

To turn back to antiquity and to the textual history of the symbols:
as far as actual content goes, there is no source from which all later
compilations of symbols derive.[27] The "corpus," such as it is, is very
malleable; and late ancient, medieval, and early modern thinkers
usually feel free to add and subtract at will. Although certain of the

---

[27] In his 1894 Kiel dissertation, *De acusmatis sive symbolis pythagoricis*, Cornelius Hölk
made a forceful case that the only real way that the Pythagorean sayings were ever
intended to be understood were as *akousmata* using his (Hölk's) understanding of the
word, i.e., things heard and used by the original Pythagoreans as religious-super-
stitious sayings, stemming from the original Pythagorean society (not, e.g., "symbola" in an ecclesiastical sense). Cf. 18: "Veram enim dictorum Pythagoricorum
originem religiosam et superstitiosam is solus perspexit, qui ἀκούσματα ea vocavit;
profundiorem quendam et a vera eorum indole alienissimum sensum cum eis coni-
unxit is qui συμβόλου notionem eis vindicavit" and 19: "Duo igitur apud veteres
inveniuntur et distinguendae sunt dicta Pythagorica interpretandi rationes: altera
qua recte acusmata explicantur ex vera vetustissimae societatis Pythagoricae forma
et indole, altera qua recta via relicta per ambages et interpretandi artificia sensus
ex eis enucleatur a vero acusmatum argumento alienisssimus." It was Hölk's conviction that anyone, even ancients, who interpreted their title differently from his
interpretation of *akousmata*—which many did—missed the mark as far as Pythagoras
and the original Pythagorean society would have been concerned. As far as the
ancient *akousmata* go, this is an interesting suggestion. But after one leaves antiquity
and the original Pythagorean context, the symbols become little more than a living, flexible configuration of sayings which changes with each interpreter. Still important for the symbols in antiquity is the 1905 dissertation of Friedrich Boehm, *De
symbolis Pythagoreis* (Berlin, 1905), who attempted a more contextualized interpretation than Hölk (see 5–6 for his investigative principles), and in so doing offered an
extensive list along with interpretations grounded in numerous ancient sources.

sayings were known before the time of Pythagoras, the symbols *qua* symbols originated in ancient, fifth-century B.C., Pythagorean communities. While they can be connected with the historical figure of Pythagoras, it would be fruitless to try to ascertain exactly which ones are authentically of Pythagoras and which not.[28] The earliest ancient textual evidence we have of the symbols comes from Anaximander of Miletus (fl. ca. 400 B.C.), who was known to Xenophon and quoted in the late tenth-century lexicon, the *Suda*. Anaximander is said to have written a Συμβόλων Πυθαγορείων ἐξήγησις, of which the *Suda* quotes three symbols.[29] There is ancient testimony for the symbols in other sources as well, the most thorough being contained in Iamblichus (c. 245–325 A.D.), though Porphyry and Diogenes Laertius are also significant.[30] Iamblichus and other Pythagoreanizing Neoplatonists are influential transmitters of the Pythagorean tradition. Because these sources are important for understanding Ficino and the late fifteenth-century Florentine appreciation of the Pythagorean tradition, I reserve detailed discussion of them until later, for comparative purposes.

With respect to the Pythagorean tradition, it was inevitable in late antiquity that patristic authors share some of the same terms of argument with pagan philosophers, especially because certain philosophers set up Pythagoras as a pagan counterpart to Christ.[31] However, given the Christian fathers' competition with the omnipresent paganism,

---

[28] It has recently been argued that these communities were just as suffused with magical preconceptions and veneration for authority as were later, post-Platonic varieties of Pythagoreanism. See Kingsley, *Ancient Philosophy*, 319 *et passim*.

[29] See the *Suda*, s.v. Anaximander, in *Lexicographi graeci*, 1.1, ed. A. Adler (Stuttgart 1928 and repr. 1971) at 1987 (p. 179) (= DK 58C6): ἔγραπσε συμβόλων Πυθαγορείων ἐξήγησιν· οἷόν ἐστι τὸ ζυγὸν μὴ ὑπερβαίνειν, μαχαίρᾳ πῦρ μὴ σκαλεύειν, ἀπὸ ὁλοκλήρου ἄρτου μὴ ἐσθίειν· καὶ τὰ λοιπά. For the Suda's list of Pythagorean *symbols*, drawn from Diogenes Laertius 8, 17–27, 34–5, and 38, see s.v. Pythagoras in 1.4, 3124 (pp. 264–7); and see Burkert, 166 and 166 n.3.

[30] On Iamblichus in general, see J. Dillon, "Iamblichus of Chalcis (c. 240–325 A.D.)" in *Aufstieg und Niedergang der römischen Welt* 36.2 (Berlin and New York, 1988) 862–909 and the studies collected in H.J. Blumenthal and E.G. Clark, *The Divine Iamblichus: Philosopher and Man of Gods* (London, 1993). For his work on Pythagoras, see below. For Porphyry's *Life of Pythagoras* see ed. A. Nauck, *Vita Pythagorae* in *Opuscula selecta* (Leipzig, 1886²) 17–52. For Diogenes Laertius on Pythagoras, along with a thorough listing of parallel passages, see A. DeLatte, *La vie de Pythagore de Diogène Laërce* (Bruxelles, 1932). The various testimonia of the symbols are collected and listed in DK 58C.

[31] Cf. H.D. Saffrey, "Allusions antichrétiennes chez Proclus le diadoque platonicien," *Revue des sciences philosophique et théologique* 59 (1975) 553–63.

which flourished in many forms throughout the Mediterranean world for the longest time,[32] the fathers' interests in Pythagoreanism were perforce delicate. Christianity was only one among hundreds of religions in the late Roman empire and its defenders had to treat profane literature—a necessary part of the cultural inheritance of all late ancient educated persons, Christian or pagan—with great care. In fact it is in the patristic era that the tendency to interpret the symbols primarily as moral maxims began, a tendency which would last throughout the middle ages.

Among patristic authors, Clement of Alexandria in his *Stromata*, Origen in his *Contra haereses*, Ambrose in a letter to Irenaeus, and most importantly Jerome, all commented on various symbols.[33] Clement offered a number of moralizing interpretations and stressed the notion that Pythagoras and his followers were acquainted with Moses' doctrines and that their work was a foreshadowing of Christ's teaching:

> By a happy utterance of divination, not without divine help, concurring in certain prophetic declarations, and seizing the truth in portions and aspects, in terms not obscure, and not going beyond the explanation of things, they honored it on ascertaining the appearance of relation with the truth. Whence Greek philosophy is like the torch of wick which men kindle, artificially stealing the light from the sun. But on the proclamation of the word all that holy light shone forth.[34]

Origen in his *Conta haereses* mentions seven symbols after touching on Pythagoras.[35] It is interesting that in the same work he gives two different interpretations of the same symbol. In the just mentioned section he discusses the symbol, "Do not eat beans," as referring to the notion that one should abstain from politics.[36] But earlier on he had interpreted the same symbol as an admonition to chastity, since beans, when split open, seemed to resemble the generative organs of human beings. As Swogger points out, the fact that a thinker felt

---

[32] Cf. G. Bowersock, *Hellenism in Late Antiquity* (Ann Arbor, 1990) and R. MacMullen, *Paganism in the Roman Empire* (New Haven, 1981).

[33] Clement: see *Stromata*, in *Die griechischen christlichen Schriftsteller der ersten drei Jahrhunderte*, 2, ed O. Stählin (Leipzig, 1906) 5.5 (pp. 342–6); Origen: Migne, *PG* 16.3, coll. 3023–3232, at 3232; Ambrose: *Ep.* 81, in Migne, *PL* 16, coll. 1095–98. Jerome: Hier., *Ep. Ruf.*, 39–40.

[34] *Strom.* 5.5, 342–6; in the quotation I have used and modified the translation of W. Wilson, 238.

[35] Origen, *Contra haereses*, 3232.

[36] Since beans had been used as a means of counting votes.

free in the same work to offer two different intepretations of the same saying is itself indicative of the symbols' flexibility.[37]

In a letter to Irenaeus, Ambrose discussed the Pythagorean saying, "do not take the public path" (known in the *Symbolum nesianum* as *viam publicam declinato*).[38] Ambrose there endorsed the notion that Pythagoras was Jewish by birth and followed Mosaic and Old Testament teaching in this precept—a notion that would later be seen as a redeeming feature of the symbols in the eyes of Antonio degli Agli.[39] Ambrose goes on to intepret the precept to mean that priests should live holy, uncommonly pure lives.[40]

Jerome, in his *Epistola adversus Rufinum*, offered brief interpretations of certain symbols.[41] His concern was to expose the ignorance of Rufinus, who, in criticizing Jerome, had asked him for the "books of Pythagoras." Jerome points out that there are no actual *volumina* of Pythagoras, only *dogmata*. He also notes that, in the letter to which Rufinus had referred, he, Jerome, had once admitted that in his adolescence he had confused doctrines of Pythagoras, Plato, and Empedocles with certain teachings of the apostles. And he mentions that he was not speaking of books in that letter but rather about the Pythagorean dogmata which could be found everywhere, even incised on bronze tablets.[42] Jerome follows this by presenting a list,

---

[37] Swogger, 43.

[38] Ambrose, *Ep.* 81, coll. 1095–98. For the *Symbolum nesianum* reference see 48 in the edition of the text below.

[39] I.e., the scholastic early mentor of Ficino, who, I argue below, wrote his own interpretation of the symbols in reaction to Ficino's, not in anticipation of it.

[40] In his *De officiis ministrorum*, Ambrose commented on Pythagorean silence (Ambr., *De off.*, 1.10.31): Numquid prior Panaetius, numquid Aristoteles, qui et ipse disputavit de officio, quam David, cum et ipse Pythagoras, qui legitur Socrate antiquior, prophetam secutus David (cf. Ps. 38.2), legem silentii dederit suis? Sed ille, ut per quinquennium discipulis usum inhiberit loquendi; David autem, non ut naturae munus inminueret, sed ut custodiam proferendi sermonis doceret. Et Pythagoras quidem, ut non loquendo loqui doceret; David, ut loquendo magis disceremus loqui. Quomodo enim sine exercitio doctrina aut sine usu profectus?

[41] See Hier., *Ep. Ruf.* and the excellent commentary of Lardet (Lardet, *Comm.*).

[42] See Hier., *Ep. Ruf.* 39 (pp. 107–8): "Pythagorae a me libros flagitas. Quis enim tibi dixit illius extare volumina? Nonne in epistula mea quam criminaris haec verba sunt: 'Sed fac me errasse in adulescentia, et philosophorum, id est gentilium studiis eruditum, in principio fidei ignorasse dogmata christiana, et hoc putasse in apostolis quod in Pythagora et Platone et Empedocle legeram'? De dogmatibus eorum non de libris locutus sum, quae potui in Cicerone, Bruto ac Seneca discere. Lege pro Vatinio oratiunculam et alias ubi sodaliciorum mentio fit, revolve dialogos Tullii, respice omnem oram Italiae quae quondam Magna Graecia dicebatur, et pythagoricorum dogmatum incisa publicis litteris aera cognosces. . . ."

with brief explications, of thirteen symbols. He took as his textual
basis the lists in Porphyry and Iamblichus and along the way mentioned also Moderatus of Gades, Archippus, Lysis, and Aristotle as
sources for information about Pythagoras and the symbols.[43] Jerome's
list became the basis for what little medieval discussion there was
concerning the symbols and can be seen as having given them a
measure of legitimacy in Christian discussion.[44] Thereafter the symbols were discussed in the *Liber de moribus* attributed falsely to Seneca
(perhaps written by Martin of Bracara), the thirteenth-century *Gesta
Romanorum*, the *Speculum historiale* of Vincent of Beauvais (c. 1190–c. 1264),
and the *De vita et moribus philosophorum* of Walter of Burley (1275–1345),[45]
the latter being a work well-known to Petrarch, Boccaccio, and
Salutati.[46] All of these medieval uses of the *symbols* are almost exclusively indebted to Jerome.[47]

To complete the medieval inheritance, there are seven Pythagorean
sayings cited in the *Picatrix*, the foreboding work of medieval magic,
originally compiled in Arabic in the eleventh century, translated into
Castilian for Alfonse the Wise in the thirteenth century, and subse-
quently Latinized.[48] This notorious work enjoyed a certain popular-

---

[43] See Hier., *Ep. Ruf.*, and the comments of Lardet, *Comm.*, *ad loc.*
[44] Swogger, 44–7.
[45] Ibid.
[46] On the manuscript and incunabular tradition of Burley's *Lives* see J. Prelog,
"Die Handschriften und Drucke von W. Burley's *Liber de vita et moribus philosophorum*," *Codices manuscripti* 9 (1983) 1–18; see also J.O. Stigall, "The Manuscript Tradition
of the *De vita et moribus* of Walter Burley," *Medievalia et humanistica* 11 (1957) 44–57.
For Burley's fortune, see G. Piaia, '*Vestigia philosophorum*' *e la storiografia* (Rimini, 1983).
On Petrarch and Boccaccio see G. Billanovich, "La tradizione del 'Liber de dictis
philosophorum antiquorum' e la cultura di Dante del Petrarca e del Bocaccio,"
Studi Petrarcheschi 1 (1948) 111–123; on Salutati see R.G. Witt, *Hercules and the
Crossroads: The Life, Works, and Thought of Coluccio Salutati* (Durham, North Carolina,
1983) *ad indicem.*
[47] Swogger, 46.
[48] See D. Pingree, ed., *The Picatrix: The Latin Version of the Ghāyat Al-Ḥakīm*, Studies
of the Warburg Institute, 39 (London, 1986) 4.9.28: "Item explanabo septem documenta que Pithagoras approbavit. Primum: pondera proporcionaliter equatis, et
ea in recta disposicione conservetis. Secundum: amicicias et amores vestros dirigite, et tamquam salutem predicta agite. Tercium: non accendatis ignem in loco
viridi quod gladio amputatur. Quartum: voluntates et appetitus vestros dirigite, et
eos recto pondere mensuretis in effectu; hec autem vestra corpora in debita sani-
tate tenentur. Quintum: recta et equali semper assuefacite; hoc autem amorem et
amicicias gencium augebit in vobis. Sextum: tempora observetis et exercitetis secundum quod domini et iudices dicunt, observando quod hoc requiritur in mundo
quantum ad vitam tuendam. Septimum: non impugnetis neque contaminetis spiritus et corpora vestra; imo observetis in debita temperancia ut ipsa semper necessitatis tempore operari possitis."

ity among Renaissance esoterists and was known in the circle of
Ficino.[49] The sayings there made their way into the *Picatrix* through
Arabic sources, derived partially from Porphyry's *Life of Pythagoras*.[50]

In the fifteenth century the possibility of investigating various aspects
of the ancient Greek philosophical heritage was augmented greatly
by the eastward voyages that humanists undertook in the generation
after the 1396 arrival of Manuel Chrysoloras in Florence.[51] For the
recovery of Pythagorean material, one of the most important of these
humanists was Giovanni Aurispa.[52] The Sicilian-born Aurispa (1376–
1459) is best known for his manifold interaction with the Byzantine
world, which included his tireless activities as a book-collector as well
as his efforts as a translator. In 1441 he made a voyage to the east
with the authorization of Tommaso Parentucelli, who became Pope
Nicholas V in 1447. Aurispa returned with a number of Greek manuscripts, one of which contained "quite a few works of Iamblichus"
("Iamblichi plura").[53] Another contained the *Commentary* of Hierocles
on the Pythagorean *Aurea verba*. Soon after, in 1449, he composed a
translation of the commentary and dedicated it to Parentucelli, who
by this time had become Pope.[54] Aurispa's appreciation of the *Aurea
verba* in his preface to Parentucelli is illustrative (App. 1.8–9):

---

[49] V. Perrone Compagni, "La magia cerimoniale del 'Picatrix' nel Rinascimento,"
Atti dell'Accademia di Scienze Morali e Politiche (Napoli) 88 (1977) 279–330; on its influence,
see also the literature cited in Marsilio Ficino, *De triplici vita*, ed. and trans. C.V.
Kaske and J.R. Clark (Binghamton, New York, 1989) 84 n.1.

[50] See the notes to the sayings in the German version of the *Picatrix*, in H. Ritter
and M. Plessner, transs., *"Picatrix": Das Ziel des Weisen von Pseudo-Maǧrīṭī*, Studies of
the Warburg Institute, 27 (London, 1962) 422.

[51] Cf. G. Cammelli, *I dotti bizantini e le origini dell'umanesimo*. I: *Manuele Crisolora*;
II: *Giovanni Argiropulo*; III: *Demetrio Calcondila* (Florence, 1941–54); and N.G. Wilson,
From Byzantium to Italy (Baltimore, 1992).

[52] On whom see E. Bigi, *DBI* 4 (1962) 593–5; A. Franceschini, *Giovanni Aurispa
e la sua biblioteca: Notizie e documenti* (Padua, 1976) esp. 3–52; D. Marsh, *Lucian and the
Latins: Humor and Humanism in the Early Renaissance* (Ann Arbor, 1998) 30–3; R. Sabbadini,
Biografia documentata di Giovanni Aurispa (Noto, 1890); idem, ed., *Il carteggio di Giovanni
Aurispa* (Rome, 1931); Wilson, *From Byzantium*, 25–9; and M.A. Gianini, "The
Manuscripts of Giovanni Aurispa (1376–1459)," Unpublished doctoral dissertation,
University of North Carolina at Chapel Hill, 1974.

[53] This might be MS Florence Bibl. Laurenziana 86.6, although this is not certain. See B.L. Ullman and P. Stadter, *The Public Library of Renaissance Florence* (Padua,
1972) 47, n.3.

[54] In Appendix one I provide an edition and translation of his preface. For the
date of Aurispa's translation of Hierocles, see Swogger, 50.

... when I was in Venice I bought on your order certain Greek books. Among them I found Hierocles on the so-called *Golden Verses* of Pythagoras, in which the whole philosophy of the Pythagoreans is contained. In these books there is so much doctrine and usefulness for the reader that even I, now an octogenarian, have read nothing either in Greek or in Latin that I understand to have benefitted me more. For other than the lack of miracles it differs from Christian faith little or not at all.

It is noteworthy that Aurispa perceives a similarity between Pythagorean practices and Christianity. With a view toward the wider intellectual context, one can observe a growth in interest among intellectuals in religious traditions which were parallel and supplemental to Christianity.

The first fifteenth-century thinker to discuss the symbols *in extenso* was Leon Battista Alberti, who in one of his *Intercenales*, the *Convelata*, had an interlocutor offer a list with very brief interpretations.[55] His appreciation for Pythagoras must have been colored by his exposure to Lucian's satirical presentation of the Samian. Alberti knew well one of the works in which Pythagoras had been sent up, *Philosophies for Sale*, and in fact used it extensively in composing his *intercenale The Cynic*.[56] There Pythagoras was described as specializing in "arithmetic, astronomy, charlatanry, geometry, music, and quackery."[57]

Alberti's approach to the symbols is indicative of this satirical attitude. One senses that for Alberti the *symbola* are mere *deliciae eruditorum*, a chance to use a little known aspect of antiquity to moralize and to demonstrate his wide learning. Even his interlocutors in the dialogue have trouble taking these *Pythagorica* seriously after he recites them.[58] And it is difficult, if not impossible, to know exactly what

---

[55] It is edited in L.B. Alberti, *Intercenali inediti*, ed. E. Garin (Florence, 1965) 77–82. On these *intercenali*—works intended to be read "inter cenam et pocula" see the considerations of Garin in his "Venticinque intercenali inedite e sconosciute di Leon Batista Alberti," *Belfagor* 19 (1964) 377–96; and for a translation and study of some *intercenali* see D. Marsh, *Dinner Pieces: A Translation of the "Intercenales"* (Binghamton, NY, 1987). For recent literature on Alberti see A. Grafton, *Commerce with the Classics: Ancient Books and Renaissance Readers*, Thomas Spencer Jerome Lectures, 20 (Ann Arbor, 1997) 53–92; and *idem, Leon Battista Alberti: Master Builder of the Italian Renaissance* (New York, 2000).

[56] Marsh, *Lucian and the Latins*, 59. Alberti may also have known the other work in which Lucian had had fun at Pythagoras' expense, *The Dream or the Cock*; cf. ibid., 60.

[57] Lucian, *Philosophies for Sale*, tr. by A.M. Harmon in the Loeb series (Cambridge, Mass., and London, 1960) 453.

[58] See ed. Garin, 81–2: "Te quidem admiramur atque ita de te iudicamus: si tam multa tamque varia, neque ea quidem iniocunda, ex tempore afferas, laudan-

Alberti's source for the symbols was. If we can accept that the "Philosophus" of the little dialogue is a stand-in for Alberti himself, he tells us, regarding the symbols: "I would not deny that I had thought out a great number of them, partly, in my leisure time and that, partly, they came to my attention extemporaneously, while I was speaking."[59] He goes on to say that he thinks his extemporizing was justifiable, whatever his fellow interlocutors and other scholarly types might think, since he did not want to seem a quitter, and since he wanted to gladden even more those who were delighted by his words.[60] This is completely in line with Alberti's style of reading—certainly *sui generis*—as Anthony Grafton has recently outlined it.[61] Alberti felt free to combine, recombine, and pick and choose at will when it came to quoting ancient texts. Thus, that his collection and usage of the precepts does not follow directly any known list should not surprise us.

Renaissance Florence and its Intellectual Currents: Marsilio Ficino and Angelo Poliziano

Alberti had approached the Pythagorean symbols relatively early in his career, probably not later than the mid-1440s. In the interim between that time and Ficino's appearance on the Florentine scene, much had occurred, so that scholars now recognize a remarkable diversity of interests in the intellectual life of late fifteenth-century Florence.[62] Numerous trends existed, but for the purposes of this

---

dum fore ingenium tuum. Si autem excogitata recitas, attribuendum id consuetudini tue censemus, quem [*leg.* quam?] nolumus ab ocio penitus abhorrere atque iccirco fieri, ut cum neque tibi semper maiora tractandi locus detur, tum te, ut liberali aliquo in negocio verseris, omnia etiam ridicula aggredi. Sed ne possumus quidem facere quin rideamus, si tu forte is es qui Pythagore dicta tuo arbitratu, rectene an inepte viderint alii, sis interpretatus, et non alios existimes seu audaces seu plane litteratos atque ingeniosos fore, qui tua aliter atque aliter sint accepturi."

[59] Ed. Garin, 82: "Non equidem negarim me pleraque istiusmodi partim in ocio excogitasse, partim mihi ex tempore inter dicendum in mentem convenisse . . ."

[60] Ed. Garin, 82: "que quidem vos, atque ceteri studiosi, quoquo pacto accepturi sitis, recte mecum actum arbitrabor, si id ero assecutus, ut et cessator minime videar, et eos qui meis rebus delectentur fecero iocundiores."

[61] Grafton, *Commerce*, 53–92, at 67–70 and *idem, Leon Battista Alberti*.

[62] Reexaminations of the "Age of Lorenzo" have been important in showing the diversity of late Quattrocento cultural life. As a start cf. Hankins, "Lorenzo de' Medici as a Patron of Philosophy" and the collected studies in ed. B. Toscani, *Lorenzo de' Medici: New Perspectives*, Studies in Italian Culture, 13 (New York, etc., 1993).

discussion, two are important. The first is represented by Ficino and his Neoplatonic approach; the second by Angelo Poliziano and his style of humanism. Ficino's approach gave dimension to Florentine prophetism and thus helped animate the Pythagorean symbols. Poliziano, however, given his radically different assumptions concerning the nature of intellectual discourse, continued the Lucianesque tendency to mock oracular symbolic discourse; he thus represents, on this score at least, a kind of anti-type to Ficino and the Ficinian tradition.

The humanist movement, with its non-philosophical focus on the *studia humanitatis*—a *mentalité* so aptly summarized in Poggio Bracciolini's remark, *philosophiae ars a me deest*—had continued, had, indeed, become central in the pedagogical formation of every educated Florentine.[63] But there was a certain strain in that movement, focusing increasingly on language and its potential, which did not appeal to all Florentine intellectuals. This is that strain—we might call it "rhetoric as a way of thought"—that the work of Valla had epitomized.[64] Poggio characterized those thinkers who partook of this strain as caring only for the "force of words." This was a dramatic step in the history of western thought, as language self-consciously became an intellectual instrument for a generation of thinkers.[65] The social con-

---

[63] On Poggio, see E. Walser, *Poggius florentinus: Leben und Werke* (Leipzig and Berlin 1914; repr. Hildesheim and New York, 1974); for Poggio and his relation with the new generation of humanists see the fine discussion in Field, *Origins*, 42–4 and the literature cited there, especially R. Sabbadini, *Storia del Ciceronianismo e di altre questioni letterarie nell'età della Rinascenza* (Turin, 1885). "Philosophiae ars a me deest" is from Poggio's letter to a certain Johannes Bartholomaeus (perh. Giovanni di Bartolomeo Guida) in Poggio, *Epistulae* 12.31 (Tonelli ed. 3.174–5; reprinted in Poggio Bracciolini, *Opera Omnia*, 3 vols., ed. R. Fubini in v.3).

[64] See R.G. Witt, "Medieval Italian Culture and the Origins of Humanism as a Stylistic Ideal," in A. Rabil, ed. *Renaissance Humanism: Foundations, Forms, and Legacy*, 3 vols. (Philadelphia, 1988) 1.31–2; for this tendency in Valla see C.S. Celenza, "Renaissance Humanism and the New Testament: Lorenzo Valla's Annotations to the Vulgate," *The Journal of Medieval and Renaissance Studies* 21 (1994) 33–52, at 33–5. On Valla in general see S.I. Camporeale, *Lorenzo Valla: Umanesimo e teologia* (Florence, 1972); and the literature in O. Besomi and M. Regoliosi, eds., *Lorenzo Valla e l'umanesimo italiano: Atti del convegno internazionale di studi umanistici (Parma, 18–19 ottobre 1984)* (Padua, 1986).

[65] Cf. N. Struever, *The Language of History in the Renaissance: Rhetorical and Historical Consciousness in Florentine Humanism* (Princeton, 1970); H.-B. Gerl, *Rhetorik als Philosophie: Lorenzo Valla* (Munich, 1974); R. Waswo, *Language and Meaning in the Renaissance* (Princeton, 1987); S. Camporeale, "*Repastinatio, liber primus*: retorica e linguaggio," in O. Besomi and M. Regoliosi, eds., *Lorenzo Valla e l'umanesimo italiano: Atti del convegno internazionale di studi umanistici (Parma, 18–19 ottobre 1984)* (Padua, 1986) 217–239; and J. Monfasani's critique, "Was Lorenzo Valla an Ordinary Language Philosopher?" in *Journal of the History of Ideas* 50 (1989) 309–323.

text of the humanist movement is important as well. From this perspective, one might argue that the humanist movement underwent
a twofold transition. First, as mentioned, it had been adopted into
standard pedagogy: all educated Florentines had wide exposure to
the *studia humanitatis*. Second, as a curricular focus, it had lost both
its novelty and its ideologically civic orientation.

Florentine humanism, that is, underwent a transition common to
many academic disciplines: it became highly specialized and more
concerned with philological minutiae. For scholars, of course, these
sorts of minutiae are of the essence—it is in the work of Poliziano
that one can see a classical philology with recognizably modern con-
tours. But for educated Florentines of the stamp of Alamanno Rinuccini
or Donato Acciaiuoli, it was not enough. They wanted an academic
discipline that would relate to the problems, real or imagined, that
they faced in their lives as leaders of the republic. And the coupling
of humanism and civic ideology had lost its edge. After a dramatic
and fractious 1450s (among whose many signal events were the peace
of Lodi, the ouster of the Medici, and their forceful reascendency
in 1458), the time was ripe for an ideology of love, friendship, and
harmony, which Marsilio Ficino helped develop.[66] It was not that
humanism "died out." Rather, it evolved in an increasingly more philologically technical direction and developed a disciplinary rivalry in the
city of Florence with Ficinian Neoplatonism. If we look ahead, the
work of Ficino itself evolved in a similar manner. As his Neoplatonism
became more and more abstract, intellectualized, and scholarly, the
clearer apocalyptic message of Savonarola grew in popularity. The
evolution of Ficino's own work was due, partly, perhaps, to political climate. As the Medici in fits and starts tightened their political
hold and widened their patronage ambitions, Ficino became more
speculative and technical and a much less public *medicus animorum*.

On the other hand, this was also partly a story of texts and of
battles over the canon. After translating only some of Plato's dialogues Ficino was led in the early 1460s to texts that would fuel a
lifelong interest in merging ritual and purely contemplative philosophy.
One of these was the *Corpus Hermeticum*, which, although it contained
little of what later ages would deem "philosophical," nonetheless gave
voice to a powerful vision of human efficacy.[67] He also encountered

---

[66] Field, *Origins*, *passim*.
[67] "Contained little": see B.P. Copenhaver, "Iamblichus, Synesius, and the Chaldaean
Oracles in Marsilio Ficino's *De vita libri tres*: Hermetic Magic or Neoplatonic Magic?"

in the early 1460s a set of texts that endorsed the notion that Pythagoras was thaumaturge, holy man, priest, and savior, and a figure
of central importance in the history of the unveiling of philosophy,
itself seen in soteriological terms; in short, Iamblichus' *De secta
Pythagorica*.[68] And this at a time when he was crafting, refining, penetrating the mysteries of the *prisca theologia*, the power of which he
was only then beginning to grasp. For Ficino's appreciation of
Pythagoras, the work of Iamblichus was especially important.[69]

The image of Pythagoras underwent a twofold evolution in Iamblichus' interpretations. First, in a multi-volume work we can call *On
Pythagoreanism*, Iamblichus (c. 245–c. 325) introduced the notion of
Pythagoras as a "divine guide." Pythagoras was sent down by the
gods with a soteriological mission: to save the souls of mankind.[70]
Second, in the same work, Iamblichus set out to provide an account
of Pythagoras and Pythagoreanism which would lead the soul from
lower to higher things, from the material to the immaterial, from the
mutable and inconstant to the constant and true: in short, from what
Iamblichus clearly believed was "less" Pythagorean to what was
"more" Pythagorean. For Iamblichus, to philosophize "in the Pythagorean manner" (Πυθαγορικῶς) meant one would "propound, not
contradictions, but firm and unchanging truths strengthened by

---

in eds. J. Hankins, J. Monfasani, and F. Purnell, *Supplementum Festivum: Studies in
Honor of Paul Oskar Kristeller* (Binghamton, 1987) 441–455; *idem*, "Scholastic Philosophy
and Renaissance Magic in the *De vita* of Marsilio Ficino," *Renaissance Quarterly* 37
(1984) 523–554; *idem*, "Renaissance Magic and Neoplatonic Philosophy: 'Ennead'
4.3–5 in Ficino's 'De vita coelitus comparanda," in Garfagnini, ed., *Marsilio Ficino
e il ritorno di Platone*, 2: 351–69; and *idem*, "Hermes Trismegistus, Proclus, and the
Question of a Philosophy of Magic in the Renaissance," in I. Merkel and A.G.
Debus, eds., *Hermeticism in the Renaissance: Intellectual History and the Occult in Early
Modern Europe* (Washington, D.C. and London, 1988) 79–110. "powerful vision": see
F. Yates, *Giordano Bruno and the Hermetic Tradition* (London, 1964); for the date of
Ficino's translation of the *Corpus Hermeticum*, 1463, see the testimonies collected in
Kristeller, *Suppl.* 1.CXXIX–CXXX.
    [68] On the early date of Ficino's paraphrases and partial translations of this work,
see the excellent study of S. Gentile, "Sulle prime traduzioni dal greco di Marsilio
Ficino," *Rinascimento*, 2nd series, 30 (1990) 57–104.
    [69] More on this in Celenza, "L'antiquité tardive"; *idem*, "Late Antiquity and
Florentine Platonism"; and *idem*, "Temi neopitagorici."
    [70] Iamblichus effected this new interpretation of Pythagoras perhaps to go one
step beyond Porphyry (234–c. 305)—the student, editor, and biographer of Plotinus
(205–269/70)—perhaps even to suggest Pythagoras as a pagan counterpoint to the
figure of Christ. See J. O'Meara, *Pythagoras Revived: Mathematics and Philosophy in Late
Antiquity* (Oxford, 1989) 213–15. O'Meara also presents a learned discussion of the
title of *On Pythagoreanism* and offers persuasive reasons for its adoption, at ibid., 30–5.

scientific demonstration through sciences (μαθημάτων) and contemplation (θεωρίας)."[71] In other words, Iamblichus strengthened the post-Platonic notion that the branches of knowledge which were concerned with immaterial reality were the most truly Pythagorean.[72]

The first four books of this (possibly) ten-volume work on Pythagoreanism have come down to us and were known to Ficino: *On the Pythagorean Life*, the *Protreptic to Philosophy*, *On General Mathematical Science*, and *On Nicomachus' Arithmetical Introduction*.[73] Books five through seven (*On Arithmetic in Physical Matters*, *On Arithmetic in Ethical Matters*, and *On Arithmetic in Theological Matters*) were known to and excerpted by the Byzantine polymath Michael Psellos (1018–78).[74] The rest of the books are lost.

To begin with the specific and move on to general considerations, the *Protrepticus* is the work which presents the fullest ancient listing of the symbols. The *Protrepticus* itself is structured as a three-stage series of exhortations. To use O'Meara's words, there is "a protreptic to philosophy in general, not restricted to a specific system (chapters 2–3); an intermediate protreptic mixing in the general with the Pythagorean (chapters 4–20); a final protreptic to the technical demonstrations of the Pythagoreans."[75] The listing of the symbols does not occur until the third stage. Iamblichus, then, saw the symbols as an important aspect of Pythagoreanism and one that was part of the inner workings of the Pythagorean tradition. (He presents the *Aurea verba* of Pythagoras, on the other hand, in the first, less advanced stage.) As noted above, Iamblichus' four-volume account of Pythagoreanism was one of the first Greek works in the Platonic tradition that Ficino approached in the early 1460s; and the prominent place Iamblichus accorded to the symbols must have been an important reason why Ficino and, consequently, Nesi became interested in them. There are

---

[71] Iamblichus, *Protrepticus*, ed. H. Pistelli (Stuttgart, 1888) 118.10–13. Trans. O'Meara, *Pythagoras Revived*, 42.

[72] O'Meara *Pythagoras Revived*, 44–52.

[73] Editions in Iamblichus, *De vita pythagorica*, ed. L. Deubner (Stuttgart, 1937). (Trans. G. Clark, Liverpool, 1989); *idem, Protrepticus*, ed. Pistelli; *idem, De communi mathematica scientia*, ed. N. Festa (Stuttgart, 1891); and *idem, In Nicomachi Arithmeticam introductionem*, ed. H. Pistelli (Stuttgart, 1894).

[74] On these see O'Meara, *Pythagoras Revived, passim* and *idem*, "New Fragments from Iamblichus' *Collection of Pythagorean Doctrines*," *American Journal of Philology* (1981) 26–40.

[75] O'Meara, *Pythagoras Revived*, 41; also cited by Thom in his *The Pythagorean Golden Verses*, 17.

also more general reasons why Iamblichus's presentation of the Pythagorean tradition is noteworthy. These have primarily to do with the soteriological resonances in the *De secta Pythagorica*, and the manner in which they fit Ficino's need to find and focus on soteriological figures in the history of the *prisca theologia*'s unveiling.

The first four books of the *De secta Pythagorica* present the first facet of the twofold Iamblichean refurbishing of Pythagoras mentioned above, i.e., the notion of Pythagoras as a divine guide sent by the gods (though, to be sure, not begotten by them). Pythagoras is spoken of as having been "sent down to men from Apollo's train," and we learn that the philosophy of the "divine Pythagoras ... was originally handed down from the Gods;" indeed, thanks to his projection of serenity and balance, all who met him in his youth and early travels were convinced that there was something of the divine in him; when his disciples wished to sleep, he could, using music, purify their minds and supply them with "pleasant, even prophetic, dreams," but he himself was far beyond the need for any such aids: "through some unutterable, almost inconceivable likeness to the gods, his hearing and mind were intent upon the celestial harmonies of the cosmos."[76]

A few things stand out, including Iamblichus' report of Pythagoras' self-identification with divinity, the oneirically soothing use of music, and especially, Pythagoras' soteriological status. If one widens the discussion a bit, one sees that among later Platonists in general, especially after Iamblichus, philosophy itself is seen to have different sorts of soteriological resonances. Hierocles, in his commentary on the Pythagorean *Golden Verses*, stressed the revelatory nature of philosophy and the notion that higher, more naturally pure souls communicated its messages to souls more weighed down by materiality.[77] Syrianus (whose views in this regard are preserved in Hermias' commentary on Plato's *Phaedrus*) presents Socrates as the figure sent down to save.[78] And in Proclus one sees repeatedly the notion that phi-

[76] See Iamblichus, *De vita pythagorica*, (I refer to chapters) 1; 2–3; and 15; trans. Clark.

[77] See Hierocles, *In Aureum Pythagoreorum carmen commentarius*, ed. F. Köhler (Stuttgart, 1974) and O'Meara, *Pythagoras Revived*, 109–18. As mentioned above, Hierocles' commentary was introduced to Quattrocento thinkers by the Sicilian born humanist Giovanni Aurispa (1376–1459). For an edition and translation of Aurispa's preface to his translation see App. 1.

[78] See Hermias, *In Platonis Phaedrum Scholia*, ed. P. Couvreur (Paris, 1901; repr. with additions by C. Zintzen, Hildesheim, 1971) and O'Meara, *Pythagoras Revived*, 119–41.

losophy is a revealed truth which "superior souls"—i.e., philosophers—are sent to reveal to the rest of humanity.[79]

Sociologically speaking, as Max Weber and, more recently, Garth
Fowden have recognized, the soteriological status which philosophy—
and often "Pythagorean" philosophy—had for the later Greek philosophers is part of an eschatological, salvationist *mentalité*, which intellectuals
removed from political power helped to create. The communities
into which these intellectuals gathered depended for their existence
on a central figure, a self-anointed holy man who through his charisma,
conviction, and miraculous deeds professed to be able to guide the
community.[80] One would shy away from making a total analogy, but
in the milieu in which Ficino lived, there was a perceived need for
a divinely inspired earthly guide, and there was a thinker, Ficino,
who sincerely believed he was that person, and who, perhaps in a
circular fashion, helped create and further the very eschatological
environment which he needed, as holy man, to have. It is hardly
stretching the bounds of historical imagination to suggest that Ficino,
in crafting his own prophetic image, looked toward what he knew
of Pythagoras, especially as this was mediated by his knowledge of
post-Plotinian Pythagoreanizing Neoplatonism, to which he had had

---

[79] See O'Meara, *Pythagoras Revived*, 142–55, esp. 155, where he cites Proclus, *In
Platonis Timaeum commentaria*, ed. E. Diehl (Leipzig, 1903–6) 3: 159.29–160.12.

[80] There is a penetrating discussion of the late-ancient environment in G. Fowden,
The Egyptian Hermes: A Historical Approach to the Late Ancient Pagan Mind (Cambridge,
1986; reissued with new preface, Princeton, 1993) esp. 186–95; following Max Weber
(cf. Weber, M., *Economy and Society: An Outline of Interpretive Sociology*, 2 vols., ed. and
trans. G. Roth C. Wittich, et al. [Berkeley, Los Angeles, and London, 1978] 1.500–06),
Fowden stresses the intellectuality of these movements (189): they taught salvation
through knowledge, so that they were not religions of the masses; and, however
acquired, this knowledge "was always the possession of an elite. Hence the tendency
within these milieux towards the emergence of a two-tier structure, with a small group
of teachers, the 'elect' or the 'zealots,' taking responsibility for the instruction of a
much larger group of what the Platonists and Manichaeans appropriately called 'listeners.'" This is similar to the distinction in ancient Pythagoreanism between the
mathematikoi, the learned, and the *akousmatikoi*, the listeners. Fowden argues that,
except for the Manichaeans, "the others were completely dependent for their coming into being, their validation and their coherence on the powerful personalities
of individual holy men. This we see most clearly among the Platonists, in Porphyry's
biography of Plotinus and in Eunapius' lives of Iamblichus and his followers." Also
see 190: "One of the reasons for this late antique obsession with the holy man was
the wide acceptance of the Pythagorean view of philosophy as a religion and a way
of life as much as an intellectual system.... In the biographies of Pythagoras written by Porphyry and Iamblichus we see the ideal which these last Platonists strove
towards, a life of worship, prayer and discussion shared among like-minded men
in what was almost the atmosphere of a religious community."

an early introduction and which, one might argue, had a formative
influence on his intellectual outlook and self-perception.[81] For a time
his prophetic self-fashioning bore fruit in the larger community. As
Vasoli has pointed out, in 1477 Ficino was seen to have predicted
the war and plague of the following year, based on the miraculous
power of certain relics; in 1480 he advised Lorenzo de'Medici on
the basis of a dangerous constellation; and he often foretold the horo-
scopes of his friends.[82] In the early part of his career Ficino saw
himself as a Iamblichean/Pythagorean holy man and was for a time
at least accepted in this self-defined role.

When he first approached the figure of Pythagoras as *vates* and
the Pythagorean injunctions, it is through this lens that Ficino saw
things. His thoughts on the symbols were colored by his deep veneration and appreciation of the Pythagorean tradition and date to
the same period, the early 1460s, which I have discussed. Important
for the purposes of this study is that Ficino took them seriously at
an early stage in his career, when he was building his reputation in
Florence. A look at his treatments of certain symbols will offer insight
to his manner of approaching them. He took them seriously as *monumenta* of the *prisca theologia* tradition, suggesting in his *De christiana
religione* that the symbols bore similarities to some of the precepts of
Moses.[83] In his commentary on pseudo-Dionyisius's *Divine Names*,
Ficino wrote that Plato suggests it is characteristic of a wise man to
understand many things with few words—"this is why Hippocrates
composed Aphorisms, Pythagoras composed symbols, and Solomon,
Proverbs."[84] For Ficino, the Pythagorean symbols are important both

---

[81] Hankins ("The Myth," esp. 443) has shown that Ficino was wary of calling
people whom he respected highly or who had risen to prominence his "students"—
auditores. One recalls that the ancient Pythagoreans were divided into two groups,
the *akousmatikoi*, or "listeners," who had to remain in that silent status for five years,
and the *mathematikoi*, or the "learned." The Latin equivalent of *akousmatikoi* would
of course be *auditores* (i.e., the word's primary meaning is "listener"); Hankins argues
(ibid.) that Ficino uses this term to refer to "those with whom Ficino had once
stood in some sort of pedagogic relationship," while reserving the term *confabulatores*
("conversation partners," loosely) for those who were older or to whom he wished to
show especial respect. It is tempting to speculate that Ficino uses the term *auditor* in
the Pythagorean manner, to refer to those who are still at a lower doctrinal level.
[82] See C. Vasoli, "L'attesa della nuova era in ambienti e gruppi fiorentini del
Quattrocento" in *L'attesa dell'età nuova nella spiritualità della fine del medioevo*, Convegni
del centro di studi sulla spiritualità medievale, 3 (Todi, 1962) 370–432, at 381–3.
[83] *De christiana religione*, ch. 34 (*Op.* 69): "Alia [i.e., praecepta Mosis] rursus ad cere-
monias, quae quidem parvi momenti sunt, nam tamquam figurae quaedam Pythagoricorum simbulorum instar, ad alium portendendum, significandumque referuntur."
[84] *Commentary to the Divine Names* (*Op.* 1049–50): "Plato in Protagora scribit, antiquo-

because they allow the communication of matters of great sapiential moment with brevity and because they are part of the venerable tradition of "veiling" wisdom and concealing secret meaning.

The Pythagorean tradition is often close by when purgation is discussed: it is "by means of Pythagorean ritual" that wise youths purge their minds of the senses and ascend the hierarchy of academic disciplines, Ficino writes in the *De christiana religione*.[85] And it was Pythagoras—"whom our Plato honored in all things"—who "used to lay the groundwork for the sacred mysteries of his teachings with a most acute purification of the mind."[86] Thus when Ficino comes across the symbols "Do not urinate against the sun" and "do not pare your fingernails during sacrifice," a discussion of purgation is inevitable:

> Urinating is purging; cutting your fingernails, too, is removing worthless superfluities from yourself. Do not put off purgation and loosening[87] till that time when you must look at the sun and contemplate sacred, that is divine, things. For it is more important to purge oneself and get rid of superfluities than it is to tire your concentration in the matters to which you are attending.[88]

The real aim of purgation, of course, for Ficino and for Neoplatonists in general, is to allow one to free the soul from the confines of the body and travel along the Neoplatonic ἄνοδος, the "way up" on the great return to divinity. This takes discipline, and Ficino's interpretation of the following symbol makes this clear. The saying runs: "Nourish the cock, but do not sacrifice him, since he is sacred to

---

rum doctrinam nihil aliud fuisse, quam breviloquium quoddam; idque esse viri absolute sapientis, paucis videlicet multa complecti. Hac ratione Hippocrates composuit Aphorismos, Pythagoras quoque symbola, et Proverbia Salomon. Quo enim altior intellectus est in angelis, eo formis paucioribus plura comprehendit et agit."

[85] From *De christiana religione*, ch. 3, "Caveant adolescentes ne facile de religione sententiam ferant." (*Op.* 3): "Alii [i.e., the wise youths] vero propter mansuetudinem et modestiam, Pythagoreo ritu mentem purgant a sensibus per morales, physicas, mathematicas, metaphysicas disciplinas, ne tanquam superiores illi, lippos adhuc oculos in divinum Solem subito dirigentes, caligari cogantur, sed gradatim progredientes."

[86] From the *Argumentum in Epistolam secundam Platonis* (*Op.* 1531): "Propterea Pythagoras, quem Plato noster in omnibus venerantur, sacra doctrinarum mysteria ab exactissima expiatione mentis exordiebatur. . . ."

[87] Of the bowels—Ficino is nothing if not holistic.

[88] *Suppl.*, 2.100–1: "Ad Solem conversus ne mingas. Iuxta sacrificium ne incidas ungues. Mingere est purgari, incidere ungues etiam est abmovere abs te superflua et vilia. Ne differas purgationem et solutionem ad id tempus, quo sol inspiciendus est et sacra contemplanda idest divina. Prius enim oportet se purgasse et incidisse superflua, quam ad ea tendas et in illis intentionem fatiges."

the sun and the moon."[89] In his treatment Ficino argues that this symbol suggests the ability of the human mind to foresee future events in dreams, and presents a comment on the powers of the soul. "There is a certain power of the soul," he writes, "which by a kind of affinity of celestial bodies and spirits is often summoned in such a fashion that it may predict the future." He goes on:

> Still, it is a recognition which is sometimes so confused and ambiguous that one can scarcely affirm what it predicts. This is the source of auguries in dreams, of various sorts of visions, of mutations of souls. For sometimes the mind, foreknowing of evil, seems to instill grief, but foreknowledge of good seems to instill a certain happiness.[90]

Ficino goes on to give examples of foreknowledge, from Socrates' intuition that Plato would be a good student to the reputed instances of prescience of Pherecydes of Syros and the Severan emperor Aurelius Alexander. From these instances, Ficino continues,

> one can easily gather that a certain power of the soul is present, a certain thinking about the heavens from which these matters must be thought to depend, by means of which thinking [the soul] may perceive all or at least most of those things which are either to come or which are far from it in the past.[91]

One does not always understand the things predicted and does not even always know one has this power. But "when the spirit is tran-

---

[89] Ficino's translation (from MS Vatican City, Biblioteca Apostolica Vaticana, Vat. Lat. 5953) f.48: "Gallum nutrias quidem, non tamen sacrifices. Lune enim ac soli dedicatus est." Ficino does not reproduce this *akousma* in its entirety in the *Commentariolus*, i.e., at ff.317–8, which Kristeller edits (*Suppl.*, 2.101–2). On cocks as solar birds, see Ficino, *De vita*, ed. and trans. Kaske and Clark, 3.13 and 14, cit. in M.J.B. Allen, "Summoning Plotinus: Ficino, Smoke, and the Strangled Chickens," in M.A. DiCesare, ed., *Reconsidering the Renaissance* (Binghamton, NY, 1992) 63–88 (now in Allen, *Plato's Third Eye* #XIV) 85 n.52; see also the literature cited there. On the antiquity of the symbolic use of the white cock, see Cumont, F., "Le coq blanc des Mazdéens et les Pythagoriciens." *Académie des Inscriptions et Belles-Lettres: Comptes rendus* (Paris, 1942) 284–300.

[90] *Suppl.*, 2.101: "Est vis quedam anime que cognatione quadam celestium corporum et spirituum sepe ita cietur ut futura presagiat. Est tamen agnitio illa interdum ita confusa atque ambigua ut vix quid presagiat affirmare quis possit. Inde somniorum auguria, inde visionum species, inde animorum mutationes. Nam interdum mali mens presaga merorem, boni autem prescientia [presentia *cod.*] letitiam quandam infundere videtur." I have translated in accordance with Kristeller's suggestion of "prescientia" for "presentia" at *Suppl.*, 2.103 n.2.

[91] *Suppl.*, 2.101: "Ex his facile colligi potest vim quandam inesse anime ex celestium unde hec dependere putanda sunt cogitatione aliqua, qua vel omnia vel saltem pleraque eorum sentiat que vel futura sunt vel ab ea longe remota . . ."

quil and removed from anxious cares and stimuli, which happens to
a great extent during sleep, the spirit thoroughly senses certain movements of related causes." "And so," he goes on, "I think that this
power of the soul is what is meant by the cock, for such is its nature.
By it, it measures time and senses changes in the times themselves
to such an extent that it is never wrong."[92]

Ficino alludes to scriptural passages from the Book of Job and from
Matthew, thus strengthening his case for the power of the cock.[93]
"Therefore," Ficino says, "it is a good thing to nourish this power."
One can do this by living "so that one's spirit is tranquil and removed
from turbulent cares, so that it can finally sense the celestial motions."
He integrates the injunction of the symbol not to sacrifice the cock
by saying that the cock "must not be sacrificed, because this power
[of the cock] is a natural power and so sacrifice [i.e., religious ritual]
would have no merit."[94] Ficino is thus careful to separate the provinces
of traditional religion and natural magic, at least at this presumably
early stage in his career. In the symbol it was said that the cock
should not be sacrificed because it is sacred to the sun and the moon.
Ficino says that the sun symbolizes "the divine power and fount of
all other light and wisdom of which prophecy is characteristic." As
for the moon, it "is the mind of the prophets which prophesies what
it does all the more exactly and certainly, the more it is filled by
the light of the sun itself."[95] Ficino uses the Pythagorean tradition

---

[92] Ibid.: "Cum tamen animus tranquillus est curis anxiis stimulisque solutus, quod
in somnis plerumque contingit, motus quosdam causarum cognatarum persentit.
Hanc anime vim per gallum significari ideo arbitror, quia galli ea natura est, qua et
tempora metiatur et ipsorum temporum mutationes ita sentiat, ut nunquam fallatur."

[93] These are: Job 38.36 (Vulgate): "quis posuit in visceribus hominis sapientiam
vel quis dedit gallo intelligentiam." Mt. 26.34 (where Jesus makes the prediction)
and 26.74–5 (speaking of Peter): "tunc coepit detestari et iurare quia non novisset
hominem et continuo gallus cantavit. Et recordatus est Petrus verbi Iesu quod dix-
erat, 'priusquam gallus cantet ter me negabis,' et egressus foras ploravit amare."

[94] *Suppl.*, 2.102: "Hanc igitur vim nutrire bonum est. Nutritur autem si ita vivamus ut sit tranquillus et a turbulentis curis solutus animus, adeo ut motus sentire
celestes denique valeat. Non tamen sacrificandus est, quia naturalis est hec vis,
quapropter nullum meritum habiturum [habitura *cod.*] est sacrificium." I have translated in accordance with Kristeller's suggested emendation of "habitura" to "habiturum," at *Suppl.*, 2.103 n.8.

[95] *Suppl.*, 2.102: "Soli quoque et lune dicatus dicitur, quia per Solem divina vis
alternique luminis ac sapientie [finis] fons designatur, cuius proprie est vaticinium.
Luna vero mens vatum est que tanto exactius certiusque vaticinatur, quanto solis
ipsius lumine plenior est." I have translated in accordance with Kristeller's suggested deletion of "finis" at *Suppl.*, 2.103 n.9.

here, then, to discuss oneiric prophecy and the seemingly prophetic, often confused inklings people have regarding the future. Along the way he engages in a discussion of the soul's power and urges moderation, which is itself achievable by Pythagorean purgation.

Ficino's approach to this and to the few other symbols he treated was colored by his overall vatic image of Pythagoras. Ficino himself did not offer any lengthy, systematic commentary on the symbols in which he had taken an early interest. Still, his influence was felt. Perhaps one can imagine the situation by making an analogy to present-day scholarship: a senior scholar might write a short article on a little-studied topic, drawing attention to its importance; his student then writes a dissertation on that topic, explicating it and fleshing out more nuances. But it is the impetus of the senior figure that is crucial in bringing the selected topic to the notice of others. Based on his reading of certain Neopythagoreanizing Neoplatonists and his absorption of their view of the Platonic tradition, Ficino helped craft a vatic sensibility in Florence, a cultural matrix where the figure of Pythagoras was one lens through which one could examine crucial intellectual issues. Yet he did not offer protracted or systematic commentary on the Samian's mysterious dicta. It was natural that Ficino's pupils and scholarly followers would develop interest in the symbols, an interest thoroughly different in kind from Alberti's lively antiquarianism. Prophecy, dreams, mysterious injunctions in need of *explicatio*: these would leave a lasting legacy in the city of Florence.

Ficino's influence was felt throughout the Florentine intellectual community. Interestingly, in a number of cases where Ficino treats the symbols, the language of his treatment and that of Antonio degli Agli in his *Explanatio symbolorum Pythagore* is too similar to be mere coincidence.[96] Agli, the Florentine prelate and eventual bishop of Volterra, is thus another possible background source for the *Symbolum nesianum*.[97] Therefore, it will be useful to enter into a brief exami-

---

[96] Correspondences discussed in Swogger, 64–75, though he assumes Agli's priority throughout.

[97] An edition and English translation of this text has been provided, as mentioned above, by Swogger, in his University of London dissertation. On Agli, see Swogger, 16–30, and N.H. Minnich, "The Autobiography of Antonio degli Agli (ca. 1400–77), Humanist and Prelate," in eds. A. Morrough et al., *Renaissance Studies in Honor of Craig Hugh Smyth*, 2 vols., Villa I Tatti Studies, 7 (Florence, 1985) 1.177–91, and the literature cited there.

nation of the interrelation of the approaches of Agli and Ficino to the symbols. In contrast to Swogger, I intend to argue that Agli's work is dependent on Ficino.

Agli, along with Lorenzo Pisano and perhaps Niccolò Tignosi, was one of Ficino's early scholastic mentors.[98] Some light can be shed on their relationship by a glance at Agli's *De mystica statera*, a treatise still present only in manuscript (in the same Naples manuscript, in fact, in which his *Explanatio symbolorum Pythagore* is contained).[99] The *De mystica statera* is a dialogue, and Agli has cast himself and Ficino in the roles of *magister* and *discipulus*, respectively. Throughout "Antonius" exhorts "Fecinus" to remember that Christian studies are to be placed before pagan studies, that Fecinus should "leave Plato and others of his sort behind."[100] Agli, like other mentors of Ficino, was worried about Ficino's deep interest in the more recondite aspects of the Platonic tradition. As to the connections between Ficino's treatment of the symbols and Agli's *Explanatio symbolorum Pythagore*, the salient question concerning the *De mystica statera* is its dating, for it appears prior to Agli's *Explanatio* in what seems to be an autograph author's copy book. Since the *De mystica statera* appears before the *Explanatio*, Swogger suggests that the date of the *De mystica statera*, if it can be established securely, is a *terminus ante quem* for the *Explanatio*. In other words, for Swogger, the order in which the treatises appear in the manuscript represents the order of their composition. As to dating, Swogger places the *De mystica statera* in the years 1455–57, though he offers no evidence for this other than that the dialogue seems to be written in a familiar tone and that the two men had to have known each other by the mid-fifties.[101] He thus

---

[98] See Field, *The Origins*, 129–74. On the lack of secure documentation for Tignosi as an early mentor of Ficino see D.A. Lines, "'Faciliter Edoceri': Niccolò Tignosi and the Audience of Aristotle's 'Ethics' in Fifteenth-Century Florence," *Studi medievali*, 3rd series, 40 (1999) 139–68, esp. 143–4.

[99] MS Naples BN VIII. F. 9; the *De mystica statera* is at ff.19–33.

[100] Ibid., f.33: "Ad hanc [*sc.* dei scientiam] itaque Platone aliisque huiusmodi relictis convertere te non differas." Cit. Field, *The Origins*, 174 n.163.

[101] Swogger, 152–3, n. 189: "Della Torre says (p. 775) [a propos of Ficino's and Agli's acquaintanceship] 'fin dai tempi di Cosimo,' i.e., about 1460–64. But our dating of the *De mystica statera*, in the discussion which follows, puts this date back into the early 1450s. The dating of the friendship between Agli and Ficino from the early 1450s (that is, approximately 1453–54) rests on the following considerations: 1. The *De mystica statera* was written between 1455 and 1457, by which time the two men had to be well acquainted, in order to account for the friendly tone of the remarks in the essay and this suggests a period of at least three years (or

suggests that Agli's comment on the symbols dates slightly prior to that period, thereby assuming that Ficino had learned Greek well enough by then to have done a preliminary translation of Iamblichus or at least of the symbols, and that Agli worked from that translation.[102]

Ultimately, however, only one positive piece of evidence is produced: the fact that Agli there uses what seems to be an early spelling of Ficino's name, *Fecinus*, as opposed to *Ficinus*. Still, barring any other evidence, it seems disingenuous to assume that the use of an early spelling means that the dialogue must itself have been written early, especially as early as the mid 1450s. The early spelling might simply be an indication that Agli set the dramatic date of the dialogue in the fourteen-fifties. What better way for Agli to reassert some authority over an errant Ficino than by using a name which would have recalled their earlier mentor/student relationship?[103]

As to the overlaps between Ficino's and Agli's treatment of the symbols, it is more plausible that Ficino's brief treatments came first and that Agli is echoing Ficino, rather than vice versa. In my view Agli's intention was to provide a more thorough, but also more

---

approximately 1452–1454); 2. The *Explanatio symbolorum Pythagore* of Agli was written about 1455, and the two men seem to have collaborated on it, so they must have talked about it for perhaps a year or so previous to its completion (or since approximately 1454 or 1453); 3. My thesis presumes that Agli got his Latin translation of Iamblichus from Ficino . . ., who according to Kristeller began his formal Greek studies . . . about 1456 or perhaps even earlier . . ., and the short gnomic sayings of Pythagoras would have made good beginning material for exercises in translation." In other words, Swogger dates the *De mystica statera* to 1455–1457 because the two men "had" to be well acquainted by then, and he dates their acquaintanceship to the early 1450s because the *De mystica statera* was written in 1455–1457 and shows by its tone that the two men must have been friends!

[102] The argument about Ficino's knowledge of Greek is difficult to accept, as is the assumption regarding the order of composition of the various treatises. What if, instead of having composed the treatises in the order in which they are present in the manuscript, Agli was simply preparing a final draft copy before having them all professionally copied by a scribe?

[103] Moreover, Agli would use this form of Ficino's name at least as late as 1464 in a letter of consolation he wrote to Piero de'Medici on the death of Cosimo il Vecchio. See MS Florence Biblioteca Laurenziana, 54.10, f.132: "En Marsilius Fecinus noster magna indole iuvenis adest testis . . .," cit. in Hankins, "Cosimo de' Medici and the 'Platonic Academy,'" 146, n.6. In addition in a later biography of Savonarola by the ps.-Burlamacchi, Ficino is referred to as Fecino; see ed. P. Ginori Conti, *La vita del Beato Ieronimo Savonarola scritta da un anonimo del sec XVI e già attribuita a Fra Pacifico Burlamacchi, pubblicata secondo il codice ginoriano* (Florence, 1937) 78–80, and 86. As support for the idea that "Fecinus" was an early spelling of Ficino's name, Swogger at 103 n.205 cites a private communication of P.O. Kristeller through Charles Schmitt. However, Kristeller later found Swogger's assignment of priority to Agli dubious; see *Marsilio Ficino and His Work*, 137.

orthodox treatment than that found in Ficino's brief, scattered musings. Agli's preface to the *Explanatio* gives us clues about his inten-
tions. He is there at pains to tell us how he feels about Pythagoras.
Having come across the *Symbola* and gone over them carefully, he
decided to explain them. But he was deterred: the symbols were
obscure, and in their construction they were fictions, unusual and
unheard of.[104] Although Pythagoras was a "man outstanding in intelligence and learning," he was a man whom Agli

> could not regard with respect and admiration. For even though, as
> blessed Ambrose testified, Pythagoras was Jewish by birth and was, in
> his soul, a worshipper of the one God, he nevertheless denied the true
> religion and began both to worship pagan gods and, finally, to preach
> countless grandiose marvels about himself.[105]

Pythagoras was not ashamed to pretend, even to lie, that he had
received the soul of Euphorbus and descended to the underworld.
The Pythagorean silence, the lecturing in the dark—all of this
Pythagorean flummery was to Agli material unsuitable for a philosopher, and characteristic rather of a vendor or actor, than of a philosopher.[106] Hating Pythagoras, as is his due, we can still study his sayings,
since by all accounts he was very learned. Moreover, if we understand that his outstanding sayings were the ones he learned from
Jewish philosophers, then studying Pythagoras' work presents us with
no insuperable problems.[107]

---

[104] I cite from the edition of Swogger and give in parentheses the folio number
of the Naples manuscript (the translations of Agli are my own, though I have consulted Swogger's); 194, 3–6 (f.1): "Cum in quedam Pithagore enigmata incidissem,
que symbola appellantur, eaque semel et bis et percurrissem et animo demum
mecum accuratius discussissem, explanare eorum aliqua postremo decrevi. Licet illorum tum obscuritas tum figurarum insolita inauditaque figmenta admodum me
absterrerent . . ."

[105] Ed. Swogger, 194, 8–14 (f.1): ". . . huc etiam accedebat, ut hominem, tametsi
ingenio ac doctrina prestantem, nec revereri possem nec diligere. Cum enim, teste
beato Ambrosio, et genere Hebreus et singularis Dei cultor anima exstitisset, vera
tum tamen religione abnegata et gentium deos colere et innumera grandiaque de
se miracula predicare denique cepit." Ficino, *Op.*, 30, also notes Ambrose's belief
that Pythagoras was born to Jewish parents. Cf. also S.K. Heninger, *Touches of Sweet
Harmony*, 229.

[106] Ed. Swogger, 194, 19–28 (f.1): "Animas enim defunctorum in varia corpora
transcribi perpetuo affirmabat; se autem Troiani Euforbii animam sortitum et assere-
bat, at ad inferos descendisse semel se fingere ac mentiri non verebatur. Silentium
quoque discere ab eo incipientibus quinquennium indicebat; in tenebris etiam ne a
discipulis cerneretur docere consuevit. Alia insuper huiuscemodi plurima faciebat,
que non philosophi, sed circulatoris potius cuiusdam atque histrionis fuisse videri
possent. . . ."

[107] Ed. Swogger, 196, 2–11 (f.1): ". . . cum omni doctrinarum genere excultum

Throughout, Agli offers interpretations of the symbols which are reflective of a traditional but learned cleric who was an "uomo dotto et di buona coscientia," as Vespasiano da Bisticci called him.[108] There is a heavy dose of biblical authorities as well as scholastic style exegesis in Agli's work; where he departs from these sorts of interpretations and ventures into more esoteric territory he almost always overlaps with Ficino or "corrects" Ficino. Two examples will suffice. Ficino examines the precept "nudis pedibus adora"—"worship with naked feet."[109] His discussion is as follows:

> Worship with naked feet. Moses was also once ordered to take off his shoes, since the place where he was, was holy land. Also, the Lord's disciples were ordered not to wear shoes when they were sent out to preach. Also Mohammed ordered his followers to enter the temple without shoes.[110]

Ficino's and Agli's first two sentences are exactly alike.[111] The first treats an Old Testament figure, Moses, who had endorsed this notion as well, the second offers a parallel from the New Testament. Ficino's third and final sentence, however, brings up a reference to Mohammed; this Agli scrupulously avoids.[112] Ficino's comment ends there, at the third sentence; Agli goes on in a moralistic vein for another page.

The second example concerns the symbol mentioned above, treated by Ficino: "Nourish the cock, but do not sacrifice him, since he is sacred to the sun and the moon." One recalls that Ficino's expli-

expolitumque fuisse constet, homine prout meritus est contempto, ad ipsius doctrine prestantiam animum intendamus. Non enim philosophorum solum, sed et Hebreorum dogmata didicisse putandus. Quo fit ut haud quaquam mirum sit, eum aliqua seu invenisse seu ab aliis accepisse, que et lectione et existimatione digna videantur; inter que nonnulla horum symbolorum eius preclara esse forsan iudicanda, que ab Hebreorum sapientibus didicisse credenda sunt."

[108] Vespasiano Da Bisticci, *Le vite*, 2 vols., ed. A. Greco (Florence, 1970) 1.295–7, at 295. Vespasiano also says that Agli (ibid.) "fu dottissimo in greco et in latino," though Agli himself admits in his autobiography that he never learned Greek well (see Minnich, "The Autobiography," 181).

[109] *Suppl.* 2.100. This is Nesi's symbol 31: "Nudis pedibus rem divinam facito."

[110] Ibid.: "Nudis pedibus adora. Etiam calciamenta deponere olim Moysi preceptum est, eo quod locus in quo tum erat terra sancta esset. Item discipuli Domini cum ad predicandum mitterentur, ne calciamenta ferrent iussi sunt. Item Machomet precepit suis ut sine calciamentis templum ingrederentur."

[111] Agli, ed. Swogger, 200 (f.2): "Calciamenta deponere a Deo olim Moysi preceptum, eo quod locus in quo tum erat terra sancta esset. Discipuli rursus Domini, cum ad predicandum mitterentur, ne calciamenta ferrent iussum accepimus."

[112] For Ficino and Mohammed see also Ficino's *De christiana religione*, 12 (*Op.* 1:17–18) on "Christi authoritas apud Mahumethenses."

cation of this symbol became a complex, extended comment on prophecy and prophetic powers which this symbol seemed to him to represent. His discussion ranged from Socrates, to Pherecydes, to the Egyptians, to scripture. Agli's treatment is an exact replica of Ficino's throughout.[113] Exact, that is, except in one respect: the sentence with which it begins. "Hoc equidem symbolum ignorare me fateor"—"I confess I really don't understand this symbol."

Agli died in 1477. In the years after his death Florentine intellectual life moved in a number of different directions. Part of this had to do with the institutional possibilities available to late Quattrocento Florentine intellectuals. During the lifetime of Bruni (who died in 1444), the rhetorically focused humanist movement had been compelled to exist outside of traditional institutions of higher learning; broadly speaking, there was no traditional place for humanist intellectuals in a university context. Their discipline being new, they were compelled to seek outside support as courtiers, secretaries, and pedagogues. Some succeeded, some did not.[114] During the fifteen-forties, fifties, and sixties, however, humanism made inroads into university life in Florence, despite the financial troubles of the Florentine *Studio*.[115] Pedagogically, by this point an education in the *studia humanitatis* was standard for all educated Florentines; it had lost its novelty.[116] And research in the fields of the humanities had changed from the early Quattrocento, primarily because of three factors: the accelerated development of semi-public libraries, the advent of printing, and the evolution of a new and different—"Gellian"—sort of commentary, whose principal exponent was Angelo Poliziano.[117]

---

[113] Agli, ed. Swogger, 232–6 (ff.7v–8v).

[114] For one who did not succeed, but documented much of the method a young humanist might employ to gain patronage at the papal court in the fourteen-thirties, see C.S. Celenza, *Renaissance Humanism and the Papal Curia: Lapo da Castiglionchio the Younger's* De curiae commodis (Ann Arbor, 1999).

[115] Cf. J. Davies, *Florence and its University during the Early Renaissance*, Education and Society in the Middle Ages and Renaissance, 8 (Leiden, Boston, Cologne, 1998) 6 (commenting on the hitherto little studied period in the history of the *Studio* from 1450–73): "It is now evident that a major shift occurred in the structure of teaching at the *Studio* with more money being spent on arts than on law and medicine." In 1473 the Florentine university was reorganized and partially moved to Pisa. For the period from 1473–1503 see the monumental study of Verde, *Lo studio*.

[116] It was in the 1430s and beyond, Davies argues, "that members of the Florentine ruling class began in earnest to arrange such educations [i.e., in the *studia humanitatis*] for their sons." see Davies, *Florence and its University*, 7; see also 106–24; and 201–5.

[117] Grafton, *Scaliger*, 1.14–22; for various developments in Renaissance styles of

We have, then, Ficino the holy man and his oracular approach on the one hand. On the other, we have the figure of Angelo Poliziano, the great philologist and for many years professor at the Florentine university. In Poliziano's 1479 preface to his translation of the handbook of Epictetus (*Epicteti enchiridion*), Poliziano suggests that the language of the *Enchiridion* is "wholly efficacious and full of energy;" he avers that the style of the *Enchiridion* is one that "shares secret knowledge [*conscius*], is pellucid, and spurns any rhetorical ornament;" in that respect, it is "wholly similar to the precepts of the Pythagoreans."[118] It is clear, at this stage—that is, at a time which is for Poliziano early in his career—that he too is taking the symbols seriously, as expressions, that is, of an ancient wisdom, even if that ancient wisdom does not resonate especially well with him.

What a difference in 1492. As the academic year began, all professors customarily gave an introductory lecture to the topic they were to treat that year. Poliziano was to teach—by his own design, one suspects—one of Aristotle's logical works, the *Prior Analytics*.[119] In his *praelectio*, he was determined to separate himself from the philosophers, who, he said, sneered at him and his style of work and

---

commentary see the studies collected in eds. A. Buck and O. Herding, *Der Kommentar in der Renaissance*, Kommission für Humanismusforschung, Mitteilung I (Bonn, 1975).

[118] From the 1498 unpaginated *Opera Omnia* (Venice: Aldus Manutius): "Sermo autem in eo omnino efficax est atque energiae plenus; et in quo mira sit ad permovendum vis. Suos enim quivis affectus in eo agnoscit. Adque eos emendandos, ceu quodam aculeo excitatur. Omnia vero ordinem inter sese mirum habent, omnibusque veluti lineis, quamvis in plura id opus capita sit distinctum, ad excitandum rationalem animum, quasi ad ipsum centrum contendunt, ut is et suae dignitatis curam habeat et propriis actionibus secundum naturam utatur. Stilus autem qualem res postularet, conscius est, dilucidus, quique omnem respuat ornatum; Pythagoreorumque praeceptis, quas illi Diathecas vocant, quam simillimus. Hoc ego opus cum latinum facere eggrederer, ut indultu a te nobis huius tam suavis ocii rationem aliquam redderem, in duo omnino mendosissima exemplaria incidi, pluribusque locis magna ex parte mutilata. . . ." For the date of the preface see I. Maier, *Ange Politien: La formation d'un poète humaniste* (1469–1480) (Geneva, 1966) 372–380 and 422, where she suggests that Poliziano translated the *Enchiridion Epicteti* between June-August, 1479.

[119] Poliziano's interest in logic dated back at least to 1480, if not earlier; in 1480 Francesco di Tommaso, a Dominican who belonged to the convent of Santa Maria Novella, dedicated his *De negocio logico* to Poliziano. The treatise, in dialogue form, was intended to explain the problem of universals as presented in Porphyry's *Isagoge* (itself an explanation of part of Aristotle's *Organon*), and was written in response to a request by Poliziano. See J. Hunt, *Politian and Scholastic Logic: An Unknown Dialogue by a Dominican Friar*, Quaderni di "Rinascimento," 25 (Florence, 1995), who edits the treatise and offers an important introduction at 3–46. For Poliziano's desire, as reported by di Tommaso, see the preface at 49–50.

thought him unqualified to teach philosophy. Concerned to distance himself from the "philosophers," he now prefers the title of "grammarian" (*grammaticus*). In this little treatise he takes aim, most assuredly, at the traditional enemies of Renaissance humanists: scholastic, Aristotelian philosophers. But his treatment of the figure of Pythagoras and the Pythagorean sayings reveals that he was trying to separate himself not only from the Aristotelians, but from the Platonists as well. "I have certainly heard," he writes with mock seriousness,

> that there was once a Samian, a certain teacher of the youth, always well-dressed and with a fine head of hair, notable, too, for his thigh of gold, who was born often, and reborn. And his name was "he himself,"—he was certainly called that by his disciples. Now he would silence these disciples, as he welcomed each one. But if you hear the sayings of "he himself," I know you're going to dissolve with laughter. But let me tell you about them anyway.[120]

He goes on to give an account replete with jokes about beans, quips about Pythagorean reincarnation, and sarcastic comments concerning Pythagoras' abilities to communicate with animals. Pythagoras, to Poliziano, is, in Lucianesque fashion, a "professor and cheap salesman of a perversely imagined wisdom."[121] It is as if Poliziano is sending up all those who would falsely claim special, supernatural powers for themselves. By the early 1490s, in the eyes of many of the intellectual elite, there is room in Florence for only one vatic individual. For Poliziano and other intellectuals, this is Girolamo Savonarola. In Poliziano's ridicule of the seriousness and veneration in which some held Pythagoras and his sayings, it is apparent that he is taking aim in a subtle way at Ficino and his style of thought as well.

We see then the "Alexandrian" maturation of the philologically sophisticated Florentine humanism on the one hand and, on the other, an increasingly sterile and intellectualized Platonism which had surpassed its socially integrative usefulness.[122] Ficino's attempt at merging the

---

[120] Poliziano, *Lamia*, 4.21–6: "Audivi equidem Samium fuisse olim quendam iuventutis magistrum, candidatum semper et capillatum, femore etiam aureo conspicuum, natum saepius ac renatum. Nomen illi erat Ipse: sic discipuli certe vocabant sui. Sed eos discipulos, ut ad se quenque receperat, statim prorsus elinguabat. Praecepta vero si Ipsius audieritis, risu, scio, diffluetis. Dicam tamen nihilo secius."

[121] Poliziano, *Lamia*, 5.18: "Hic igitur Ipse, tam portentosae sapientiae professor ac venditator. . . ."

[122] On Poliziano's "Alexandrian" tendency see Godman, *From Poliziano to Machiavelli*, 31–79.

ritually rich post-Plotinian Neoplatonic tradition with Christianity
had played itself out in the day to day context of Florentine intellectual and political life. In the late 1480s, Giovanni Pico della
Mirandola consciously distanced himself from Ficino, going so far,
in his *De ente et uno*, to suggest that Plato had really agreed with
Aristotle that Being and One were convertible.[123] And Savonarola
was not interested in Plotinus, Porphyry, Iamblichus, Proclus, ontological hierarchies, or any other such thing. Ficino continued his
immensely productive labors, and remained one among many different
sorts of artists, intellectuals, and institutions under the broad wing
of Medici patronage. However, as the adamantly fideistic Savonarola
gained influence in Florence, it was he whom almost all of the members of Ficino's circle chose to follow, as Ficino, increasingly isolated
yet still a convinced adept of the Orphic theology, searched relent-
lessly for the true nature of the mysteries.[124]

One such follower was Giovanni Nesi, the Florentine diplomat,
university official, active preacher in a number of Florentine lay confraternities, Neoplatonist, apocalyptic thinker, and *piagnone*. Instead
of a break with Ficino, Nesi maintained a middle way: a Savonarolan,
he sought none the less to preserve certain aspects of the philosophical heritage bequeathed to Florence by Ficino.

Giovanni Nesi and Pythagoras: Between Ficino and Savonarola

The *Symbolum Nesianum* represents a noteworthy but exceptional position in the context of the mentioned divisions in Florentine intellectual life. Neither wholly Ficinian nor wholly Savonarolan, its author
attempts, here and elsewhere, to find a middle way. The context of
the work is complex: to understand it thoroughly, attention must be
paid to a number of aspects, from the codicological to the political.

---

[123] See M.J.B. Allen, "The Second Ficino-Pico Controversy: Parmenidean Poetry,
Eristic and the One," in ed. Gian Carlo Garfagnini, *Marsilio Ficino e il ritorno di
Platone: Studi e documenti*, 2 vols. (Florence, 1986) 2: 417–455, now in Allen, *Plato's
Third Eye: Studies in Marsilio Ficino's Metaphysics and its Sources* (Aldershot and Brookfield,
1995) as study number X; E. Garin, *Giovanni Pico della Mirandola: Vita e dottrina*
(Florence, 1937); L. Valcke and R. Galibois, *Le périple intellectuel de Jean Pic de la
Mirandole, suivi du Discours de la dignité de l'homme et du traité L'être et l'un* (Sainte-Foy,
1994); and S. Toussaint, ed., *L'esprit du Quattrocento: De l'être et de l'un et Réponses à
Antonio Cittadini* (Paris, 1995). For the text see Giovanni Pico della Mirandola, *De
hominis dignitate, Heptaplus, De ente et uno, e scritti vari*, ed. E. Garin (Florence, 1942).
[124] Cf. Allen, *Synoptic Art*, 145–7.

Over a year after Savonarola's death, in the first week or so of January 1500, Giovanni Nesi joined in a meal of the Camaldolese monks in Santa Maria degli Angeli in Florence. He was intrigued by the fact that they had been doing exercises, which the Prior of Santa Maria degli Angeli, then Guido da Settimo, called *gymnastica monachorum*—"exercises for the monks." These consisted of collections of short phrases that the monks were supposed to expound upon and interpret. There had been one *gymnasticon* written by a certain Luca and another by a certain Marco. Having heard these and their expositions, and having been pleased by them, Nesi said (Introductio.1):

> Well I'm delighted with you, reverend father, that you take up these little gifts from your charges and friends. But I—that I might dine as an equal with them—want also to present my "symbol."

The prior asked what this "symbol" was, and Nesi replied (ibid.): "A kind of 'ordering' in which I have interpreted almost all of the apophthegms that Pythagoras proposed." Three days later—we are told at the end of the treatise's narrative framework—Nesi brought his commentary to the Prior (Epilogus.5–6).

> Upon accepting it the father handed it to the monk Raphael, who read through it in front of everybody in a loud voice. And it pleased everyone: they praised it in the highest degree and preferred it by far to the already set out *Symbols* of Luca and Marco. They admired in this way a layman who at the same time was versed in such a fruitful way in the world but was also abundantly versed in sacred scripture, so that he did not harm scripture; far from sprinkling it about, rather, he ornamented everything he said with it.

All of this we know from one, inherently deceptive source, a manuscript in the Biblioteca Nazionale Centrale in Florence, which contains the *Eptathicum* of Paolo Orlandini, twice prior of Santa Maria degli Angeli, and twice vicar general of the Camaldolese order.[125] The title *Eptathicum* refers to the seven main sections which the manuscript contains. There are treatises on virtue, the divisions of theology, biblical hermeneutics, the spiritual struggle, the soul, there is

---

[125] On whom see G. Farulli, *Istoria cronologica del nobile ed antico monastero degli Angioli di Firenze del sacro Ordine Camaldolese dal principio della sua fondazione al presente giorno* (Lucca, 1710) 69–71; G.B. Mittarelli and A. Costadoni, *Annales Camaldulenses Ordinis Sancti Benedicti*, vii–ix (Venice, 1762–73) *passim*; E. Garin, *La cultura filosofica*, 213–23; Weinstein, *Savonarola and Florence*, 362–71; and Polizzotto, 149–53 and *ad indicem* (Polizzotto cites Farulli and Mittarelli and Costadoni at 150 n.53). Many of Orlandini's works are unedited; cf. Kristeller, *Iter*, 1 and 2 *ad indicem*.

a treatise against astrologers and, finally, there are the *Gymnastica monachorum*.[126] Nesi's work, one of the *gymnastica*, is a listing of and commentary on the Pythagorean sayings, putatively a letter of Nesi himself to then Prior Guido da Settimo.

The *Eptathicum* and the manuscript in which it is contained are deceptive for a number of reasons. First, the manuscript was copied in 1518,[127] presumably also the date of the final redactions of the works it contains by Paolo Orlandini. The *Eptathicum* on the whole is a patchwork of writings, some of which are contained in other manuscripts,[128] and, though original works by Orlandini are there, it is not just an anthology of discrete writings. This is especially so when one comes to the *Gymnastica monachorum*. There, Orlandini presents an idealized portrait of life at Santa Maria degli Angeli during the priorate of Guido da Settimo. In the interstices of the various works are authorial comments, fragments of dialogues about the works, notes on guests who visited the monastery: the image projected is that Santa Maria degli Angeli was a *contubernium sacrum et philosophicum*, a republic of letters embedded in an idealized, active, and often humorous religious context. To contextualize the *Symbolum Nesianum*, a deeper look at the *Gymnastica* is in order.

Orlandini begins the *Gymnastica* with an *Epistola nuncupatoria* praising Guido da Settimo, who was the "best of fathers and teachers," whose tenure as prior represented "the best of days."[129] This might seem surprising to say, since Guido was harsh and unloved by some;[130] but in the end he was worthy of admiration. Orlandini himself has always "admired most of all those in whom a certain evidence of wisdom and virtue shines forth. This is just the sort of man our ven-

---

[126] After this there are four miscellaneous works; cf. App. 3:III. A–D.

[127] See App. 3.

[128] Especially important are MSS Munich, Bayerische Staatsbibliothek Clm 172 and 173, for descriptions of which see Kristeller, *Iter* 3.613 and C. Halm, G. Laubmann, et al., eds., *Catalogus codicum latinorum Bibliothecae Regiae Monacensis*, 2 vols. in seven parts (Munich, 1868–81); pt. 1.1–2 published in a second edition (1892–4) 1.1 (1892): 38. For the correspondences of the works with MS Florence BN II. I. 158, see App. 3.

[129] MS Florence BN II. I. 158, f.236: "Audisti saepenumero Reverende Domine quam sim solitus magnis afferre laudibus Reverendum in Christo Guidonem olim utique optimum patrem et preceptorem meum simul et felicissimos appellare dies eius. . . ."

[130] Ibid. (to the dedicatee): "Hinc admirari soles, quem enim plerique omnes odere monachi sui, quid ego eundem laudare contendam?"

erable Guido was."[131] Guido emphasized in the healthiest of ways
the place of literary studies for monks: "Both by word and by example he used to keep after us all, so that we would incline toward
the study of literature; he used to say that it was an outstanding
provision for monastic life and its proper nourishment."[132] His encour-
agement bore fruit in the day to day life of the monastery and as
time went by enough interesting things happened that Orlandini
decided to write them down. Like an ant, he "gathered his trea-
sures, not into a catalogue, but rather, digested into his own ordering [*syntagma*]."[133] If some of the chapters lead to laughter, others
will edify.[134] What is certain is that if Pucci, the dedicatee, reads
patiently and attentively, he will find a lot to like.[135]

As the work proceeds we see that the learned guests who came
to visit, both lay and religious, were made welcome and were encour-
aged to partake in the monks' discussions. Many interesting things
were discussed—the four ancient academies, the differences and similarities between Plato and Aristotle, where Aristotle contradicts himself, etc. Moreover, it becomes clear that symbolic and proverbial
wisdom, if possible arranged in alphabetical order, was much appre-
ciated.[136] In chapter twenty-three, "On the four types of speech and
questions of men," the logician Oliviero da Siena is a guest at Santa
Maria degli Angeli, as he has been in other chapters.[137] At one point
"he took note of individual men and went through them by type;
he used these things that were almost like hieroglyphs and symbols,
so that they would be recognized by those who had grasped this

---

[131] Ibid., ff.236–236v: "Dilexi autem apprime illos in quibus aliquod //236v//
specimen sapientiae et virtutus eluceat. Qualis extitit hic noster Venerabilis Guido. . . ."

[132] Ibid., f.236v: "et verbo et exemplo nos angebat omnes ut incumberemus litterarum studiis, autumans hoc esse viaticum praecipuum et pabulum singulare pro
monastica vita. . . ."

[133] Ibid.: "Propterea iam demum animum ad scribendum appuli, profecto quaedam
quae in tempore illo quod felicissimum appellare consuevi veluti formica aggregavi
equidem et thesaurizzavi mihi, atque idipsum non in catalogum certum, sive in proprium syntagma digestum."

[134] Ibid.: "Si quod capitulum ridenda contineat, alterum continuo ediscenda
praestabit. . . ."

[135] Ibid.: "Placebunt autem multa si haec et patienter leges et attente."

[136] Cf. e.g., ibid., ff.258–259v, i.e., ch. 24, "De variis enygmatibus et figuratis
verbis," where the sayings there reported are arranged in alphabetical order.

[137] Ibid., ff.257v–258. Oliviero da Siena was the author of, i.a., the *Tractatus rationalis scientiae* (Siena, 1491). Cf. C. Vasoli, *Profezia e ragione: Studi sulla cultura del
Cinquecento e del Seicento* (Naples, 1974) 422.

sort of doctrine of his."[138] Soon thereafter, chapter twenty-five is devoted to the "apophthegms and witty sayings of prior Guido," who, we learn, "sprinkled his conversation with sayings and witty remarks."[139] In that same chapter, short anecdotes are reported, in the style of Diogenes Laertius but with a contemporary, religious touch. Orlandini writes, e.g., "Once when I was complaining about preaching publicly in church, he [i.e., Guido] said, 'A preacher needs four things: devotion, reading, discrimination, and pronunciation. Have these and you will preach well.'"[140]

Proverbial wisdom, sayings, alphabetical order: the stage is set for the *Symbolum Lucianum*, the *Symbolum Marcianum*, and, finally, the *Symbolum Nesianum*. In chapter twenty six, "on the origin of the symbols of Luke and Mark," Orlandini tells how these texts came about, informing the reader about "a certain new idiom that has just recently come to light in our *contubernium*."[141] Two of the monks, Marco and Luca, were arguing about the merits of Cassian versus those of Cicero. Eventually the arguments reached such a pitch that Guido instructed them each to write something on the topic, "like the Athenians," echoing the contemporary Gellian vogue for elegant, miscellanistic discourse which Poliziano's *Miscellanea* had well illustrated.[142]

Luca's brief prefatory epistle to Guido stresses that, for mnemonic reasons, he has arranged the various sayings drawn from Cassian in alphabetical order, "both so that your cenobites might be trained in the monastic life by the use of certain of these new characters, and so that they might commit them to memory more easily, even if it

---

[138] Ibid., f.257v: "Sicque notabat hic noster autor homines singulos et censebat eos per sua genera et his q[uas]i heroglyphis utebatur et symbolis, ut ab his dignoscentur duntaxat, qui tale eius dogma ex eo percepissent." On hieroglyphics in the Renaissance see R. Wittkower, "Hieroglyphics in the Renaissance," in his *Allegory and the Migration of Symbols* (London, 1977) 113–28; and P. Castelli, *I geroglifici e il mito dell'Egitto nel Rinascimento* (Florence, 1979).

[139] Ibid., f.259v: "Capitulum 25. De apothegmatibus et salibus patris prioris Guidi. Erat utique dicax admodum hic noster pientissumus Prior, qui et scommata et sales passim loqueretur. . . ."

[140] Ibid., f.260: "Recusanti mihi ut concionarer publice in ecclesia, ait, 'Predicatori quattuor debentur: devotio, lectio, delectus, et pronunciatio. Habeto isthaec et bene praedicabis.'"

[141] Ibid., f.261v: "Minime censeo ab re fore ut referatur de novo quodam idiomate nuperrime edito in nostro contubernio."

[142] Ibid.: "Decertabant illic quenque praeceptores duo, quorum alter nobis Cassianum, alter Ciceronem interpretabatur, dum se vicissim alterutri praeferrent, ac de linguae ipsius ornatu quisque pro suo autore certaret. Die vero quadam, eo iurgiorum tandem deventum est ad iussum patris, ut ambo inscriptis ederent, quicquid pulchri atque etiam novi atheniensium instar sibi in sua facultate suppeteret."

is done with a certain artifice."[143] There is a brief conclusion, notable in that it gives a date: "the third day of January, 1499 [Florentine style, so: 3 January, 1500]." Orlandini's narrative account then continues: After Luca's "symbols" were read out to the monastic community, "some smiled, some laughed, and not a few praised the work. The father [i.e., Guido] commended them all in the highest degree and gave the paper [*schedam*] which he had taken to me, with the charge of preserving it."[144]

It is noteworthy that Orlandini refers to the work he was charged to preserve as a "scheda," which he here uses as a collective singular.[145] As Silvia Rizzo has noted, in contemporary philological and editorial parlance this word could signify "the first redaction of a work, while it was still in individual folia, before its definitive transcription into a codex."[146] One recalls that the final version of the *Eptathicum*, of which the *Gymnastica* are a part, was itself put together in 1518, almost two decades after these *Symbola* were being publicly read at Santa Maria degli Angeli. It is likely, then, that Orlandini had a significant part in the final redaction of the individual texts of which the *Gymnastica* are composed, even as he provides the narrative continuity between them. Much of what we hear would seem to be his voice.

As the narrative continues this becomes clearer. That night, after Luca's text had been read aloud to the whole community, the monks went to their cells, Marco having been given the charge of writing down his "symbol." A few days later he returned, "offering his symbol to the Father." In offering it to Guido, Marco writes in his prefatory letter (reported by Orlandini) that he noticed how Luca had presented his work in alphabetical order;[147] and Marco stresses that

---

[143] Ibid., f.261v: "Reverentiae tuae, pater amantissime, collegi quaedam quasi apopthegmata ex autore meo eademque perbrevia, et inserire alphabeto digesta, tum ut eis veluti caratheribus quibusdam novis instituantur hi coenobitae tui in monastica vita, tum ut illa ab eis queant facilius ac si artificiosae memoriae commendari."

[144] Ibid., f.266v: "Luciana haec symbola coram patre et monachis ac si per conctionem die quadam lectitata fuere sub cella prioris a suo autore. Hinc surrisere nonnulli, arrisere quidam, laudavere non pauci. Pater autem apprime omnia commendavit, schedamque acceptam mihi tradidit, ad nutum eius conservandam."

[145] The length of the work prevents us from thinking of it as only one folium.

[146] S. Rizzo, *Il lessico filologico degli umanisti* (Rome, 1973) 306. See there for further evidence.

[147] MS Florence BN II. I. 158, f.266v: "Vidi equidem, Reverende in Christo pater et domine, quemadmodum *in alphabeti seriem* disposuerit commentariolum suum venerabilis Lucas."

his own work was one that had been "dispersed... in separate pages" but one that he too has "reduced to the same form of the alphabet."[148] Again, in the same section, we see a reference to what are apparently separate sheets of paper.[149] And once more, at the end of the little work, in the peroration, Marco says that he has gathered together "these sayings... which were dispersed in my papers," even as he emphasizes that he has done so "as quickly as possible and, as a result, without any elegance whatsoever."[150] As we approach the *Symbolum Nesianum* putatively authored by Giovanni Nesi, it is through this lens that we should see the treatment. While there is nothing to make one think Nesi did not have a large, even exclusive hand in the original version of the *Symbolum Nesianum*, one must also recognize that, almost twenty years later, Orlandini was probably heavily involved in the final redaction.[151]

Nesi's Oraculum de novo saeculo, *its reception, and the* Symbolum Nesianum

As to Giovanni Nesi himself, it was in the summer of 1496 when he had first approached the symbols in an organized fashion. This was in his *Oracle of a New Age* (*Oraculum de novo saeculo*), dedicated to Gianfrancesco Pico della Mirandola.[152] The work was printed and

---

[148] Ibid.: "ut luce ipsius instar tractatum reducens omnem, *quem habeo in excartabulis usque quaque dispersum ad hanc eamdem alphabeti formam.*"

[149] Ibid., "Quae igitur exhaurire valui *e nostris carthulis....*"

[150] Ibid., f.270: "Peroratio. Haec habui *dicteria*, pater Reverende, *quae in carthulis dispersa meis redigi impugillarer, idque quam celerrime, qua propter et inconcinne* admodum ut possem hodie quoquomodo et ipse hoc ceu minervale munus ad te referre."

[151] In addition it is noteworthy that Pythagoras is used or cited in the *Eptathicum* at other locations (i.e., at least, f.2v, f.23v, f.31, f.35v, f.37, f.43v, f.51, f.211, f.217, f.219v, f.229v, f.234) and that there are other, more direct correspondences, for which see the Commentary below, at Introductio.1, Introductio.2, 25.1, and 44.1. Also, there are sources used and cited which either appear or would be in general circulation after the original version. See the Commentary, at 8.1, 12.2, and 45.7.

[152] Iohannis Nesii Florentini *Oraculum de novo saeculo*. I cite from the copy in the Biblioteca Riccardiana, Edizioni rare 554. For date and place of publication cf. the colophon: "Impressit ex archetypo Ser Laurentius De Morgianis Anno Salutis M.CCCCLXXXXVII. Octavo idus maias, Florentiae." (Hain 11693) There is also an important autograph manuscript of this work (presumably a final authorial redaction) in MS Florence, Biblioteca Riccardiana 383, and a copy in MS Florence, Biblioteca Riccardiana 384, both of which I have consulted. Vasoli, 1973, edits the second half of the *Oraculum* at 161–79 and offers a discussion at 116–22. See also S. Toussaint, "Un cas de 'Theologie Poetique': Le portrait mythologique de Jean Pic de la Mirandole e l'*Heptaplus*," in *Momus, studi umanistici* (Lucca, 1994) 75–89, esp. 82–6; and D.P. Walker, *The Ancient Theology* (London, 1972) 51–8.

published in May 1497, shortly before Alexander VI's bull against
Savonarola was publicly promulgated in Florence.[153] The Florentine
concern for the prophetic figure—part of a mentality inherited from
Ficino's reading of the Iamblichean Pythagoras—is apparent. Nesi
has read that someone will come who is "holier than man." He will
"brighten the earth . . . open to all the font of truth . . . [he is some-
one] whom all, finally, will follow."[154] Later in the treatise, it is
revealed that this person is none other than the "Socrates from
Ferrara," Girolamo Savonarola.[155] Along the way, in a strange monument to late Quattrocento oneirology, Nesi presents a dream vision
in which *inter alia* the figure of Pythagoras appears, golden thigh and
all, offering certain of his symbols; Nesi gives them no extended comment.[156] After he gives the list, Nesi writes that these and many other
similar ones were read out. "But," he writes, "I cannot expatiate
longer on this topic, since I am circumscribed by the limitations of
time and by what I have proposed to do."[157]

It is in the *Symbolum nesianum* that he finally gets around to "expa-
tiating." In his introduction he says [Introductio.10]:

> In any case, I have collected almost all [of the symbols] into that one
> work I published, the *Oracle on the New Age*, as well as certain [sym-
> bols] in my dialogues. However, for your sake and that of your monks,
> I have brought every one into a kind of alphabetical order, along with
> certain of their interpretations.

Before examining the *Symbolum Nesianum*, however, it will be useful to
examine the reception contemporaries accorded Nesi's *Oraculum*. This
will help decipher the *Symbolum Nesianum*'s meaning and importance.

---

[153] Polizzotto, 86.

[154] I cite sigla numbers and in parentheses give the folio number. A.ii (1): ". . .
elucescat in terris sacratior quam homo aliquis, qui fontem omnibus veritatis ape-
riat, quem denique sequantur omnes." Ficino had earlier used these words, though
certainly not in reference to Savonarola, in his *In epistolas divi Pauli 3*, in his *Vita
Platonis*, under "Quae Plato affirmavit" and in a letter to Braccio Martelli now in
the 8th book of his *Epistolae*; see *Op.*, 1.431; 1.769–70; 1.867; the Ficino citations
are noted in Allen, *Synoptic Art*, 71, n.55. Allen (ibid.) suggests Plato's *Laws*, 4.711E
as possible source.

[155] B.v (13): "Ferrariensis igitur Socrates philosophiam quae de moribus agit, diutius exulantem, revocavit in urbem civitatique restituit, vitiorum castigator acerrimus, virtutum laudator gravissimus." On the perception of Savonarola as "Socrates,"
see Godman, *From Poliziano to Machiavelli*, 134–79.

[156] A.vii–a.vii[v] (7–7v).

[157] A.vii[v] (7v): "Sed non possum in hac re spaciari longius, temporis angustiis et
meo instituto circumscriptus."

In fact, it seems at times as if the *Symbolum* is a response to the reception of the earlier work as well as, subtextually at least, a *piagnone* response to the execution of Savonarola.

We can first look at the work of an author who was favorably inclined towards Nesi's general position concerning Savonarola, i.e., that the Ferrarese Socrates was sent by God to cure Florence's ills. In his 1497 work, the *Dialogo della verità della doctrina predicata da Frate Hieronymo da Ferrara nella ciptà di Firenze,* the *piagnone* Domenico Benivieni accepted this premise in general and offered specific approbation to Nesi's *Oraculum.*[158] Savonarola is spoken of as "truly a divine man, granted by God to these times and especially to us, not without great mystery."[159] His learning is "true and sent by God in these times to men."[160] And people "ought firmly to believe in those sent by God."[161] Benivieni does go on to say, however, that these men "are not always recognized by miracles . . . but by their good life and the good fruit of their learning."[162] He offers twelve reasons why Savonarola is good, centered around the notions that his preaching has been good and lasting, that most of his prophecies have come true, and that good people follow him.[163]

Following on this, Benivieni's interlocutors discuss those good men of high repute who have written on Savonarola. Among them is

---

[158] Domenico Benivieni, *Dialogo della verità della doctrina predicata da Frate Hieronymo da Ferrara nella ciptà di Firenze* (Florence, 1497) = GW 3846; the work has been edited with modernized Italian orthography by Gian Carlo Garfagnini in his "'Lumen propheticum' e 'lumen fidei' nel *Dialogo* de Domenico Benivieni," in eds. A. Fontes, J.-L. Fournel, and M. Plaisance, *Savonarole: Enjeux, débats, questions* (Paris, 1997) 149–71; the *Dialogo* is edited at 157–71. I cite from Garfagnini's edition.

[159] Ed. Garfagnini, 157: "*Domenico.* Io stimo che tu vogli dire de' casi della città nostra, e massime del nostro padre, frate Ieronimo da Ferrara, veramente uomo divino concesso da Dio a questi tempi e a noi spezialmente, non senza grande mysterio."

[160] Ed. Garfagnini, 158: "*Domenico*: . . . . Io non solamente credo che la dottrina di questo padre sia vera et da Dio mandata in questi tempi agl'uomini per reformazione della sua santa chiesa. . . ."

[161] Ed. Garfagnini, 159: "*Domenico*: Dopo questo, io demonstro la utilità e la necessità della predicazione et della prophezia nella chiesa di Dio, e come gl'uomini debbono fermamente credere a quelli che sono mandati da Dio. . . ."

[162] Ed. Garfaginini, 159: "e quali si conoscono non sempre per miracoli, come apertamente demostro, ma per la loro buona vita et per el buono frutto della loro dottrina." As Garfagnini has emphasized, defining what was and was not "miraculous" was obviously of prime importance in the polemics surrounding Savonarola's legitimacy. Cf. 154–5; and *idem,* "Savonarola e la profezia: tra mito e storia," *Studi Medievali,* 3rd series, 29 (1988) 173–201; *idem,* "La polemica antiastrologica del Savonarola ed i suoi precedenti tomistici," in eds. G. Federici Vescovini and F. Barocelli, *Filosofia scienza astrologia nel Trecento* (Padua, 1992) 155–179.

[163] Ed. Garfagnini, 159–60.

"our Giovanni Nesi," who, "using the literary device of a vision, in his new treatise which he calls the *Oracle of a New Age*, elegantly and eruditely demonstrates the poor state of the world and of the city of Florence and further that God has sent this father [i.e., Savonarola], with his salubrious learning, for its reformation." The other interlocutor answers: "I have always known Giovanni to be a man of intelligence, both well-learned and a lover of virtue."[164] Both before and after the discussion of Nesi, the interlocutors consider other authors who have written in Savonarola's favor. The others are treated at the same length and in the same depth as Nesi. The interlocutors mention Giorgio Benigno Salviati, Bartolomeo Scala, Paulino da Nola, Bartolomeo Fonzio, Gianfrancesco Pico della Mirandola, and others. Benivieni clearly understands Nesi's message, even if, as in the case of the other authors treated, he does not go into great depth. Moreover, in stressing the notion that Savonarola was sent by God, Benivieni accepts at least implicitly part of Nesi's overall scheme regarding Savonarola's importance.[165]

On the other hand, in his *Contra Johannis Nesii Oraculum de novo seculo*, Giovanni Caroli wrote against Nesi's *Oraculum*.[166] This anti-Savonarolan Dominican belonged to the convent of Santa Maria Novella, and lived from 1428–1503; he was ordained a priest by Saint Antoninus himself at the age of twenty.[167] The manner in which

---

[164] Ed. Garfagnini, 161: "*Domenico*: El nostro Giovanni Nesi elegantemente et eruditamente, in un suo nuovo trattato el quale lui inscrive Oraculum de novo saeculo, sotto figura d'una sua visione dimonstra el male stato del mondo et della città di Firenze, e Dio avere mandato questo padre per reformazione di quello [*leg.* quella ?] con la sua salutifera doctrina. *Filalete*: Sempre conobbi Giovanni per uomo d'ingegno e litterato e amatore delle virtù."

[165] This modifies slightly Polizzotto's view that Nesi's *Oraculum* was damned by faint praise by *piagnoni*, especially Benivieni (cf. Polizzotto, 106, with n.16).

[166] The work is present in the following manuscript, from which I cite: MS Florence, BN, Conv. Sopp. C. 8. 277, ff.137–174v. On this manuscript see G.C. Garfagnini, M.R. Pagnoni Sturlese, G. Pomaro, S. Zamponi, eds. *Catologo di manoscritti filosofici nelle biblioteche italiane*, v. 3 (Florence, 1982) 35–7. On Caroli see S. Orlandi, *Necrologio di Santa Maria Novella: 1235–1504. Testo e commenti biografici*, 2 vols. (Florence, 1955) 1.203–205; 2. 353–380; at 2.376 there is a description of this manuscript (though he reports the old foliation). On Caroli's other works see the studies of S.I. Camporeale, "Giovanni Caroli e le 'Vitae fratrum S.M. Novellae.' Umanesimo e crisi religiosa (1460–1480)," *Memorie dominicane*, n.s., 12 (1981) 141–267; *idem*, "Giovanni Caroli: Dal 'Liber dierum' alle 'Vitae fratrum,'" *Memorie dominicane*, n.s., 16 (1985) 199–233; and *idem*, "Humanism and the Religious Crisis of the Late Quattrocento: Giovanni Caroli, O.P., and the *Liber dierum lucensium*," in eds. T. Verdon and J. Henderson, *Christianity and the Renaissance: Image and Religious Imagination in the Quattrocento* (Syracuse, 1990) 445–466.

[167] Orlandi, *Necrologio*, 2.354; on his death date see *Necrologio* 2.359.

Caroli wrote to Nesi is instructive. Rather than harsh invective against Nesi himself, we see a call back to the fold. This call is not occasionally without its sinister side, and is always balanced by very stern warnings against the content of Nesi's message. The import is clear: Nesi has gone too far in his praise of Savonarola, recalling the days of ancient prophecies in his pro-Savonarolan rhetoric, when present day circumstances do not warrant it. Caroli's spirited work shows that Nesi's *Oracle*, far from falling on deaf ears, was powerful enough to inspire fear that certain of its positions might be taken too seriously.

In the preface Caroli reminds Nesi not to forget "how dangerous it is to have praised a living man exceedingly."[168] "Love your 'Socrates,'" Caroli exhorts Nesi, "but do so only as you might a learned man; respect and admire him, but place a restraint on your love."[169] To Caroli, one of Savonarola's problems was that he, a foreigner to Florence, preached against Florentine morals. Nesi should realize this. "For your homeland," Caroli writes, "has not been lacking good morals; rather, it loves and cultivates them."[170] Savonarola is a new man in Florence, and he leads a new army. Despite initial, fleeting strength, "a new and untried army is almost always confounded by the craft and skill of veterans."[171]

The rest of the treatise echoes the themes outlined in the preface. Nesi has claimed too much; what he reports "surely, must not be called 'oracles' but 'dreams.'"[172] Even Nesi's use of the Pythagorean sayings was incomplete, according to Caroli. He cites five of the "sayings of that Samian," which Nesi had used, then goes on:

> I myself would add some others: never place your scythe in a foreign pasture; judge no one if you do not wish to judged; do not pretend that a wolf, or one who seems like one, is a reasonable man; what you would not want for yourself, do not to another. If you should do these things, believe me, my dear Nesi, you will not err.[173]

---

[168] f.138: "Neque enim fugere debet quam periculosum sit viventem hominem nimium collaudasse."

[169] f.139: "Ama igitur Socratem illum tuum, sed quam maxime peritum; observa illum et admirare, sed frena amori tuo imposito."

[170] Ibid.: "Patria enim tua non mores amisit, sed eos amavit et coluit."

[171] Ibid.: "... nova et inexercitata militia plerumque solet veteranorum solertia et arte confundi."

[172] f.145v: "sunt aut certe non oracula sed sompnia appellanda."

[173] f.149: "Magis autem *Samii illius precepta* que scribis, mente recondito, quibus inter cetera dicit: de misteriis divinis absque lumine sileto; ne novum lumen effingito; adversus solem ne loquito<r>; stramenta semper colligata teneto; stateram ne tran-

The malleability of Pythagorean "symbolic" discourse, then, is proven once again.

Arguments in favor of Florence continue to crop up. Here too, Nesi has gone too far. Caroli knows that some of the negative things Nesi has said about Florence, he has expressed with a license that poets or painters might use, to gratify men. "But didn't the Apostle say 'All things are allowed to me, but not all things are useful; all things are allowed to me, but not all things edify?'"[174] Even if there were flaws in Florence, could this "Ferrarese Socrates" really be counted as an authority? "Harshest castigator of the vices, gravest praiser of the virtues: What a bombastic name! What a presumptuous sentiment! What vain praise and most prideful pride! So Florence has come to such a point of poverty that it is necessary to accept in turn this new 'Socrates' from the swamps of Ferrara!"[175] Even if Savonarola were not a foreigner to Florence, Nesi's exceeding praise was simply inappropriate. In the end, it is clear: "Men, my dear Nesi, should be praised for their merit, but not with the praises reserved for God, not for a prophecy of which you are ignorant, and they should not be extolled above the human condition. . . . So, especially while they are alive, restraints must be placed on the praises of men."[176] Caroli is seeking to bring the image of Savonarola from the realm of the supernatural to the natural, from the divine to the human, from the realm of the oracular to the realm of the purely wise. The *Symbolum Nesianum*, written in early 1500, can be seen almost as a response to these concerns.

It is in the interpretations of the Pythagorean symbols, as I suggested above, that each commentator's agendas are revealed. The *Symbolum*

---

silito. *Addam ipse et alia: falcem in alienam messem nequaquam immittito; si non vis iudicari* [*cod*: ius iudicarum; *cf.* Mt. 7:1–2] *neminem iudicato; racionalem hominem lupum vel visum non fingito; quod tibi nolles alteri ne facito. Hec si feceris, non errabis, crede mihi, O Nesi.*"

[174] Ibid.: "fingere vero ut poetis ac pictoribus licet et ea licentia gratificari hominibus tuis velle. At inquiebat Apostolus nonne 'Omnia mihi licet, sed non omnia expediunt, omnia mihi licet sed non omnia hedificant.'"

[175] f.152v: ". . . vitiorum castigator acerrimus, virtutum laudator gravissimus. O inflatum nomen! O tumidissimam sententiam! O ventosam laudem et superbia<m> superbissimam! Ergo florentia ad tantam devenit inopiam ut novum Socratem op. . . . at a Ferrarie paludibus mutuo accipere."

[176] f.167: "Laudandi sunt ergo, O Nesi, pro meritis homines, at non dei laudibus, non de prophetia quam nescis, non supra hominem extollendi. . . . Itaque frena laudibus hominum ponenda sunt, quamdiu presertim vivunt."

Nesianum is no exception. The fundamental hermeneutic poles are Savonarolan and Ficinian, though it seems that Nesi's primary ideological leaning is as a *piagnone*. To generalize: Anyone who looks at a pre-Socratic figure, Pythagoras included, looks at him in a mediated way. So in order to understand a thinker who might be researching a pre-Socratic, it is important to determine the type of mediation he is using—the lens through which he reads. I have argued that Ficino views Pythagoras through a late ancient, Iamblichean, soteriological lens. Nesi, while struggling to preserve some of the Ficinian heritage, views the symbols of Pythagoras through a *piagnone* lens, through the lens, that is, of a Savonarolan, deeply affected by recent events in Florentine history. When he approaches the symbols, the echoes of both Savonarola and Ficino reflect this.

The *Symbolum Nesianum* presents a collection of forty-eight symbols with comment, offering a patchwork of interesting materials and citations.[177] A glance at the *index locorum* reveals that Nesi's two most important sets of sources were biblical and ancient, "profane" literature. With respect to biblical literature especially, Nesi utilizes a highly allusive, subtextual style of discourse. By quoting one line he often seems to allude to a surrounding scriptural location, depending, reasonably, on the likelihood that his audience knew much scripture by heart. The *Psalms* are especially important to him, as are, unsurprisingly, the prophetic books of the Old Testament, especially Isaiah and Jeremiah. Often Nesi seems to evoke the notion that Florence is a deserted Jerusalem; images of destruction, fire, and

---

[177] For the sake of convenience I shall speak of Nesi as the author of the work, though, owing to the considerations offered above, it is impossible to determine the extent of Orlandini's collaboration in the work's final redaction. Cesare Vasoli offers an interesting and fundamental discussion concerning the authorship possibilities of the *Symbolum Nesianum* in his "Pitagora in monastero." To clear up possible confusion, I should mention that the date given for Nesi's letter to Orlandini which frames and accompanies Nesi's commentary is, on f.280, as follows: "Florentiae, die decimo Januarii 1499 [*Florentine style; so: 1500*]"; however, it is important to note that on f.270v, after the above discussed *Symbolum Marcianum*, the date given is "die vi. Januarii 1489." But since the date given at the end of the *Symbolum Lucianum* (which comes before the *Symbolum Marcianum*) was 1499; since the date after the *Symbolum Nesianum* is 1499; and since there are, as I believe, numerous allusions in the *Symbolum Nesianum* to Savonarola and his fate, it is reasonable to assume that the date of 1489 given after the *Symbolum Marcianum* represents a *lapsus calami* on the part of the scribe. Thus we can assume that Orlandini wants us to think that the *Gymnastica* took place in the early days of January, 1499, Florentine style, so, 1500. Because of this confusion in the manuscript, Garin, *La cultura*, 214, reads the date as 1489, an error occasionally followed by other scholars.

death are not absent. If it is true that these symbols and their interpretations were read to the monks, "to the delight of all," one must
be prepared to acknowledge a darker side as well, filled with regret
and lamentation at Florence's woes.

With respect to ancient literature, the message is clear: Nesi is *au
courant*, in step with fashionable Platonizing texts and well aware of
Poliziano's Gellian tendencies. He also knows Aristotle's *Nicomachean
Ethics* well, which is unsurprising, since Nesi had written a dialogue
which had the *Ethics* at its heart and was thinking of preparing a
new redaction for publication.[178] There is ample use of the Church
fathers, especially those who had to do with the Pythagorean sayings. Medieval authors are few, though the ample use of canon law
is an exception; here perhaps one senses the later collaboration of
Orlandini, who wrote an introductory treatise on canon and civil
law.[179] Nesi is also conscious of the work of *moderni*, citing works of
Ficino, Pico, Poliziano, and Pietro Crinito.

Certain specifics reveal both Savonarolan and Ficinian concerns.
First, there are numerous occasions when the allusions in the treatise refer, sometimes obliquely, to Savonarola's fate, and seem to be
a set of criticisms directed at the city of Florence for having treated
Savonarola the way it did. Symbol 22 is illustrative. Here Nesi discusses the symbol, *gallis albis parcito*, or, "spare white cocks." Nesi
begins by discussing the opinion of Proclus that suggests cocks partake to a great extent in solar virtue and thus cause lions (also solar)
and even solar demons themselves to flee (22.1–2). It is noteworthy,
though, that his citation of Proclus is a paraphrase of Ficino's translation.[180] Then he refers us to Pico's *Oration*, to the opinion that
"white cocks" are "the messengers of truth and preachers of the
word of God." (22.3) He goes on to say that "those who speak the

---

[178] Nesi's *De moribus* is in MS Florence, Bibl. Laurenziana 77.24. See R. Bonfanti,
"Su un dialogo filosofico del tardo '400: Il *De moribus* del fiorentino Giovanni Nesi
(1456–1522?)," *Rinascimento*, 2nd ser., 11 (1971) 203–221 and Field, *The Origins*, 229.

[179] Dedicated to a certain Bernardo da Pistoia, present in MS Munich, Bayerische
Staatsbibliothek Clm 173, ff.109v–120v; cf. Kristeller, *Iter*, 3.613; moreover, later in
the *Gymnastica monachorum*, chapters 41–48 all concern canon law.

[180] Ficino also used Proclus in his own *De vita*; cf. B.P. Copenhaver, "Hermes
Trismegistus, Proclus, and the Question of a Philosophy of Magic in the Renaissance,"
in I. Merkel and A.G. Debus, eds., *Hermeticism in the Renaissance: Intellectual History
and the Occult in Early Modern Europe* (Washington, D.C. and London, 1988) 79–110,
esp. nn. 41 and 44 for lions and cocks. Beyond the Proclan/Ficinian allusion, one
wonders whether, in mentioning the flight of the lion, Nesi is alluding to the
Florentine *Marzocco*. I thank Felicia Else for the suggestion.

truth are from time to time brought to ruin, so that the Lord's
prophets have been stoned, cut to pieces, tempted, and killed by the
blow of the sword!" This kind of thing happened in the ancient
world, too, as Philostratus and Aulus Gellius testify (22.4). According
to Nesi, what Pythagoras really meant when he added that the cocks
in question were white, was that these messengers of truth have in
them an intellectual light. In fact (22.6–7):

> it is necessary that we applaud messengers of this sort, enemies of
> demons, allies of God and the angels, and let us rejoice with them as
> well, lest we harm them in some fashion in the meantime. Besides,
> those white cocks who disclose things to us are placed in the front
> rank; they plead with us, and they scold us. . . . We must spare them,
> so that we never injure them, so that, rather, we always and every-
> where obey them.

It is hard to imagine that Nesi is not thinking here of Savonarola.

Not that Nesi is always and everywhere necessarily a Savonarolan
apologist: rather, it is Savonarola's haunting, penumbral presence
in the text that is noteworthy. From this perspective symbol 1 is
worth a look, where Nesi comments on the famous *abstine a fabis*, or,
"Do not eat beans." The allusion here shows the complexity of
Nesi's relationship to Savonarola and the Savonarolan legacy. This
Pythagorean prohibition on beans had always been the subject of
lively interpretation. To live chastely (since beans when split open
seemed to resemble both male and female genital organs); to abstain
from politics (since beans were used to cast votes); to abstain from
luxury; to abstain from beans because the intestinal disturbances they
caused were not suitable to those of a scholarly cast: all these had
been offered by various ancients as interpretations, and Nesi goes
through them *seriatim*.[181] However, the manner in which he begins
his treatment is interesting. Nesi cites Plutarch's opinion that "beans"
stand for "banquets, from which," Nesi writes, "philosophers and
holy and religious men should abstain." He goes on (1.1): "For the
Apostle says, 'No one fighting in the cause of God mixes himself up
in worldly affairs.'" (*Nemo militans deo implicat se negociis secularibus.*)

His use of this phrase from Paul's second letter to Timothy is
striking, since, as Lorenzo Polizzotto has shown, it was used by the
above-mentioned Giovanni Caroli in the pamphlet war of 1495.

---

[181] See symbol 1, with commentary. For the ancient literature on the beans prohibition see Burkert, 183–5.

Caroli had employed it as the basis of a two-pronged attack against both Savonarola's prophesying and his propensity to get involved in Florentine politics.[182] Yet, despite the fact that Caroli had written and campaigned not only against Savonarola but also against Nesi himself, Nesi none the less saw fit to adopt this Pauline pronouncement into his interpretation. He could not have been ignorant of its sub-textual import. On the other hand, at the end of his comment on this symbol, the interpretation he winds up favoring is the one that would make this symbol an admonition to chastity. If Nesi some-times stresses themes similar to those of Savonarola and deplores the fact that he was executed, in other places perhaps he is trying to come to terms with just where Savonarola trangressed the limits to which he should have held himself. Here and elsewhere, the *Symbolum nesianum* offers witness to the inner workings of the *piagnone* move-ment, when it was still recovering from the shock of the loss of its prophet. Savonarola's memory lives on in the text, through the dense web of biblical allusions and elsewhere: in the interpretation of var-ious symbols, numerous quotations are drawn from the prophetic books of the Old Testament which resonate with Savonarolan ten-dencies (8.5; 13.4; 17.8; 25.2; 27.6; 38.3; 39.1); an Old Testament passage used by Savonarola in a particularly vehement sermon is quoted (7.3); and so on. Whether the references to Savonarola and his fate are subtextual and highly allusive or whether they are more apparent, they are there.

Also interesting, however, are the legacies of Ficino in the *Symbolum nesianum*, interesting because of their nature: scattered, loose, and only broadly similar to the kind of philosophical depth that Ficino's work represented and to the kind of later Platonic imagery that had filled Nesi's earlier work, the *Oracle*. There is, of course, the general similarity to Ficino in the field of discourse: the springboard for the work consists of the sayings of a *priscus theologus*, Pythagoras, who was quite important to Ficino.[183] Throughout the treatise, Nesi feels free to call Pythagoras "our prophet"—*vates noster*. It is clear that Pythagoras' status as a Ficino-endorsed *priscus theologus* is enough to allow con-centrated work on him. Some distinctions, however, should be made.

---

[182] Polizzotto, 61. The treatise is in MS Firenze BN Conv. Sopp. D. 9. 278, ff.46–53v, which I have examined in person. See also Orlandi, *Necrologio*, 2.371 and 2.378 on this text.

[183] See Celenza, "Pythagoras in the Renaissance."

As I suggested above, the *Symbolum Nesianum* presents the symbols of
Pythagoras seen through a *piagnone* lens; the legacy of Ficino's thought
and work reflects this.

Nesi quotes, for instance, Ficino's religious works as much as anything else, taking an apt metaphor from Ficino's *Commentary on Paul*
(Introductio.2); and when he deals with the Pythagorean saying that
one should "honor the figure and the altar above all things," Nesi
alludes to the famous first chapter of Ficino's *De christiana religione*,
quoting the argument that "Religio maxime homini propria est et
veridica."[184] (21.2)

When Nesi comes to more properly Platonic philosophical arguments
or approaches more recondite Neoplatonic material, he leans heavily
on Ficino—very heavily. Writing, for example, about the Pythagorean
saying, "do not speak against the sun," he touches on Proclus,
Iamblichus, Plotinus, Plato, and Julian—but he does this all by quoting Ficino's *De sole* (3). In treating the symbol alluded to above,
"Spare white cocks," Nesi cites Proclus's *De sacrificio et magia* by para-
phrasing Ficino's translation of same (22.1–2). Most revelatory is his
treatment of the symbol (29), "lacking light, treat not of light." Once
again, he takes a long quotation from Ficino's *De sole*. He argues
that "light" symbolizes "God," so that what this symbol really means
is that we should not speak of God without God, that is, we should
not speak irreligiously of religious matters. As his treatment of this
symbol progresses Nesi cites Plato's *Cratylus*; he writes that Plato says
that, "One must beware lest we talk about God without God, and
lest we wish to measure what is immeasurable with the aid of our
own nature." However, if one scans the *Cratylus* diligently, this quotation is nowhere to be found. Upon further investigation one finds
that Nesi has cited not the *Cratylus*, as he claims, but Ficino's *Epitome*
thereof—Nesi has read the condensed version of Plato that Ficino
had prepared.[185]

The presence of Ficino in the *Symbolum* meshes well with the other
aspects covered here. This work, the *Symbolum Nesianum*, is much less
"radical" than Nesi's earlier work, the *Oracle*, in the sense that the
Symbolum is further from the (admittedly malleable) boundaries of
orthodoxy than had been the *Oracle*. The *Symbolum* represents a post-

---

[184] On Ficino as theologian, see Jörg Lauster, *Die Erlösungslehre Marsilio Ficinos*,
Arbeiten zur Kirchengeschichte, 69 (Berlin and New York, 1998).
[185] See the commentary, *ad loc.*

Savonarolan moment in the *piagnone* movement, when Nesi has been chastened by the criticism of his earlier work, and when all the *piagnoni*, obviously, were chastened by the hanging and public burning of Savonarola's body in 1498. If Nesi did maintain a dual loyalty to Ficino and Savonarola, the echoes of Ficino that we see in the *Symbolum nesianum* represent loyalty to a friend rather than an attempt to evolve a system that would find an intellectual compatibility between the thought of Ficino and Savonarola.

One recalls that the *Symbolum Nesianum*, which in its original redaction was authored in very early 1500, is sandwiched within the much larger *Eptathicum* of Paolo Orlandini, itself redacted almost twenty years later. Above I suggested that in crafting his work, Orlandini was attempting to create an imagined community, an image of Santa Maria degli Angeli as a *contubernium sacrum et philosophicum* where laymen participated as well as monks. Again, after the *Symbolum*, one senses Orlandini's *genius*. He records Nesi as apologizing, after the symbols had been read before the prior Guido da Settimo, that he had not gathered more material, but then averring that on the other hand (Epilogus.2) "I also didn't have to, since I am addressing those men who are also your most learned monks, extremely quick to learn everywhere all the learned opinions." He goes on (Epilogus.3): "Therefore take this little book, a work of three days time, which I put together because of your kindness toward me . . ." One is struck by the notion that the work would be later redacted (ibid.): "I have placed the parchment sheets within the little book [*membranis intus positis*], so that you might delete whatever you do not wish to publish."

Thereafter Orlandini's narrative resumes. Nesi was praised by all, since even though a layman, he was none the less admirably familiar with sacred texts (Epilogus.6). Then Orlandini, questioned by the Prior about his own literary production, revealed that he had written down the Prior's own witticisms and hoped to discuss them with him at some other time.[186] The Prior agrees, and the monks withdraw, *hilares quidem*; and Orlandini retires more anxious than the rest, left to meditate on the Prior's charge to him. We are left, in the end, with an esoteric monument to an esoteric practice. While Santa Maria degli Angeli itself appears in the *Eptathicum* as an open, fluid community made lively by the presence of outsiders, it is in reality

---

[186] See the Commentary below, [Epilogus].10: stridoneos sales.

the insiders who shape the community's practice and wisdom, as a guest like Nesi and a text like the *Symbolum Nesianum* serve to highlight. In a sense, the traditionally esoteric side of the Pythagorean inheritance—the notion that there exists a body of wisdom which is to be transmitted by insiders, to insiders, and in a veiled fashion—is preserved here. This would not always be the case when other European thinkers approached the symbols of Pythagoras, and, as we shall see, their various approaches serve to individuate the *Symbolum Nesianum* even as they reflect well a number of larger tendencies in the developing intellectual life of early modern Europe.

The European Context

The *Symbolum Nesianum* is a Florentine document. It is tied to a specific, *piagnone* context and should be understood within that context. Still, one may legitimately ask what is the work's place on a wider European landscape. Did it have any influence on other interpretations of the symbols? Does it show reciprocal influences or connections? How is it situated within the larger, emerging sixteenth-century context of classical scholarship? To suggest answers to those questions, this chapter examines other treatments of the Pytha-gorean symbols contemporaneous to, or later than, the *Symbolum*. Given the complex authorial circumstances of the work—i.e., the fact that it was in all probability a work of Giovanni Nesi but was then modified during its later redaction by Paolo Orlandini—a wider examination is necessary to understand the work's overall place. I shall examine the work of Filippo Beroaldo the Elder, Erasmus, Johannes Reuchlin, and Lilio Gregorio Giraldi, in order to come to a sense of why and how their treatments of the Pythagorean symbols differ from those in the *Symbolum*.

Filippo Beroaldo the Elder

Filippo Beroaldo the Elder (1453–1505), Bolognese humanist, was known widely in his era.[187] A prolific editor and commentator,

---

[187] For recent literature on Beroaldo see L.A. Ciapponi, "Introduction," in Beroaldo, Filippo, *Annotationes centum*, ed. L.A. Ciapponi (Binghamton, N.Y., 1995) 1–52.

Beroaldo spent time in France and was well known in French humanist circles. More importantly, he was the epicenter of late fifteenth-century Bolognese humanism, who spent the years of 1472–1475 and 1479–1505 teaching poetry and rhetoric at the *studium generale* of Bologna.[188] He was one of that first generation of humanists who made extensive use of the new art of printing, as the comparatively scanty manuscript remnants of his literary production show.[189] In his

Important contributions there cited include M.T. Casella, "Il metodo degli umanisti esemplato sul Beroaldo," *Studi Medievali*, 3rd. ser. 16 (1975) 627–701; D. Coppini, "Filologi del Quattrocento al lavoro su due passi di Properzio," *Rinascimento* 2nd ser. 16 (1976) 219–229; C. Dionisotti, "Calderini, Poliziano ed altri," *Italia medievale e umanistica* 11 (1968) 151–85; V. Fera, "Tra Poliziano e Beroaldo: l'ultimo scritto filologico di Giorgio Merula," *Studi umanistici* 2 (1991) 7–88; L. Frati, "I due Beroaldi," *Studi e memorie per la storia dell'Università di Bologna* 2 (1911) 209–228; E. Garin, *La cultura filosofica degli umanisti*, 359–87; idem, *Ritratti di umanisti* (Florence, 1967) 107–29; idem, "Note in margine all'opera di Filippo Beroaldo il Vecchio," in eds. G. Bernardoni Trezzini et al., *Tra latino e volgare. Per Carlo Dionisotti*, Medioevo e umanesimo, 18 (Padua, 1974) 2: 437–60; M. Gilmore, "Beroaldo, Filippo, senior," in *Dizionario Biografico degli Italiani* 9 (Rome, 1967) 382–384; K. Krautter, *Philologische Methode und Humanistische Existenz: Filippo Beroaldo und sein Kommentar zum Goldenen Esel des Apuleius* (Munich, 1971); idem, "Angelo Poliziano als Kritiker von Filippo Beroaldo," *Res publica litterarum* 4 (1981) 315–330; idem, "Der Grammaticus Poliziano in der Auseinandersetzung mit Zeitgenössischen Humanisten," in *Die Antike-Rezeption in den Wissenschaften während der Renaissance*, Mitteilungen der Kommission für Humanismusforschung, 10 (Weinheim, 1983) 103–16; P.O. Kristeller, "The University of Bologna and the Renaissance," *Studi e memorie per la storia dell'Università di Bologna* n.s. 1 (1956) 313–23; I. Mariotti, "Lezioni di Beroaldo il Vecchio sulla *Thebaide*," in eds. R. Cardini, E. Garin, et al., *Tradizione classica e letteratura umanistica. Per Alessandro Perosa* (Rome, 1985) 2: 577–93; F. Pezzarossa, "'Vita mihi ducitur inter paginas': la biblioteca di Filippo Beroaldo il Vecchio," *Schede umanistiche*, N.s. 1 (1997), 109–130; E. Raimondi, *Politica e commedia: Dal Beroaldo al Machiavelli* (Bologna, 1972); idem, *Codro e l'umanesimo a Bologna* (Bologna, 1950); A. Renaudet, *Préreforme et humanisme à Paris pendant les guerre d'Italie, 1494–1517* (Paris, 1916, repr. 1953), *ad indicem*; F. Rizzi, "Un maestro d'umanità: Filippo Beroaldo," *Archiginnasio* 48 (1953) 77–111; J.B. Wadsworth, "Filippo Beroaldo the Elder and the Early Renaissance in Lyon," *Medievalia et Humanistica* 11 (1957) 78–89. The most important Renaissance lives of Beroaldo are those of Jean de Pins and Bartolomeo Bianchini; for de Pins, I use Jean de Pins, "Vita Philippi Beroaldi Bononiensis," in ed. J.G. Meuschen, *Vitae summorum dignitate et eruditione virorum ex rarissimis monumentis literato orbi restitutae* (Coburg: J.G. Steinmark, 1735) 1: 123–51, originally published in Jean de Pins, *Divae Catherinae Senensis simul et clarissimi viri Philippi Beroaldi Bononiensis vita* (Bologna, 1505); and for Bianchini, "Philippi Beroaldi vita," in *Commentationes conditae a Philippo Beroaldo in Suetonium Tranquillum* (Bologna, 1506). Fullest published bibliography to date of Beroaldo's works is in Krautter, *Philologische Methode*, 188–192.

[188] See U. Dallari, *I rotuli dei lettori legisti e artisti dello Studio bolognese dal 1384 al 1799*, vol. 1 (Bologna, 1888) 90–188.

[189] In Kristeller, *Iter* (*ad indicem*), one sees that the lion's share of material on Beroaldo consists of manuscripts of letters to or from other humanists in various of their *epistolari*.

day he was known widely for his erudition, and seemed a wonder
to his contemporaries. In Pico della Mirandola's eyes, Beroaldo's
biographer de Pins reported, Beroaldo seemed to be "a kind of living, speaking library of all the good arts and things, so that nothing ever seemed too abstruse or difficult, nothing so recondite because
of its antiquity."[190]

Two things characterized Beroaldo and his work. First, as a scholar
and writer he took part in a new, annotative, miscellanistic commentary style, whose high point we see in Poliziano.[191] In some ways
this was tied to the development of printing: as "comparative" philology became more international, philology grew more focused, more
virtuosic, and less broad. Instead of a commentary on one author,
humanists focused on various individual, troublesome passages, on
cruces that they could resolve, to the admiration of their colleagues
in the republic of letters, and, sometimes, to the detriment of their
rivals. Second, as both Krautter and Ciapponi have noted, Beroaldo's
literary production was strongly influenced by his pedagogical practice.[192] Many of his works are dedicated to his former pupils, and
in them one sees that Beroaldo, even at his philologically most virtuosic, pays concerted attention to the moral philosophical lessons
that the texts under study can offer. "Just as parents make the bodies of their children," he wrote to Martinus Boemus, "so too a teacher
fashions the minds of his students."[193] His most characteristic works,
his short commentaries, reflect this twofold emphasis, and his *Symbola
Pythagorica moraliter explicata* is no exception.[194]

The short treatise is dedicated to a powerful Hungarian cardinal,
Tamás Bakócs, 1442–1521, then archbishop of Esztergom; he was
a counsellor at the court of Mathias Corvinus and chancellor under

---

[190] De Pins, cited in Krautter, 25 (my emphasis): "*Philippum nil sibi magis quam
vivam quandam bonarum omnium artium et rerum loquentem bibliothecam videri, quod nihil
usquam tam vel abstrusum vel difficile, nihil tam vetustate reconditum,* quod non ille recens
promptum facile expeditum ac velut apud se domi natum haberet."

[191] Cf. Grafton, *Scaliger,* 1.14–22 and *idem,* "Renaissance Readers and Ancient
Texts: Comments on Some Commentaries," *Renaissance Quarterly* 38 (1985) 615–649.
On the Renaissance commentary see also the studies in Buck and Herding, eds.,
Der Kommentar in der Renaissance.

[192] Krautter, *Philologische Methode,* 10–21 and 41; Ciapponi, "Introduction," 24.

[193] See the letter to Martin in *Varia Philippi Beroaldi opuscula* (Basel: Gregorius
Bartholomeus, 1509) 1v: "Nam sicuti parentes filiorum corpora effigiant, ita prae-
ceptor discipulorum mentes format."

[194] I cite from Philippi Beroaldi *Symbola pythagorica moraliter explicata* (Bologna:
Benedictus Hectoris, 1503).

Wladislaw II.[195] Beroaldo notes that the prince sent his two nephews to him, as if "to the market of the liberal disciplines . . . so that they might be colored with the pigments of our learning."[196] In introducing the work to the prince, Beroaldo writes:

> Now I don't deny that this is a trifling little gift—if you look only at the exterior shell. However, should you look within, at the marrow, you will judge it precious. The task is to explain the *symbola* of Pythagoras with an understanding both tropological and moral, doubtless a succulent thing, and no less fruitful than it is pleasurable.[197]

In so characterizing his little work, he employs a typical Beroaldan *topos*, suggesting that the critic, the interpreter, must penetrate beyond the outer shell to arrive at the fruitful, "juicy" center. In his *Annotationes centum*, Beroaldo, in a Gellian vein, suggested that a reader who wanted to "look within, not at the poet's outer layer, but even at the blood itself, at the marrow," would be persuaded by his interpretation of a particular passage in Lucan.[198] In the epilogue to his *Proverbial Oration*, Beroaldo suggests that "the learning contained in proverbs is grave and fruitful . . . and the marrow even juicier."[199]

---

[195] On whom see E. Koltay-Kastner, "L'umanesimo italiano in Ungheria," *La rinascita* 2 (1939); Krautter, 16–7.

[196] Beroaldo, *Symbola*, A1r (my emphasis): "Tu nuper Bononiam ad me tamquam *ad mercatum ingenuarum disciplinarum* duos nepotes tuos Ioannem et Paulum iuvenes probos, modestos studiosos destinasti, eosque in contubernio meo esse voluisti, *ut doctrinae nostrae pigmentis colorarentur*, nec non dolatorio eloquentiae levigarentur."

[197] Ibid., A1v: "Munusculum est oppido pusillum, nec inficior, si corticem exteriorem tantum spectes. Sed si medullam interiorem introspexeris, pretiosum iudicabis. Opusculum est quo symbola Pythagorae per tropologiam moralemque intellectum explicantur: res haud dubie succulenta, nec minus frugifera quam voluptifica." Beroaldo goes on immediately thereafter to show that he is aware of the conditions of the printed word and the power of print culture to augment the name and reputation of a patron: "So that, moreover, my reverence toward you be made more widely known and more attested, I have seen to it that this little book, composed and printed in a thousand copies, be published, a book which bears on its outer page and in its title your sacred name." ["Ut autem mea erga te observantia fieret celebratior testatiorque curavi ut hic libellus per mille exemplaria formatus excus<s>usque divulgaretur, qui in liminari pagina ac titulo gestat nomen tuum sacrosanctum."]

[198] Ed. Ciapponi, 42.3: "Qui non cutem poetae sed sanguinem quoque ipsum ac medullam, sicuti dici solet, introspicere voluerit, is profecto cognoscet hanc nostram interpretationem poeticae adamussim convenire sententiae." Also see ibid., 104.4, and Ciapponi, "Introduction," 8–9, who discusses this *topos* in Beroaldo and points to its antecedent in Aulus Gellius, at Gell., *Noct. Att.*, 18.4.2.

[199] Beroaldo, *Varia*, 47r: "Proverbiorum doctrina seria est et frugifera . . . et medulla succosior."

Earlier he had cited with approval Jerome's approbation of Solomon's proverbs, since with them Solomon taught moral discipline using, as was fitting, succinct, brief sentiments.[200] The Pythagorean symbols themselves are valuable in Beroaldo's eyes for the same sort of reason: they strike the perfect balance of being brief but at the same time communicative of matters of great moment. They are "sparing of words, fruitful in wise sentiments."[201] This all means that, not only with respect to symbols, but generally, the *interpres* has a great responsibility in Beroaldo's eyes, for, as Beroaldo wrote in his 1487 *Commentary on Propertius*, the critic "unwraps the packages, illuminates the obscurities, and reveals what is hidden; it is he who expounds carefully and copiously what the poet touches briefly, in passing."[202]

Beroaldo also manifests a strong interest in moral philosophy, one typical of many humanists.[203] In designating his style of interpretation of the symbols as "tropological and moral," Beroaldo refers hendyadically to one of the four characteristic medieval modes of hermeneutic, the "moral" or "tropological" sense.[204] His moralizing predilection is reinforced when, explaining why he chose to expound the sym-

---

[200] Ibid., 38r: "Non credis hoc mihi? Crede divo Hieronymo scribenti quod Salomon in libro proverbiorum moralem docuit disciplinam, succinctis, ut decuit, brevibusque sententiis vitae instituta componens."

[201] Beroaldo, *Symbola*, A4v (my emphasis): "Et plane haec symbola leges quadam tenus imitantur, quarum scriptum angustum est, interpretatio diffusa, *parca sunt verborum, fecunda sententiarum*, foris corticosa, intus succosa, aliud sonantia, aliud significantia, quibus praecepta quaedam catholica hoc est universalia sunt involuta ad vitam sancte beateque degendam valde congruentia."

[202] Beroaldo, *Commentarii in Propertium* (Bologna: Benedictus Hectoris and Plato de Benedictis, 1487) A2r, cited and translated in Ciapponi, "Introduction," 9. This sort of attitude toward the weighty responsibilites of the hermeneut was shared—albeit with very different fundamental assumptions concerning the nature of interpretive inspiration—by Marsilio Ficino. See Allen, *Synoptic*, 93–124.

[203] For a survey of Renaissance moral philosophy see J. Kraye, "Moral Philosophy," in C.B. Schmitt and Q. Skinner, eds., *The Cambridge History of Renaissance Philosophy* (Cambridge, New York, etc., 1988) 303–386. Kristeller insisted that this was the only major area of philosophy in which the humanists consistently made major contributions. For a statement of his view see his "Humanism and Moral Philosophy," in Rabil, ed., *Renaissance Humanism*, 3.271–309. Krautter, *Philologische Methode*, 29–30, emphasizes Beroaldo's taste for moral philosophy versus metaphysics.

[204] The other three were the literal (where the reader took the sense *ad verbum*), the allegorical (where the reader interpreted with an eye toward right belief), and the anagogical (which signalled "the way up," and led the reader toward the *eschaton* of interpretation). A nice medieval statement is the high medieval distych: "Littera gesta docet, quid credas allegoria,/moralis quid agas, quo tendas anagogia." See H. de Lubac, *Exégése médiévale: Les quatres sens de l'Ecriture*, 4 vols. in 2 parts (Paris, 1959–1964) 1.1.23–24, for the cited passage and *passim* on the fourfold sense of interpreting scripture.

bols he did ("since they are innumerable"), he chose those which seemed "more conducive and beneficial to the life of mortals."[205] This is important in understanding Beroaldo: he is not a revolutionary, not an avatar of the modern world, despite the manner in which his Latin is nicely *au courant*. Like most Renaissance thinkers he manifested continuity as well as novelty and was an institutional man who sought his originality within a flexibly articulated framework of hermeneutic rules and techniques. To use the categories of Hankins, one might say that Beroaldo's style of reading is a "doctrinal" one, whose aim is "to use the text of the *auctores* as an armature upon which to hang moral lessons and an encyclopedic knowledge of all the arts and sciences."[206] Beroaldo's style of interpretation and his preferred genre of philosophizing are of a piece, then, with his fundamentally pedagogical aims. In addition, as we shall observe, the miscellanistic commentary, as a relatively open and flexible genre, offered him an opportunity to bring various personal touches to his Pythagorean musings, as he laments the death of a friend, frankly discusses sexuality, and promotes his own work.

Beroaldo begins his treatment by introducing the figure of Pythagoras (A2r–A3r). Then, as does the *Symbolum Nesianum* (Introductio.6–11), Beroaldo continues with a discussion of the word "symbol," and its possible meanings, citing among others Terence, Aulus Gellius, Pliny, Plautus, and the Suda (A3r–A5r). Thereafter, as Beroaldo himself mentioned (see above), he is selective in choosing his symbols, and in fact only discusses a total of nine.[207]

---

[205] Beroaldo, *Symbola*, A4v: "Caeterum, cum innumera sint symbola Pythagorae, pauca quaedam ex divini philosophi secretariis selecta deprompsi, quae hodierna narratione a nobis latissime explicarentur: quae vitae mortalium conducibiliora salubrioraque esse credidimus."

[206] Hankins, *Plato*, 1.19; cf. 1.18–26 for Hankins' typology of Renaissance reading.

[207] They are, with my numeration and with Beroaldo's brief definitions: [1] (Beroaldo, *Symbola*, A5r; = Nesi's 44): "ζύγον μὴ ὑπερβενειν [i.e.,ὑπερβαίνειν], quod latine significat 'stateram ne transilias.'" [2] (A6v; = Nesi's 12. No Greek given; discussed within the framework of the first symbol): "coronam urbium non carpendam, hoc est leges urbium esse servandas." [3] (B2r; = Nesi's 11): "καρδίαν μὴ ἐσθίειν, idest, cor non comedendum." [4] (B8v; = Nesi's 7): "μὴ γεύεσθαι μελανούρων, id est, non oportere gustare ex melanuris, hoc est, habentibus caudas nigrantes." [5] (C2v; = Nesi's 20): "τὸ πῦρ μαχαίρᾳ μὴ σκαλεύειν, hoc est, ignem gladio ne fodias." [6] (C4v; = Nesi's 8) "μὴ φόρειν στένον, hoc est anulum angustum non gestandum." [7] (C6r; = Nesi's 23): "ὁμωροφίους χελίδονας μὴ ἔχειν, id est, hirundines sub eodem tecto non habendas." [8] (C6v; = Nesi's 10): "ἐπὶ χοίνικος μὴ καθέζειν, id est, super chenice non sedendum." [9] (C8r; = Nesi's 1): "κυάμων ἀπέχεσθαι, id est, a fabis abstinendum esse."

Here I shall concentrate on two, since they are both representative of Beroaldo's style of thought, and of the possibilities his hermeneutics allowed him. As the first I choose Beroaldo's third, "καρδίαν μὴ
ἐσθίειν, idest, cor non comedendum:" "Don't eat your heart." Although
Krautter devoted a number of excellent pages to this symbol by way
of background to his larger study of Beroaldo's Apuleius commentary, Beroaldo's treatment is so illustrative of his approach that it
must be discussed at length.[208] Its first noteworthy feature, vis à vis
Beroaldo's other symbols, is its length—it takes up over twenty per-
cent of the commentary.[209] This is largely because Beroaldo uses his
comment on the symbol to offer an extended lament for the death
of his best friend, Mino de' Rossi. The traditional interpretation of
the symbol, he is aware, is that "one must rid the soul of grief."
But, he goes on, how many mortals really can do this? "Who is
there, that does not 'eat his heart' every day, who does not waste
away with grief, who isn't overwhelmed with anguish?"[210] Beroaldo
takes an extreme position in a traditional humanist anti-Stoic debate,
i.e., that the idea of ridding one's soul entirely of perturbation (thereby
achieving the state of *apatheia*) is impossible. To stress how foreign
the lack of perturbation is to the known human condition, Beroaldo
writes that there are some who point to certain Ethiopians, "who
neither grieve, nor become angry, nor are moved by any human
emotion, whom on account of this they call *apathes*, almost, you might
say, impassible, that is, they live without any perturbation of their
spirits."[211] "But in my view," Beroaldo continues, "when I ponder
carefully the human condition, and human life, it seems barely possible to find a man who is 'apathes,' who doesn't now and again
'eat his heart,' who doesn't taste of grief and sadness—indeed, even
till he is full of it."[212]

---

[208] See Krautter, *Philologische Methode*, 31–33.

[209] It is approximately thirteen pages in a work of fifty-six pages.

[210] Beroaldo, *Symbola*, B2r: "Sequitur symbolum Pythagorae quo vitae beatitudo
consistit, quod sic infit καρδίαν μὴ ἐσθίειν, idest, cor non comedendum, quod signat
moerorem ex animo eiiciendum, quotus quisque mortalium est? Qui cor quotidie
non edat, qui moerore non tabescat, qui egritudine non conficiatur?"

[211] Ibid., B2v: ". . . qui neque doleant, neque irascantur, neque ulla humana
affectione moveantur, quos ob id ipsum apathes vocant, quasi dicas impassibiles,
hoc est, sine ulla animorum perturbatione degentes. . . ."

[212] Ibid.: "Mihi humanam conditionem ac vitam solerter pensitanti vix possibile
videtur inveniri hominem qui sit apathes, qui cor subinde non edat, qui moerorem
tristitiamque non gustet vel ad satietatem."

The immediate cause for these meditations, he tells us, is the death of his friend Mino de' Rossi, whom he had known for thirty years, ever since they had both studied with Francesco dei Pozzi, and with whom he had shared throughout the years a love of Latin literature (B2v–B3r). The honored Mino's death, as he succumbed to a violent fever, was enough to make Beroaldo forget the message of the symbol.[213] Beroaldo then makes a transition in his discussion of the symbol, to move toward an exposition of its traditional meaning. In this bridging section Beroaldo invokes traditional precepts praising moderation, especially the well-known μηδὲν ἄγαν ("nothing too much"), and suggests that we follow it "if we want to live well and blessedly, for whoever does nothing excessively or rashly will never exult overmuch in happiness, or be overly vexed by sadness."[214]

Beroaldo then moves on to an attempt to find a means of conforming to the symbol's message, which he finds in the humanities— "the *studia humanitatis*, founded by the liberal muse, they have 'juice,' they have charm." "This," he goes on, "is that sun which lightens the clouds of the human spirit, this is that siren which mollifies the hearts of men with life-giving song, this is that *nepenthes* by which sadness is beaten away."[215] The humanities are the best way to lighten one's cares, for

> literate discourse is the greatest ornament in fortunate conditions, the greatest solace in adverse conditions. There is nothing so sad that through them does not become less sad, nothing so happy that does not become happier. So let us flee, then, to the one most powerful relief of grief, studies; let us flock to the solace of writing and reading, to a solace that wipes the stain of sadness from our brow, that calms our spirit. . . .[216]

---

[213] Ibid., B4v: "Cuius acerba mors fecit me oblivisci symboli pythagorici quod precipit cor non esse gustandum meroremque ex animo proiiciendum."

[214] Ibid., B6r: ". . . si bene beateque vivere velimus, nunquam enim nimis aut letitia exultabit aut tristitia vexabitur qui nihil quicquam nimis faciet atque intemperanter . . ."

[215] Ibid., B7r: "Verum studia humanitatis et liberali musa condita, ea habent succum, habent suavitatem. Hic est ille sol qui nubila humani animi serenat, haec est illa syren quae cantu salutari mortalium corda commulcet, hoc est illud nepenthes quo tristitia discutitur." Nepenthes is a drug known to remove all sorrows; Beroaldo is probably drawing on Pliny, *Nat.*, 21.159: "nepenthes illus praedicatum ab Homero, quod tristitia omnis aboleretur." Cf. *Oxford Latin Dictionary*, ad loc. For Beroaldo's love of Pliny see Krautter, *Philologische Methode*, 28.

[216] Beroaldo, *Symbola*, B7r: "Litterae litteratae in secundis rebus sunt maximo ornamento, in adversis maximo solatio. Nihilque tam triste quod per has non fiat minus triste, nihil tam letum quod non sit his letius. Ergo igitur ad unum moeroris levamentum potentissimum studia confugiamus, ad scribendi legendique solatia

Perhaps indicating the extent of his grief, Beroaldo suggests that certain other remedies should not be spurned; there is *helenium*, which, he writes, lightens the spirit when taken with wine, as well as *buglosson*, which has much the same effect.[217] Beroaldo goes on to praise music as lightening cares as well (B7r), there is more discussion of wine (B7v–B8r), and he closes with an exhortation to drive grief from the spirit, "so that interior joys might match a serene face."[218]

The second symbol for discussion is the ever-lively "do not eat beans," Beroaldo's ninth. He is certainly correct to say that there have been numerous and discordant interpretations,[219] and in naming authorities he goes through Cicero, Pliny, Varro, Horace, and others (C8r). One of the traditional interpretations of this symbol, one recalls, was that it was an admonition to chastity. Beroaldo pauses with this interpretation for a while, and dilates. Those who have thought about this carefully, he writes, know that one interpretation is that Pythagoras meant to advise abstaining from the venereal act, since beans look like testicles and are even similar to glands in the genital area.[220] After establishing this as authoritative, however, Beroaldo argues that we should not believe Pythagoras meant us completely to abstain from sexual intercourse, which would be more unhealthy than healthy: there are ancients who advise sexual release—for men—for medical reasons.[221] He relates the tale of

---

convolemus quae tristitudinis maculas abstergebunt frontem, serenabunt animum. . . ." Perhaps an echo of Cicero, *Pro Archia*, 7.16: "Studia . . . secundas res ornant, adversis perfugium ac solacium praebent. . . ."

[217] Ibid.: "Verum enim vero sunt et illa ad moerorem explodendum parva quidem non tamen aspernanda remedia, videlicet ut helenium nobis praesto sit, sic appellatur herba ex helenae lachrymis nata, quae in vino pota effectrix est hilaritatis eaque tristitia omnis aboletur. Habeamus et buglosson quae in vinum deiecta animi voluptates auget et ob id vocatur euphrosynon, sic enim graeca voce hilaritudo atque letitia significatur." Beroaldo is certainly working once again (see penultimate note) from Pliny, *Nat.*, 21.159, whom he cites almost verbatim in the case of *helenium*, and for *buglosson*, from Pliny, *Nat.*, 25.81, also more or less a verbatim citation.

[218] Ibid., B8v (my emphasis): "Ergo igitur pro virili parte elaboremus ut symboli pythagorici bene memores cor minime gustemus, meroremque ex animo propellamus, vitam agentes hilariorem iucundioremque, *ut fronti serenae gaudia interiora respondeant*, ut intus et foris, nubilo tristitiae discusso, serenati simus. Nam alioqui vita non est vitalis, nisi cum hilaritate contingat, et vacuitas ab angoribus adhibeatur."

[219] Ibid., C8r: "Discordes sunt variaeque sententiae eruditorum cur Pythagoras a fabis abstinendum esse censuerit."

[220] Ibid., C8r–v: "Quidam diligentius scitiusque arcanam Pythagorae doctrinam pensitantes autumant symbolice et operte eum voluisse homines non a fabulo edendo abducere, sed a rei veneriae proluvio submovere, nam κυάμους et fabam et testiculos significare tradunt, et re vera fabae genitalibus maximeque virili balano, hoc est, glandi sunt perquam similes, quod et graeci scriptores prodiderunt."

[221] Ibid., C8v: "Non tamen credamus in totum nobis concubitu interdictum esse

Diogenes the Cynic, who, having become most continent after seriously taking up philosophy, still had to use sexual release as a purgative medication, more for reasons of health than of pleasure. One day, goaded by desire, he called for a prostitute, but, when she was late, he masturbated; when the prostitute finally arrived, he said that his hand was his concubine and had served the function of the prostitute.[222] When it comes right down to it, Beroaldo argues, even serious and philosophical men have to release built-up semen, which needs to be excreted like other excrement.[223]

Having finished this aspect of the symbol's interpretation, Beroaldo goes on to others. He treats another traditional interpretation, that one should abstain from politics because beans were used in voting, citing Plutarch and others. He gives ancient examples of authors who advise keeping away from politics (Dr–Dv). He then argues against this opinion, suggesting that we are born as social beings. What glory could be greater than helping in the administration of one's republic? Human beings were born to act, and one has to help one's fellows. Even though there are two cities, a higher and a lower, there are those who have succeeded in philosophizing and living a life of political action.[224] Even Pythagoras lived a life of

---

et venere, quod pernitiosum magis esset quam salutare. Nam concubitus sicut frequens soluit corpus, ita rarus excitat, et si veneri modus absit, nihil perniciosius, ita bonae valetudini, nihil pene utilius, si modice rarenter exerceatur. Galenus maximus medicorum refert se novisse viros virtute et sanctitate venerabiles, qui abstinentia coitus ultronea adeo contristarentur, ut appetentia et concoctio et bona valitudo afficeretur."

[222] Ibid., C8v–Dr: "Hinc scitum illud Cynici Diogenis memoratur, qui cum ex instituto philosophiae esset continentissimus, tamen concubitu quasi purgatorio medicamento utebatur, non voluptatis causa sed bonae //D// valitudinis. Qui olim tentigine satyriove extimulatus, scortum continuo iussit per internuntium evocari, quo serius adventa<n>te factus est mastuprator. Mox cum meretrix advenisset, 'manus,' inquit, 'fuit mihi pro concubina implevitque vicem meretricis.'"

[223] Ibid., Dr: "Ex quo satis liquet venerandos et graves et philosophicos viros uti venere non ob voluptatem sed ob valitudinem, ut ita exuberantia noxii seminis releventur, et enim non minus ex desiderio naturali excrementa geniturae quam stercoris et urinae foras egerenda sunt."

[224] Ibid., Dv–D2r: "Cum ad tuendos conservandosque homines hominem natum esse videamus, consentaneum esse huic naturae ut sapiens velit gerere et administrare rem publicam. Et cum ad laudem et decus nati institutique simus, una laus maior et decus homini esse potest quam ex administratione rei publicae? Et cum homines ad agendum esse natos constet, cumque actionum plura sint genera inter maximas actiones hominis est rerum publicarum administratio. Nempe ab homine hoc exigitur cur prosit hominibus si fieri potest multis, si minus paucis, si minus proximis, si minus suis. Quomodo ergo prodesse homo hominibus poterit? Si se seiunxerit a negotiis in ociumque proiecerit. Scitote duas esse res publicas, altera magnam et vere publicam qua dii atque homines continentur, alteram pusillam,

governance, Beroaldo suggests—alluding to the settlement at Croton—
where he passed on to his disciples the highest learning and discipline.[225] Beroaldo is then led to discuss the rustic life and *otium*, which
leads him to a consideration of Columella, bees, Vergil, Hiero,
Achelaus, and Xenophon, and finally back to Columella and some
self-promotion, where Beroaldo advertises his upcoming work of annotations on Columella.[226]

Comparing Beroaldo's extended and variegated comments to those
in the *Symbolum Nesianum*, one observes that, beyond the general traditional interpretations of the two symbols, there are few direct similarities, both in the source material used by both authors and in
general tone. If, however, we move beyond a superficial comparison and extend our analysis to the styles of commentary represented,
the differences between Beroaldo and the *Symbolum Nesianum* are all
the more illustrative. For the *Symbolum Nesianum* is much more in
line with the traditional "Pythagorean" focus on esoteric styles of
transmitting knowledge and of engaging in intellectual discourse. It
is a more or less closed community for which the work is intended,
a community enclosed by the walls of Santa Maria degli Angeli and
including both the official inhabitants—the Camaldolese—and the
extended community of scholars who are guests in the *contubernium
philosophicum* which Orlandini's *Eptathicum* on the whole is at pains
to present. Beroaldo, on the other hand, is enthusiastically exoteric:
he announces openly in his preface that a thousand copies of this
work are being printed, and even hopes to see it in the hands of
many readers, as a handbook—an *enchiridion*.[227] In addition, Beroaldo
uses the openness and malleability of the Pythagorean symbols to
their fullest extent, employing the apparent impenetrability of the

cui nos conditio nascendi assignavit. Haec autem exempli causa est Romanorum
Atheniensium et ut meos quoque attingam Bononiensium, quae non ad homines
omnis pertineat sed ad certos. Sunt quidam qui utri rei publicae operam dant maiori
scilicet et minori, qui philosophantur simul et negotiantur."

[225] Ibid., D2v: "Ipse Pythagoras regendae rei publicae disciplinam suis discipulis
ultimam tradebat iam doctis iam perfectis, iam sapientibus, iam beatis."

[226] Ibid., D3v–D4r: "Nos itaque Columellam scriptorem primae tribus primaeque
notae classicum eloquentem copiosum, graphicum hoc anno publice enarrare dec-
revimus, ex cuius enarratione mentes auditorum erudiantur, aures commulceantur.
Ego, qui in ocio negotiosus, in feriis occupatus esse soleo, composui Annotationes
in hunc scriptorem compendiariam atque intervallatas, quibus salebrosa levigantur,
tortuosa corriguntur, quas opinor non improbabit quisquis nostra qualiacunque sunt
probare consuevit."

[227] Ibid., A1v: ". . . in manibus quotidie habebunt tamquam enchiridion."

uninterpreted saying ecphrastically, as a stimulus to thought and as a means of teaching. When Nesi, on the other hand, wishes to allude to contemporary events, as he does, I have argued, in his symbol 22 (on the beans) and elsewhere, the meaning is much more concealed, hidden behind a densely allusive web of biblical citation. Beroaldo laments the loss of a friend, openly discusses his views on sexuality, and engages happily in self-promotion. It is a different world in which he lives and moves, and a different style of comment is appropriate. Beroaldo's emphasis on moral philosophy, didacticism, and proverbial learning is important and significant on a Europe-wide level, as we shall now see by focusing on Erasmus.

Erasmus

It is with Erasmus that we see the fullest and most extended development of a culture of proverbial learning, specifically connected to pedagogical aims.[228] Teachers, in Erasmus's eyes, should be well-versed in many authors, and should gather choice tidbits from as many authors as possible; they ought to have a system at hand to do so, as he advises in his *De ratione studi*, first printed in full in 1512.[229] Erasmus outlines how even the general reader who is concerned with his own elegance and moral betterment might do this in the *De copia verborum ac rerum*, first printed in the same year, and stresses that the commonplaces one collects "will ensure both that what you read will stay fixed more firmly in your mind and that you will learn to make use of the riches you have acquired by reading. . . ."[230]

In their focus on the benefits of a proverbial style of learning, one senses a basic reciprocity of interest between Erasmus and Beroaldo; but Erasmus goes much further, for in his *Adagiorum Chiliades*—the

[228] For recent synthetic studies on Erasmus see C. Augustijn, *Erasmus: His Life, Works, and Influence*, tr. J.C. Grayson (Toronto, 1991); L. Jardine, *Erasmus, Man of Letters: The Construction of Charisma in Print* (Princeton, 1993); J. Tracy, *Erasmus of the Low Countries* (Berkeley, Los Angeles, and London, 1996). Enlightening on the historiography on Erasmus from his own day to the early twentieth century is B. Mansfield, *Phoenix of his Age: Interpretations of Erasmus, c. 1550–1750* (Toronto, 1979) and *idem, Interpretations of Erasmus, c. 1750–1920: Man on his Own* (Toronto, 1992).
[229] See *ASD* 1.2.120 and 129 (=*CWE* 24.672 and 678) Cf. A. Moss, *Printed Commonplace-Books and the Structuring of Renaissance Thought* (Oxford, 1996) 101–115. Unless otherwise noted, when citing Erasmus in this section I use with occasional modifications the translations in *CWE*, giving also the relevant location and sometimes the Latin passage in *ASD*.
[230] *ASD* 1.6.260–1, tr. in Moss, *Printed Commonplace-Books*, 111.

Adagia—he had developed a theory of the proverb. The work first appeared in 1508, and was itself a greatly expanded and revised version of his 1500 *Collectanea* of proverbs. It would become a lifelong concern: he continued revising and expanding his *Adagia* until his death.[231] At the outset, Erasmus takes care to define a proverb, a *paroemia*; in his view it is "a saying in popular use, remarkable for some shrewd and novel turn."[232] He stresses that if one is looking for the authority of antiquity, as he knew many of his contemporaries were, there seems to have been no type of learning more ancient than proverbs, for it is in these "symbols" that almost all the learning of the ancients was contained.[233] The modern scholar must study them carefully, because they contribute to four things especially: "philosophy, persuasiveness, grace and charm in speaking, and the understanding of the best authors."[234]

Proverbs possess a "kind of natural and genuine power of truth" (*nativa quaedam et genuina vis veritatis*), they are adaptable, and they are engimatic. Because of this latter factor, they need much study: an ancient author might only allude to one, and the reader might miss the concealed meaning.[235] Still, proverbs should not be overused. As Aristotle recommended in his *Rhetoric*, writing on epithets, "we should treat them not as food but as condiments, not to sufficiency but for delight." If one uses too many proverbs in one's writing, the writing seems stilted and disconnected.[236] Elsewhere, he writes, he gives more detailed consideration to the question of how to use proverbs.[237] Then, before dividing them into various types, Erasmus offers another general comment:

---

[231] See M.M. Phillips, *The "Adages" of Erasmus: A Study with Translations* (Cambridge, 1964); M.L. van Poll-van de Lisdonk et al., eds., *Adagiorum chilia prima, pars prior* (*ASD*, 2.1.5–19).

[232] *ASD* 2.1.46 (=*CWE* 31.4).

[233] *ASD* 2.1.58 (=*CWE* 31.13): "Quodsi quem movet antiquitatis autoritas, nullum doctrinae genus antiquius fuisse videtur quam paroemiarum. In his ceu symbolis tota ferme priscorum philosophia continebatur."

[234] *ASD* 2.1.60 (=*CWE* 31.14).

[235] *ASD* 2.1.62–64 (=*CWE* 31.17–19).

[236] *ASD* 2.1.65–66 (=*CWE* 31.19–20).

[237] *ASD* 2.1.68 (=*CWE* 31.21). Erasmus refers to his *De copia*. The sentence was written in 1508; thus the original reference, as the editors of the *Adagia* in *ASD* point out (2.1.69, note to line 481), must refer to a manuscript version of the *De copia*, which was first printed in 1512.

> The nature of proverbs does not rule out an enigmatic obscurity, which is otherwise not recommended; on the contrary, the obscurity is welcome, as though there was some family relationship.... So too is it the case both that many oracular responses have mingled with the code of proverbs, and that the symbols of Pythagoras clearly belong to the nature of proverbs.[238]

Again, he uses the term "symbol," here connected specifically with the Pythagorean *symbola*. They become for him a very small but consistently theorized part of a larger enterprise: his construction of a learned, subtle, and paleochristianized culture which—even if the version he imagined never emerged and even if he could not have foreseen the separate Christianities which would become part of Europe's history from his day on—remained his guiding passion from his early years until his death.

Erasmus begins his *Adagia* with a Pythagorean precept: "To friends, all things are common." Since, he writes, "there is nothing more wholesome or more generally accepted than this proverb, it seemed good to place it as a favorable omen at the head of this collection." He offers a brief discussion, which he closes by citing Cicero and Gellius, and their attribution of this saying to Pythagoras. He goes on to mention that Pythagoras founded a society where all things were held in common, exactly what Christ wants Christians to do.[239] Erasmus then discusses two symbols together, "Friendship is equality," and "a friend is another self," both of which he also suggests are ascribed to Pythagoras.[240] He then makes a transition to the Pythagorean precepts at large, "which," he writes, "circulated among the Ancients with the force of oracles." Some might seem superstitious and laughable at first glance, but if one removes the allegory ("si quis allegoriam eruat"), one sees that they are nothing more than precepts for living correctly ("quaedam recte vivendi praecepta"). Certainly, there is no need to follow them literally, as Plutarch said some superstitious Etruscans have done.[241]

---

[238] *ASD* 2.1.72 (=*CWE* 31.24). I depart slightly from the *CWE* translation; here is the Latin: "Neque respuit adagiorum ratio aenigmaticam obscuritatem, quanquam alias improbatam, imo veluti familiarem libenter amplectitur.... Proinde et oracula pleraque in ius proverbiorum abierunt et Pythagorae symbola ad paroemiarum naturam videntur pertinere."

[239] *ASD* 2.1.84–86 (=*CWE* 31.29–30).

[240] *ASD* 2.1.86 (=*CWE* 31.31).

[241] *ASD* 2.1.88 (=*CWE* 31.32). The Plutarch reference is to *Moralia* 727c (i.e., *Table Talk* 8.7).

Erasmus's culture of proverbial learning, we can see, is accompanied by a rigidifying trend, as he openly stigmatizes the ritualistic, i.e., literal, use of the precepts, and absorbs them into a wider, moral/didactic proverbial context. Of course, the *Symbolum Nesianum* as well as Beroaldo's treatise both presented mainly moralizing treatments. In the former, however, there is still a vestige of an older ritualistic significance to the precepts, infused by the partially Ficinian programme underlying them. They are weighty, important, and despite the diffuse style of the *Symbolum Nesianum*, richly signifying. Although Beroaldo's treatment is exclusively and explicitly moralizing, he does at least devote a separate treatment to the *symbola*, preserving them as something integral. In Erasmus, instead, the symbols are absorbed into an encyclopedic collection of proverbs reflecting Erasmus's own transformation of the *enkyklios paideia*, a standard Renaissance aim, as well as a look forward to a new kind of *collezionismo*, where the ancient world had to be possessed, classified, and categorized.[242] Erasmus's treatment of the two precepts we examined in Beroaldo—"Do not eat your heart" and "Abstain from beans"—reflects these themes.

The first is brief and suggestive of Erasmus's deeper research into Greek sources than his predecessors'. He gives the symbol's traditional interpretation, i.e., that one should not torment oneself with excessive worry. He takes full advantage of his knowledge of Athenaeus's *Deipnosophistae*, and cites, beyond that text, Aristotle's *De partibus animalium*, Aristophanes, Theognis, and four different *loci* in Homer, all of which have a variation on the saying embedded in them.[243] As to the beans, Erasmus like Beroaldo acknowledges that many interpretations of this symbol have been given. Then, in a virtuosically thorough fashion, Erasmus enumerates and discusses the different sources, and goes through the various traditional interpretations. He employs an interesting, somewhat dialectical method in his exposition, consistently posing questions and amassing contradictory ancient testimony to flesh out his answers. Plutarch and Cicero say the prohibition on beans is about avoiding flatulence. But

---

[242] Cf. P. Findlen, *Possessing Nature: Museums, Collecting, and Scientific Culture in Early Modern Italy* (Berkeley, Los Angeles, and London, 1994); T.C. Price Zimmermann, *Paolo Giovio: The Historian and the Crisis of Sixteenth-century Italy* (Princeton, 1995).

[243] *ASD* 2.1.96 (=*CWE* 31.37). Erasmus cites Athenaeus, *Deipnosophistae*, 10.452; Aristotle, *De partibus animalium*, 3.4.666a7–11; Aristophanes, *Clouds*, 1369; Theognis, 910; Homer, *Iliad*, 6.201–202, 24.129, 1.243, and *Odyssey*, 9.74–75. Cf. notes in *ASD* 2.1.97.

Aristoxenus in Aulus Gellius disagrees, and thinks the Pythagoreans loved beans above all things, for their purgative value. But Gellius also inteprets a line of Empedocles to mean that the word for beans, *kyamoi*, meant "testicles," and thus reports that the symbol enjoins chastity. Diogenes Laertius comes into play; in this section, Erasmus mentions one of the traditional interpretations, that Pythagoras had proscribed beans as a way to discourage people from seeking public office, since beans were used in voting. "For myself," Erasmus adds, "I prefer the explanation added by the writer who collected the incidents referred to by Gregory of Nazianzus: that those who 'eat beans' are men corrupted by bribery in the casting of their votes." Here he refers to the exceedingly rare Nonnos of Panopolis, some of whose work had been known to Filelfo and Poliziano. Erasmus's learning is as always impressive, and his didactic and cultural imperatives are manifest. His goals and his style of exposition, however, did not lead to a different or unique style of understanding the symbols and their place. Lelio Gregorio Giraldi's method of approach did, and it is to his sophisticated and interesting treatment that I shall turn momentarily. Before Giraldi, however, it will be useful to glance briefly at the thought of Johannes Reuchlin, who saw in the Pythagorean tradition a particularly important manifestation of what he believed was an age old, Hebreo-Christian tradition of religious wisdom.

Johannes Reuchlin and the Hebraica veritas

Reuchlin has no extended commentary on the Pythagorean *symbola*, though he does list them and sees them as an important part of Pythagoreanism. His thoughts on the Pythagorean tradition are most fully expressed in his 1517 work, the *De arte cabalistica*, dedicated to Pope Leo X; there, Reuchlin suggests a fundamental similarity and relation between the Kabbalah and Pythagoreanism.[244] The date of

---

[244] On Reuchlin see L. Geiger, *Johann Reuchlin, sein Leben und seine Werke* (Leipzig, 1871; repr. Nieuwkoop, 1964), which is still unsurpassed; see also *idem*, ed., *Johann Reuchlins Briefwechsel*, Bibliothek des litterarischen Vereins in Stuttgart, 126 (Tübingen, 1875; repr. Hildesheim, 1962); M. Brod, *Johannes Reuchlin und sein Kampf* (Stuttgart, 1965); the studies in M. Krebs, ed., *Johannes Reuchlin, 1455–1522: Festgabe seiner Vaterstadt Pforzheim* (Pforzheim, 1955); and S. Rhein, "Johannes Reuchlin (1455–1522). Ein deutscher 'uomo universale,'" in P. Gerhard Schmidt, *Humanismus im Deutschen Südwesten: Biographische Profile* (Sigmaringen, 1993) 59–75. For Reuchlin and his ties to Renaissance occultism, see the fundamental study of C. Zika, *Reuchlin und die*

the work's composition is important, for it signalled a time of crisis for Reuchlin. He had been involved for some time in the set of circumstances which has come to be known as the "Reuchlin affair." Reuchlin, asked for his expert opinion in 1510 by the town council of Cologne, had refused to endorse the opinion that all Hebrew books should be confiscated, and wrote an opinion stating this. In 1511 he wrote a treatise defending his opinion, the *Augenspiegel*. Thereafter, his own work, the *Augenspiegel*, came under investigation. The work was condemned by the theology faculty of the University of Cologne in 1512 and in 1514 by a University of Paris commission of theologians. Controversy arose, and in the aftermath the famous work, the *Letters of Obscure Men* (*Epistolae obscurorum virorum*) was written, in which a number of well-known humanists, among them Crotus Rubeanus and Ulrich von Hutten, skewered Reuchlin's scholastic critics.[245] A series of polemical writings ensued, and, at the behest of the Master of Heretical Depravity, the Brabant Dominican Jacobus Hoogstraeten (who would later critique Luther's *De libertate christiana*), a papal investigation was undertaken.[246] The original papal investigation ended in a *mandatum de supersedendo*, i.e., an official postponement, in 1516, despite the fact that the majority of investigators had decided in Reuchlin's favor. Thus the *De arte cabalistica*,

---

okkulte Tradition der Renaissance, Pforzheimer Reuchlinschriften, 6 (Sigmaringen, 1998). The *De arte cabalistica* was printed in 1517 in Hagenau; the standard modern version is a reprint contained in Johannes Reuchlin, *De verbo mirifico (1494). De arte cabalistica (1517)* (Stuttgart, 1964); for this study I have used the reprint in Johann Reuchlin, *On the Art of the Kabbalah/De arte cabalistica*, tr. Martin and Sarah Goodman, with introductions by M. Idel and G. Lloyd Jones (Lincoln, Nebraska and London, 1993); throughout I employ the abbreviation *DAC* and cite the sigla numbers. For a general bibliographical study of Reuchlin's works, see J. Benzing, *Bibliographie der Schriften Johannes Reuchlin im 15. und 16. Jahrhundert* (Vienna, 1955); see there, 28–30, for the printing history of the *De arte cabalistica*. New editions of Reuchlin are: Johannes Reuchlin, *Briefwechsel*, Band I, 1477–1505, Unter Mitwirkung von Stefan Rhein, bearbeitet von Matthias Dall'Asta und Gerald Dörner (Stuttgart-Bad Cannstatt: Frommann-Holzboog, 1999) and Johannes Reuchlin, *Schriften zum Bücherstreit, 1. Teil Reuchlins Schriften*, eds. W.-W. Ehlers, L. Mundt, H.-G. Roloff, and P. Schäfer, in Johannes Reuchlin, Sämtliche Werke, 4 (Stuttgart-Bad Cannstatt: Fromann-Holzboog, 1999). I rely here somewhat on my study, "The Search for Ancient Wisdom in Early Modern Europe: Reuchlin and the Late Ancient Esoteric Paradigm," *Journal of Religious History* (2001), where more bibliography is given.

[245] For recent literature on this problem, with new discoveries, see W. Ludwig, "Literatur und Geschichte—Ortwin Gratius, die Dunkelmännerbriefe und 'Das Testament des Philipp Melanchthon' von Walter Jens," *Mittellateinisches Jahrbuch* 34 (1999) 125–67.

[246] Hoogstraeten's critique of Luther: H.A. Oberman, *The Dawn of the Reformation* (Grand Rapids, Michigan, 1986) 45.

written at a time of particular religious controversy in Reuchlin's life, was a bold attempt to transcend apologetics and win the Pope to an opinion in which Reuchlin passionately believed: that there was an important overlap between Hebrew and Pythagorean tradition that could help further the interests of true Christianity.

The work itself is a dialogue with three interlocutors, Philolaus, a "Pythagorean," Marranus, a Moslem, and Simon, a Jewish Kabbalist. On the first day, which coincides with the first book, Simon explains some basic principles of Kabbalah to the other two. On the second day, given that it is the Jewish Sabbath, Simon is absent, and Philolaus explains the principles of Pythagoreanism to Marranus. They wind up the second book noting certain similarities between the Pythagorean tradition and Kabbalah, and on the third day they seek out Simon, who goes on in the third book to give them an in-depth explanation of a number of Pythagorean principles.

Reuchlin's Pythagoreanism is clearly identifiable as Neopythagorean in the Iamblichean and post-Iamblichean mold. The main locus of similarity is that Reuchlin believes, as had Ficino, that there is a place within the philosophical life for religious ritual. In the *DAC*, Reuchlin's approach to the question of how to merge his interests in religious ritual with philosophical concerns stresses a number of interrelated features, which form a recognizable complex of esoteric concerns.[247] First, there is a characteristic approach to allegoresis. Just as, for Ficino, Plato had been the figure he felt himself obligated to save from charges of impiety, for Reuchlin it is Pythagoras. Thus, one of the most damaging, consistently attested portions of the Pythagorean legacy (for someone writing from a Christian perspective) was that Pythagoras had believed in the transmigration of souls. Reuchlin turns rhetorical cartwheels to show that, despite all ancient, late ancient, and medieval tradition to the contrary, this was not true. Second, and connected to the first feature, Reuchlin, as Iamblichus had done much earlier, links Pythagoreanism with soteriology, suggesting that Neopythagorean philosophizing, for Reuchlin combined with Kabbalistic teaching, was something that could contribute to individual salvation.

Third, Reuchlin, like other Platonic esoterists in the Iamblichean mold, stresses efficacy. The rituals described and the signs used are

---

[247] The following fivefold interpretation is more fully developed in Celenza, "The Search for Ancient Wisdom."

not just means to deeper contemplation; they bring results.[248] The Pythagorean Kabbalist, for Reuchlin, is someone who is the friend of angels; who calls down angels into his service by means of the correct ritual behavior; and who, because of this great friendship with angels, performs what the crowd calls miracles.[249] Fourth, Reuchlin, like many Renaissance thinkers in the early sixteenth century, shares a conviction that human ratiocinative capacity is insufficient as an instrument for seeking divine truth. There is so much mystery in the world that we need divine illumination to reach divinity, an illumination activated by Kabbalistic and "Pythagorean" practice. This practice centered on the use of language in such a way that one could plumb divine mysteries and have an access to divinity otherwise unthinkable.

Fifth, Reuchlin's approach highlights a certain type of information transfer in an atmosphere of religious uncertainty. Pythagoreans and Kabbalists agree, since both want to bring mens' minds to perfect blessedness. To do so, they both engage in information transfer by means of symbols, signs, adages and proverbs, numbers and figures, letters, syllables, and words. Pythagorean Kabbalistic illumination creates communities of insiders by helping the practioner know not only what texts to read but also what to exclude. With the boundaries of knowledge being burst open—by printing, by careful, ever more intense philological scholarship, by debates and by an increasingly rigid seeming religious atmosphere, manifested paradoxically in a burgeoning plurality of orthodoxies whose outer limits no one was sure of—coded, veiled wisdom was appealing, as a short cut, as a means to combine learning and inspired wisdom, an epistemological bypass to knowing the truth.

Understood within this framework, the Pythagorean *symbola* fit seamlessly into Reuchlin's world-view. They are bearers, for Reuchlin, of secret meaning; they are mnemonic tools which encapsulate larger moral truths; they are signs of community, of initiation, of friendship, of recognition. Reuchlin recognizes Erasmus (perhaps partially facetiously) as a fellow-Pythagorean (*DAC*, I iii verso), because of the *Adagia*, and thus provides a convenient link to his treatment of the *symbola*. The Erasmian overtone is useful, because Reuchlin's brief

---

[248] Excellent on this mentality is S. Clark, *Thinking with Demons: The Idea of Witchcraft in Early Modern Europe* (Oxford, 1997) 281–93.
[249] *DAC*, Eiii verso.

treatment of the symbols is primarily moralizing, despite the intricate web of Pythagorean/Kabbalistic esoterism within which Reuchlin sees the symbols as operating. Reuchlin divides them into three categories, those that deal with the worship of god and divinity, those that deal with the individual's duty to himself, and those that deal with his duty toward others. He offers no extended comment on any of them, and simply presents brief interpretations for each.[250] Philolaus concedes that there are certainly more and avers that he did not want to go through them all on this occasion. He is also careful to state, at the conclusion of his treatment of the symbols, that "almost all Pythagorean philosophy is full of signs of words and coverings of things," which Pythagoras was the first to bring to the Greeks from the Hebrews and the Egyptians, and about which Pythagoras stressed the need for silence and reticence.[251]

Reuchlin is caught in the esoterist's dilemma, always a part of the Pythagorean tradition: on the one hand, one must keep certain important truths only for a tightly controlled group of initiates, who have the requisite training to use them well. On the other, one must defend and at times create one's social position when hostile orthodoxies threaten to intrude on one's well-being; thus, to create this social space, the truths must be presented with due reverence but nonetheless revealed, thereby simultaneously compromising the posture of secrecy even as one functions as the "revealer" promising secret knowledge. This tension inherent in Reuchlin's Neopythagorean Kabbalism was part of an outlook radically different from that of Beroaldo and Erasmus; so, too, was it from that of Lilio Gregorio Giraldi, whose scholarly and exhaustive treatment of the *symbola* complements his forward looking, anthropological interest in the history of western religion.

Lilio Gregorio Giraldi

— Here you see the tomb of Lilio Giraldi, who bore both sides of fortune's page.[252]

---

[250] *DAC*, Iiii verso–Iv verso.

[251] *DAC*, Iv recto.

[252] ". . . Tymbion/vides Gyraldi Lilii, Fortunae utramque paginam/qui pertulit . . .," from Giraldi's gravestone, cited in G. Barotti, *Memorie istoriche di letterati Ferraresi*, second edition, 2 vols. (Ferrara, 1792) 1:328–64. Also cited in K. Wotke, "Einleitung,"

Lilio Gregorio Giraldi (1478–1552) was a tremendously erudite Fer-
rarese scholar, who indeed bore both sides of the page of fortune.[253]
Having been educated by Battista Guarino, among others, he travelled
widely and spent time in Naples, where he met Sannazzaro and
Giovanni Pontano. Thereafter he went to Lombardy and came into
the orbit of the Pico family. He became, eventually, the tutor of
Giantommaso Pico, the son of Gianfrancesco Pico della Mirandola.
In 1507 he went to Milan and perfected his Greek, studying with
Demetrios Chalkondylas. He then went to Modena, where he was in
the Rangoni household, becoming the tutor of Ercole Rangoni, who
himself would become a Cardinal. In 1514 Giraldi joined Rangoni
in Rome, and was in the Eternal City for the Sack of 1527, where
he lost all of his personal wealth, property, and books. He fled to
Bologna, but found no patronage there, and then moved back to
his native Ferrara. He came into the circle of Renée de France, the
Calvinist sympathizing wife of Ercole II; during the 1540s she would
distance herself more and more from Catholic ritual and openly sup-
ported Protestants passing through Ferrara.[254] Tormented by gout,
Giraldi was in his last years unhappy and sometimes on the verge
of penury, though he remained impressively productive through it all.

Giraldi was a learned commentator on contemporary as well as
ancient affairs, writing a popular book *De poetis nostrorum temporum*, a
work *De deis gentium*, a set of *Dialogismi XXX* in the tradition of
Poliziano's *Miscellanea*, a work *Adversus literas et literatos*, and numerous other, comparatively little studied works.[255] What impresses about

in Lilius Gregorius Gyraldus, *De poetis nostrorum temporum*, ed. K. Wotke, in Lateinische
Litteraturdenkmäler, 10 (Berlin, 1894), reprinted in *La storiografia umanistica*, eds. A.
Di Stefano et al., 2 vols. in 3 parts (Messina, 1992) 2: final text (I cite from the
pagination in the original), ix.

[253] This paragraph relies on Barotti, cited in previous note, as well as L. D'Ascia,
"Humanistic Culture and Literary Invention in Ferrara at the Time of the Dossi,"
in eds. L. Ciammitti, S.F. Ostrow, and S. Settis, *Dosso's Fate: Painting and Court Culture
in Renaissance Italy* (Los Angeles, 1998) 309–332; F. Bacchelli, "Science, Cosmology,
and Religion in Ferrara, 1520–1550," in *Dosso's Fate*, 333–354; and R.A. Pettinelli,
Tra antico e moderno: Roma nel primo Rinascimento (Rome, 1991).

[254] On Renée and the Ferrarese environment see C.J. Blaisdell, "Politics and
Heresy in Ferrara," *Sixteenth Century Journal* 6 (1975) 67–93.

[255] For the *De poetis nostrorum temporum*, see the edition of Wotke, cited above; for
the *De deis gentium* I use Lilio Gregorio Giraldi, *De deis gentium varia et multiplex his-
toria, in qua simul de eorum imaginibus et cognominibus agitur, ubi plurima etiam hactenus multis ignota explicantur et pleraque clarius tractantur* (Basel: Joannes Oporinus, 1548; reprint
New York, 1976); for the *Dialogismi XXX* see the edition in Giraldi's *Opera Omnia*
(Basel: Thomas Guarinus, 1580); as well as the piece of L. D'Ascia, "I *Dialogismi*

his *oeuvre* is its high level of sophistication, both from the source-based perspective of the history of classical scholarship, and from the more subjective but none the less interesting viewpoint of theoretical vivacity. Many times in his work one senses a glimmer of comparative approaches of a later age, as if he is foreshadowing the development of an Enlightenment-era comparative cultural history. Particularly noteworthy is his interest in comparative religious history. In his prolific, tormented later period, i.e., the 1540s and very early 1550s, one can imagine an intimate link between his scholarly interest in religion and the cultural environment in which he found himself. In a city, Ferrara, whose dynastic rulers had earlier in the century been enemies of Julius II and of the two Medici popes, Leo X and Clement VII; in a city which had gone so far in recent years as to engage in war with the papacy; in a city which in the 1540s developed into a strong refuge for Protestantism without officially converting, one might say that there was more ideological space for Giraldi's interest in comparative religious practice than there would have been in the rigid environment of Rome in the 1540s, or in the Florence of the same era. Before moving to his commentary on the Pythagorean *symbola* I shall look at his *De deis gentium*, to establish a context for his views on religion.

In that work Giraldi intends, he writes in the preface, to be encyclopedic in his coverage and portrayal of the ancient Greek and Roman gods. Moreover, unlike Boccaccio in his *Genealogiae deorum*, Giraldi wishes to cover all aspects of the ancient gods: "I have covered in this work all the credulous religions about the gods of almost all the ancient pagans—not, I say, the genealogies of the gods, but also their *nomina* and *cognomina*, appearances, distinguishing features, and which homeland each has, also what sacred rituals and religious rites are appropriate for each."[256] His aim, in other words, is encyclopedic and exhaustive. The work is structured in seventeen *syntagmata*,

XXX di Lilio Gregorio Giraldi fra Bembo, Erasmo, Valla," *Rivista di letteratura italiana* 10 (1992) 599–619; for the *Progymnasma adversus literas et literatos*, see the *Opera Omnia*, 2:422–443.

[256] A2 recto (from the preface, unpaginated, to Ercole II d'Este): "Ego quoque dum volo hoc quicquid est reliqui cadentis ac prope iacentis vitae producere, non valde horum dissimile opus hoc tempore confeci; quo opere sum omnes omnium pene gentium de deis superstitiosas religiones complexus—non genealogias deorum dico, sed et nomina et cognomina, effigiesque, insigniaque, et quae patria cuique est, sacra quoque ac cerimonias." Boccaccio comes in for some gentle criticism on A2 verso.

and each covers a different aspect of a god or set of gods. Each *syntagma* carries a separate dedication. At the work's outset, Giraldi is careful to say that there should be no question of his piety. He is well aware that many who are devoted to the *studia humanitatis* come under suspicion of impiety; he is also cognizant of the fact that it is dangerous to discuss many gods; and thus he offers a profession of faith. The first *syntagma* is interesting for its synthetic ambition. Giraldi discusses the different attitudes among pre-Socratic philosophers toward divinity. Thereafter he goes on to a wide-ranging survey of the divisions of the gods, and what functions the gods served.

Here and elsewhere he is aware of the inherent translatability of polytheistic systems. For example, the second *syntagma* is devoted to Jupiter, among other gods, and Giraldi clearly recognizes that different ancient cultures shared a concept of Jupiter and used different names for him to describe his different aspects. The names *Jupiter optimus maximus, Jupiter stator*, etc., all fulfilled different functions, while describing different facets of the god's might. The successive *syntagmata* go on in this vein, discussing first the different names of the divinities under examination and what those names represented, then describing the rites performed to honor the divine beings.

Along the way, the prefaces to the various *syntagmata* testify to Giraldi's social and cultural contacts during a time, the late 1540s, which was difficult for him from the perspective of finding patronage. One, to Bernardo Barbuleo, is particularly poignant. In it, Giraldi summarizes the high and then many low points of his ill-starred career; he touches on his early studies together with Bernardo, the dedicatee, his time with Celio Calcagnini, his time in the environment of the papal court, including his happy period of service to Ercole Rangoni. He then moves to the sack of Rome and his subsequent struggle with gout, which has left him so incapacitated that he cannot even lie on his side without assistance, let alone walk around. Despite this current hardship, however, with the aid of an amanuensis he writes every day.[257]

---

[257] *De deis gentium*, 179–80 (it is the preface to the fourth *syntagma*, "de Saturno, Rhea, Vesta, Iano, Vertuno"): "Lilius Gregorius Gyraldus Bernardo Barbulaeo s.p.d.

Amavi ego te, mi frater Bern. Barbulaee, a primis usque nostrae adolescentiae annis, cum ambo nos operam daremus bonis literis et moribus, sub doctissimo et integerrimo viro Bap. Guarino, ex cuius ludo tot ex omni ferme Europa viri excellentes in omni literarum et optimarum disciplinarum genere, tanquam ex equo (quod dicitur) Troiano effluxerunt. At nostrum uterque in humanitatis studiis tan-

Things had not always been so difficult, however. Giraldi's work on the Pythagorean *symbola* owes its origin to an earlier period in his life, when he was at the outset of the first, privileged part of his career. At that time, he had come into the orbit of the famous skeptic and nephew of Giovanni Pico della Mirandola, Gianfrancesco Pico della Mirandola.[258] To Gianfrancesco's son Giantommaso, Giraldi dedicated his two-fold work on enigmas and on the Pythagorean symbols.[259] The work was printed only in 1551, though he had originally written it in 1507, while in Carpi, where he spent time at the court, as he tells Prospero Pasetti in a prefatory letter. Now in his elder years the work still lies unpublished, and Giraldi has come to Pasetti,

tum profecit, quantum vel natura nostra, et ingenii vires patiebantur: vel quantum tenues admodum facultates permisere, et angusta domi res, quibus quidem difficultatibus haud facile homines (ut ait poeta) emergunt, et virtutibus insignes ac illustres evadunt. Hinc est, quod nos nostra gloriola contenti, quam in Mustaceo (ut ait Cicero) quaesivimus [cf. Cic., *Epist. ad Attic.* 5.20.4]; donec tu quidem hic Ferrariae subsistens, iuventutem cum Coelio nostro instituisti, adeo ut tu dignus iudicarere qui sacerdotio divi Petri praeficereris. Ego vero procul a patria peregre profectus, ea<m>dem de me expectationem concitaram, ut omnes me crederent in aliquem procerum sacrorum ordinem cooptandum, et praesertim sub Leone, Adriano, et Clemente, pontificibus, apud quos me ita domestica familiaritas accepta visa fuit, ut a me nihil unquam ab eis frustra petitum sit, quinimmo et pleraque ultro oblata, praecipue meo in humanis adhuc agente alumno et discipulo Hercule Rangonio, Romae divae Agathae Diacono. Post cuius immaturum obitum et urbis direptionem, ita reflantem habui fortunam ut ab eo tempore non tantum res meae deteriore loco esse coeperint, sed et corporis vires ita debilitari, ut in eam articulorum omnium adversam valetudinem inciderim, ut non modo ambulare (ut tu quidem frater optime nosti) sed nec etiam in latus decumbere possim, nisi sim a valente aliquo ministro adiutus. Nec tamen cum ita morbis affligar, cesso, quin aliquid indies per ammanuensem puerum vel scribam, vel dictem. Sicut superioribus his diebus faciebam, cum de Deis gentium manum opus confeci, cuius tibi duo syntagmata mittere constitui, in quorum altero Saturnum et Magnam deûm matrem, et Vestam, tum etiam Ianum et Vertunum, sum complexus, in altero Neptunum, et deos caeteros marinos, nymphasque varii generis, ad haec et Aeolum et ventos. Accipe igitur amantissime frater ab aegroto tuo Lilio et pene conclamato qualecunque munus, non quod ex me aliquid tibi ignotum et reconditum habere possis, vel quod ex tua illa refertissima de omni librorum genere bibliotheca non facile haurire queas, sed ea duntaxat ratione, omnibus ut constet, mutuam inter nos amicitiam ex multo fuisse tempore constitutam. Di faxint ut et per scripta nostrum utriusque nomen posteritati notum esse contingat. Vale."

[258] Gianfrancesco Pico's fideistic (and Savonarolan) skepticism is best expressed in his *Examen vanitatis doctrinae gentium et veritatis Christianae disciplinae, distinctum in libris sex* (Mirandola: Ioannes Mazochius, 1520), a work structurally modeled on Sextus Empiricus. Cf. W. Cavini, "Appunti sulla prima diffusione in Occidente delle opere di Sesto Empirico," *Medioevo* 3 (1977) 1–20; G.M. Cao, "L'eredità pichiana: Gianfrancesco Pico tra Sesto Empirico e Savonarola," in ed. P. Viti, *Pico, Poliziano e l'Umanesimo di fine Quattrocento* (Florence, 1994) 231–45; C.B. Schmitt, *Gianfrancesco Pico della Mirandola (1469–1533) and his Critique of Aristotle* (The Hague, 1967).

[259] Giraldi, *Aenigmata/Symbola*.

in the hopes that Pasetti, who has always been Giraldi's *patronus acer-*
rimus, would accept the work, and help him in any way possible.[260]
In the actual dedication letter to Giantommaso, written in 1507,
Giraldi stresses that he does not wish in any way to compare his
own work to that of Giovanni and Gianfrancesco Pico, but rather
wants Giantommaso to turn, by means of these jesting diversions,
to serious and greater matters. He signs the letter from Carpi, 1507.[261]

The book is in two parts; the first deals with various brief *aenig-*
mata, the second with the symbols. His handling of the *Aenigmata*
(8–65) reminds one very much of Erasmus's *Adages*. The sayings
Giraldi treats are often no more than a word or two, and it is clear
in his treatments of them that what we might call the hermeneutic
obligation—where the creative burden of scholarly interpretation falls
heavily on the critic—is strong. He brings to bear his vast erudition
in solving the various riddles of which his *Aenigmata* are composed.
He treats *Aenigmata* of Cleobulus (13), Heraclitus (15), the Sphinx
(18), and Apollonius of Tyana (31), among many others; as sources
of his explications we find the *Suda* (43) and Athenaeus (54) among
relatively rare authors, as well as near contemporaries like Ficino
and Crinito (32–4).

Giraldi's work on the *Symbols* follows (71–181). The preface, again
to Giantommaso Pico, shows wide, systematic learning, as well as a
definite theoretical perspective concerning the problem of symbols
and enigmatic discourse. He writes that the most ancient poets, who
were also called theologians, always spoke in figurative discourse
when they were talking both about divine as well as natural things,
as he hopes to show in a work on poets.[262] As he does elsewhere in
his *oeuvre*, he develops his interest in comparative religious practice,
discovering a realm of similarity in symbolic discourse among different
religions. Those, he writes, who have either founded new religions
or laws, or accepted them from the immortal gods, imitated poets

---

[260] Giraldi, *Aenigmata/Symbola*, 3–5.

[261] Ibid., 7: "Tibi autem, Pice, utrunque libellum non ea ratione misi, ut mea
cum iis conferas quae domi tibi nascuntur, hoc est, cum iis quae quotidie a pa-
rente tuo scribuntur, a quo omnis est tibi vita perdiscenda, sed ut his Saturnalibus
pro strenis a magistro manus habeas, ut per haec iocosa et ludicra, ad seria et
maiora te convertas. Vale: ex Castro novo Carpensi. M.D.VII."

[262] Giraldi, *Aenigmata/Symbola*, 71: "Qua puto ratione factum ut antiquissimi illi
poetae, qui et theologi vocati sunt, omnis (ut sic dicam) sapientiae antistites, res
ideo divinas et naturales fabularum quibusdam figmentis involutas cecinerint, quod
in Dialogis de Poetis pluribus, ut spero, ostendemus."

and their style of symbolic, aphoristic discourse.[263] Ancient pagan
figures, Mohammed, Moses, and Christ are counted among these
religious thinkers.[264] The basic message is that many ancient authorities agree that it has pleased divinity to hide itself in fables. From
the very beginning, then, both Pythagoreans and Platonists employed
enigmas and symbols, since they knew that unadorned, open exposition was inimical to God and nature. (72–3) As his preface continues, Giraldi uses two words to describe the style of discourse which
symbols imply, *cuniculus* (here, "subterranean passage") and *labyrinthus*,
thus suggesting that he saw the precepts as mysterious, certainly, but
also connected, as if they are somehow inherently linked.[265]

After these general remarks concerning the style of discourse,
Giraldi moves on to a discussion of the Pythagorean symbols and
the figure of Pythagoras. Textually speaking, he gets right to the
heart of the matter, citing Iamblichus's *De secta pythagorica*, which as
we have seen contains the fullest ancient listing of the symbols, along
with various other writers, including Jerome—*noster Hieronymus*.[266] He

---

[263] Giraldi, *Aenigmata/Symbola*, 71–2: "Hos poetas imitati sunt, qui religiones
novasque leges, vel ipsi primi instituerunt, vel a deis immortalibus acceptas, mor-
talibus attulerunt, vel posuerunt. Nam et ipsi obscuris plerunque, opertisque ser-
monibus usi sunt, adeo ut nec aenigmatum involucris, metaphorisque ac parabolis
quas vocamus et iis interdum longe repetitis abstinuisse videamus."

[264] Ibid., 72: "Quem sane loquendi morem, ut iam vetustate desitos mittamus,
Zoroastres, Zamolxes, Zaleucos, Dardanos, Charondas, Numas, alios: nonne et
Magmed, quem vulgo Mahometen vocamus, cum in suo Dialogo, tum in eo etiam
quem a Deo sibi datum suis persuasit, Alchorano usurpasse videmus? Sed et, si
inter impios meminisse licet, num Mosem, caeterosque Hebraeorum vates, qui
Graeca voce prophetae dicuntur, iis saepe usos esse conspicimus? Et parcius quidem CHRISTUM Deum, Dominum, et servatorem nostrum?"

[265] Cf. Ibid., 73: "Sic ipsa mysteria figurarum quasi cuniculis operiri volebant, ne
vel haec adeptis nudam rerum talium se divina natura praeberet, sed summatibus
tantum viris sapientia interprete, veri arcani consciis, contenti ut sint reliqui ad ven-
erationem figuris et involucris defendentibus, a vilitate secretam"; and also 74: "Hinc
ergo factum reor, ut in prodendis sacris, vel Deorum vel naturae arcanis magni illi
inter scriptores heroes, tenebris plerunque, plusquam Cimmeriis, flexuosisque Maeandris,
et (ut sic loquar) labyrinthis usos esse videamus."

[266] Ibid., 74–5: "Iamblichus ex Chalcide Syriae philosophus, θεῖος, hoc est divinus cognominatus, inter alia multa quae in omni philosophia monumenta reliquit,
de secta et vita Pythagorae libros edidit, in quibus Pythagoram ait, griphis et aenig-
matis, quae Symbola dicuntur, usum fuisse. Idem scribit Demetrius Byzantinus, et
Naucratia Athenaeus, idem Olympiodorus et Hierocles et Cyrillus, Alexandrini; et
in iis quae contra Ruffinum noster scripsit Hieronymus. Idem et Porphyrius philosophus, in iis libris quos de vita Pythagorae scripsit." Giraldi here shows his learning: Iamblichus was recognized by Platonists who followed him as so important to
the history of the Platonic religious and philosophical tradition that his successors
routinely (as opposed to exceptionally) referred to him as θεῖος—divine; cf. G. Fowden,

leans heavily on the notion that Pythagoras learned much from the
Hebrew prophets, and mentions (without affirming or denying it)
Ambrose's opinion that Pythagoras was born a Jew.[267] Since as the
leader of an ancient community Pythagoras taught how to live well
and in a holy fashion, he offered his disciples short opinions, which
the Greeks call *diathecae* (here he echoes Poliziano, whom Nesi also
had cchocd), by which they might move their minds from the busy
content of their thoughts to tranquillity.[268]

In addition, here as elsewhere in his *oeuvre*, Giraldi demonstrates
a consciousness of recent and current work, demonstrating as well
that he has updated this specific treatise between 1507 and 1551.
After listing ancient figures who have commented on the Symbols,
he writes that,

> in our time, two Germans, most learned men, began this task [*i.e.*,
> *interpreting the symbols*], though they did not complete it: namely, Erasmus
> of Rotterdam and Johannes Reuchlin. And before them, from our peo-
> ple, Beroaldo the Elder collected together certain things in a little book
> of his. Because of this I, although I am unequal to them, am going
> to try now to expound these same symbols to you with greater care
> and scholarship.[269]

It is interesting to observe a Renaissance scholar positioning himself
vis à vis his immediate predecessors. We are entering the world of the

---

"The Pagan Holy Man in Late Antique Society," *The Journal of Hellenic Studies* 102
(1982) 33–59, at 36.

[267] Giraldi uses sophisticated sources: *Aenigmata/Symbola*, 75: "Pythagoras igitur, qui
vulgo quidem Samius, a plerisque Syrius, ab aliis Tyrius, a Graecis quibusdam Tyr-
rhenus, a nonnullis (ut scribit Divus Ambrosius) ab Hebraeis originem duxisse exist-
imatus est: et perinde etiam, ut ait Theodoritus, a circumcisione non abstinuit, ab
Hebraeorum prophetis et in primis a Mose multa desumpsisse facile videri potest: id
quod et Iosephus contra Appionem, et Aristobolus philosophus Peripateticus, Hebraei,
et Eusebius et Hieronymus Christiani prodidere, quod nec negat Iamblichus, et aperte
ostendit Hermippus, diligentissimus historiarum perscrutator. . . ." See also 79.

[268] Ibid., 76: "Cum, inquam, ille ad bene beateque vivendum institueret, sententias quasdam perbreves, diathecas a Graecis dictas, illis occultius proponebat,
quibus eorum mentes a cogitationum intentione ad tranquillitatem traducebat." For
diathecae, cf. the *Symbolum Nesianum*, Introductio.7.

[269] Ibid., 77: "Haec, inquam, symbola antiqui<u>s Anaximander Milesius, is qui
iunior dictus est, et Alexander Polyhistor, interpretati sunt—quorum, quod sciam,
interpretationes ad nos non pervenerunt. Plutarchus quidem, et Athenaeus, et Laertius,
aliique ex parte et hinc inde interpretati sunt. Sed nostro tempore Germani duo,
viri doctissimi, id quidem potius incepere quam perfecere: Erasmus videlicet Rhote-
rodamus, et Ioannes Phorcinus [*i.e.*, *of Pforzheim: Reuchlin*]. Nam ante hos ex nostris
senior Beroaldus, pauca quaedam suo quodam libello collegit. Quamobrem nos im-
pares iis licet, tibi maiore cura et studio ea ipsa nunc symbola exponere tentamus."

erudits, where a specific scholarly problem, here that of the Pythagorean Symbols, must be treated *cum cura et studio* to be satisfactory. Giraldi is correct to recognize the learning of Erasmus, Reuchlin, and Beroaldo, but he is also right in distinguishing his treatment, to follow, from theirs. It is more dispassionate, more informed, less ideologically committed, and more wide-ranging in its conclusions.

After mentioning different religious systems which use symbols in various guises and forms (78–81), and after discussing the possible etymological meanings of the term symbol (81–83), Giraldi goes a step further than any of his predecessors and develops a theory of authenticity. How does one know if a symbol is truly Pythagorean or not? Those which are uncontroversially Pythagorean are wrapped up, their obscure meanings twisted into a cover. "As you shall see," Giraldi writes, "there are some symbols which, because they were not written with the same reason as others, have come into doubt as to whether they are legitimate." Moreover, Demetrius of Phalerum suggests that what is to be expected in symbols, authentic ones, is that with gravity and a certain brevity we understand the manifold senses under them.[270] Some symbols forbid things, some symbols have the nature of adages.[271] Following divisions reported by ancient writers, Giraldi suggests that the Pythagorean symbols can be best understood as falling into two different threefold arrangements: moral, natural, and theological, on the one hand, and, on the other, as answering the questions "what is," "what is greatest," and "what is best."[272] In short, followers were warned using the symbols about what to do, and what to flee.[273] His reader should not be surprised,

---

[270] Ibid., 83–4: "Illud tantum non omiserim, Symbolorum id proprium esse, ut maeandris obscurisque sententiarum involucris involuantur, quod in iis mire est observatum, quae sine controversia Pythagorica sunt. Nam, ut videbis, aliqua sunt, quae quoniam ea non sunt ratione conscripta qua caetera, propterea plerisque dubitatum an sint legitima. Illud quod Demetrius Phalereus in symbolis attendendum ait, ut cum gravitate et brevitate quadam plurimum sensus sub his intelligamus. Dat ille exemplum, ut si dicamus, Humi nobis cicadae canunt: cum intelligamus, Arbores nobis excisas esse. Est ergo symboli propria et peculiaris brevitas cum gravitate quadam, quae plura uno significatu comprehendat."

[271] Ibid., 84: "Sed nec minus illud attendere oportet quod est a Plutarcho traditum: pleraque esse in symbolis, quae prohibita videri possint, quae ab ipsis tamen Pythagoricis nec aversata nec formidata sunt, verum per ea deterrentur, ab iis quae per ipsa significari volebant. . . . Nec illud te lateat volo, symbolorum pleraque proverbiorum naturam habere, cum et ideo Pythagoram adagiis non abstinuisse legamus."

[272] Cf. Iamblichus, *Vit. Pyth.* 18.82–87; tr. Clark, 34–38.

[273] Giraldi, *Aenigmata/Symbola*, 84–5: "Ad haec quae per symbola traduntur, nos ad mentem intellectumque per corporeos sensus transferunt, et ea trifaria[m] esse

he suggests, if during his exposition he suggests multiple or even contrary meanings for certain symbols, since even the Pythagoreans themselves did not agree among themselves about the different possible meanings. In his exposition he will explain some simply and look for the deeper meaning in others; in ordering them he has followed his own system, since different ancient authors order them differently.[274]

Giraldi's lengthy hermeneutic preface is ambitious and richly textured. He attacks the problem of the symbols from a number of different angles, and seems conscious of wanting to know *how* they worked. In what social context, with what constellation of *discipuli*, with what sort of central figure did the symbols make sense: these are his concerns. He is aware of the malleability of the corpus itself, and recognizes as well the notion that he might not be able to wring one consistent meaning out of each symbol. The basis of his interpretive method is the use of antiquity and ancient authorities. But Giraldi's method is not an ateleological antiquarianism—rather it is antiquarianism in the service of a larger hermeneutic goal: the integrative understanding of a series of difficult, decontextualized fragments. More and more one senses that the burden of creative understanding is on the critic, that the critic must weave together a tapestry consistent, informed, and conscious of a wealth of detail. Let us turn to a specific example, to see how Giraldi applies his method.

Giraldi's treatments of the two symbols we have been following in other authors, "Do not eat your heart" and "do not eat beans," while noteworthy, do not demonstrate some of the more interesting tendencies just highlighted. Both are full of erudition and both show

---

dicuntur, hoc est moralia, naturalia, theologica: id quod et tibi ex horum interpretatione liquido constabit. Verum quoniam Pythagoram sua acroamata, hoc est, auditiones, trifariam divisisse accepimus, in eo videlicet quod quid est, ut quid quae ternarius numerus, quid ternarius; et in eo quo quid maxime, ut quid iustissimum, quid optimum, et in quid agendum, quid non, ut An piscis et faba in cibis sint habendi. In omnibus his tribus symbola reposuisse creditur. His etenim, uti praeceptis quibusdam, ut dixi, discipulos quid agendum fugiendumve monebat."

[274] Ibid., 85: "In his vero interpretandis minus tibi mirum videndum, si varias plerunque sententias attulero, et nonnunquam fere contrarias ac oppositas, cum et Pythagoricos ipsos in iis non convenisse videamus. Eorum enim aliquos nude ea et simpliciter exposuisse accepimus, alios altiores et in iis occultiores sensus indagare et perscrutari voluisse: id quod de aliquibus omnino contenderim, et a me quoque fiet. Ordinem autem in recensendis his meum ipsius, non aliorum, ea ratione secutus sum, quod varie a veteribus digesta videmus, immo plerunque confuse allata."

his scholarly thoroughness. However, his version of the symbol "one must sacrifice with bare feet" exhibits, in addition to thoroughness, a characteristic Giraldian interest in comparative religious practice. It is edited and translated in appendix two. Regarding this symbol, Giraldi's position on Pythagoras's meaning is that it is an exhortation to purgation before the enactment of religious rites (App. 2.6). To arrive at that opinion, however, Giraldi frames his cautious assertion interestingly. He begins by embracing the notion that Pythagoras picked up this precept from the Jews, using examples from the Old Testament, Josephus, and Pope Leo the Great (App. 2.2–4). He is also willing to cite the Moslem custom of entering temples with bare feet, though he does not dilate upon it (App. 2.5). In order to make the precept understandable in Christian terms, Giraldi suggests that "washing the feet" can be understood in a mystical way, as "cleansing the mind." This he buttresses with biblical examples and a citation from Cassiodorus (App. 2.7–8). He then returns to pagan antiquity, suggesting that the Spartans worshiped with bare feet, perhaps taking this practice from Jews, their allies according to Josephus (App. 2.9–10). Finally, Giraldi affirms that Christians are prohibited from taking the Eucharist with bare feet and cites a number of sources to explain why this might be (App. 2.10–13).

His treatment here is noteworthy and emblematic of his detached, scholarly approach in general. He is committed to discovering a meaning rooted in antiquity, and is dispassionately interested in understanding the ramifications of the symbol. In contrast to Ficino, Nesi, and especially Reuchlin, one senses no ideologically driven need to make the symbols "relevant." In contrast to Beroaldo, Giraldi does not feel obliged to turn them into didactic moral exempla. And in contrast to Erasmus, Giraldi's breadth of historical vision is less confined, since he does not feel himself compelled to force the symbols into the framework of a larger didactic enterprise. Instead, there is a theoretical yet creative mission shaping Giraldi's purview, that of a detached scholar enmeshed in the concerns of his chosen field. In this sense, one observes a difference even with respect to Poliziano. While Giraldi and Poliziano are easily comparable with respect to their wide philological learning and their handling of a specific textual problem, Giraldi has a more focused interest in the history of religion per se, so that his erudition is put to the service of a larger, more synthetic overall goal.

Conclusion

In these introductory sections I have attempted to survey significant writings on the *symbola* from antiquity through the middle sixteenth century. The aim has not been encyclopedic; rather, my examination of each author's treatment of the symbols situates the author's work in an intellectual context and tries to evaluate the manner in which the author's interpretation and style of approach to the symbols is part of a larger whole. Since one of the book's primary goals, however, is to present a thorough edition, translation, and commentary to the *Symbolum Nesianum*, perhaps it is appropriate at this juncture to return to late fifteenth-century Florence and offer some concluding general comments. In this respect, certain questions come to mind regarding the second half of the fifteenth century in Florence. Why and how did prophetic figures become so important? When we arrive in the late 1480s, that is, in the years immediately preceding the ascendency of Savonarola, what was the structure of the Florentine intellectual community? And can we even say that "it" had "a" structure at all?

I have argued for the importance of Ficino's encounter with late ancient, Neopythagorean varieties of Neoplatonism and the appreciation for prophetic figures which he found there. This suggests that there are some cases where newly discovered texts actually help *shape* ideology and even social practice. When this happens, it is never monocausal: there is always a dialectical push and pull of individual agendas, social forces, the changing structure of interpenetrable intellectual communities, and patronage relations, all of which interact with the reception of texts. But the texts are there. Using them, Ficino created a vatic mantle for himself which he could not continue to bear, given his intellectual interests and his social circumstances. This, combined with the evolution of the humanist movement and the fideistic reaction to "vanities" fueled by Savonarola's ascendancy, caused Florentine intellectuals to split off in different directions. When one speaks of elites moving in different directions, however, it is always tempting to oversimplify, creating *ex post facto* factional divisions which were perhaps never so clearly, or so rigidly, drawn in reality. Philologically oriented humanists, bawdy poets, Aristotelians, Platonists, unification theorists: all of these were part of Florence's cultural matrix in the 1480s and 90s, and one did not have to adhere exclusively to one or the other sect.[275]

Giovanni Nesi's experience shows this in the case of late Quattrocento Florence. In his *Oracle* Nesi the *piagnone* wrote of a "new Socrates," a prophetic figure imbued with God-given powers who would bring Florence from darkness into light. He made this claim in his treatise utilizing esoteric imagery which was accepted by *piagnoni* to a degree, though Nesi had gone so far that Savonarola himself could not praise the treatise beyond only a few words.[276] But, *Stateram ne transilias*: perhaps in his *Oracle* Nesi did indeed "leap over the scale," transcending acceptable *piagnone* limitations. The very language of his treatment of that Pythagorean symbol (44) reflects this. He writes (44.1):

> Certainly this sentiment points toward moderation of soul. Now there is a moderation of natures, a certain restraint of desires, which does not allow the emotions to roam too freely, but rather like a chariot-driver for the other virtues, composes man's spirit in such a way that whatever he should do or say wholly lacks censure.

"A certain restraint of desires"—*cupiditatum quaedam quasi refrenatrix*. It recalls the language of admonishment with which Giovanni Caroli had castigated Nesi in reproval of Nesi's *Oracle*: "*frena* amori tuo imposito;" "*frena* laudibus hominum ponenda sunt."[277] *Frena, refrenatrix*—restraint: this is what Florentine *piagnoni* were compelled to exercise in the tumultuous years after 1498, and this is what underlies the *Symbolum Nesianum*'s delicate Savonarolan subtextuality. Considered diachronically, the *Symbolum* is no timeless masterpiece of literature, and seems to have had no great European diffusion. If, however, we attempt to deepen our synchronic sense, the *Symbolum* appears movingly *in* time, and helps to flesh out a controversial and subtle era, whose outward literary masks often concealed dense webs of meaning.

[275] On this point cf. Hankins, "Lorenzo de' Medici as a Patron of Philosophy."
[276] Cf. Polizzotto, 106 n.16.
[277] See above.

THE *SYMBOLUM NESIANUM*

LATIN TEXT AND ENGLISH TRANSLATION

Note on the Text

The text is drawn from the *codex unicus*: MS Firenze BN II. I. 158, fols. 270v–280. I have preserved the orthography as it is in the manuscript, expanded abbreviations, and punctuated for sense. The scribe shows a consciousness of diphthongs, sometimes writing them out, sometimes using an "e-caudata." I have simply used classicizing orthography in those cases. I have refrained from using "sic" in the text. In the few times I make a change from the manuscript reading, I do so silently but give the manuscript reading in a note. I have added section numbers to the text, to facilitate reference.

In the text itself the symbols are numbered, as in the manuscript, from 1–48. In the manuscript there is a section 49, but this is also labelled "Epilogus," and does not treat a symbol. Thus, in order to preserve the numeration of the list of symbols, I have dropped the number 49 from the last section (noting this, however, in a footnote).

//270v// ... Cap. 29: De symbolo nesiano: ubi et quid sit symbolum explicatur.

[Introductio] [1] Interfuit his, forte cum agerentur, spectabilis vir Johannes Nesius, florentinus civis, et is apprime doctus, qui gavisus quam plurimum eiuscemodi contionibus similiter ac omnia probans, inquit: "condelector equidem tibi, Pater reverende, qui isthaec munuscula sumas a filiis et familiaribus tuis. Ego vero, ut possim pariter cenare cum istis, et meum symbolum dare volo."
    Pater: "Quidnam?"
    Nesius: "Syntagma quoddam in quo digessi apophthegmata fere omnia quae tulit Pythagoras."
    [2] Pater: "Perquam velim adiici duobus istis et Nesianum symbolum, ut numero deus impare gaudeat. Habes hic?"
    Nesius: "Nequaquam. Habeo domi. Perendie afferam."
    Pater: "Ita obsecro."
    Nesius: "Faciam prorsus."

[3] Epistola proemialis ad Symbolum Nesianum.

Johannes Nesius Florentinus reverendo patri Angelorum Priori salutem:
    Nudius tertius cum in cenobio tuo essem, reverende Pater, gavisus sum—equidem gaudio magno valde—ubi repperi Reverentiam tuam in medio monachorum tuorum, audientem solerter illos et interrogantem pro symbolis suis. [4] Symbola autem, ut video, ea censes quae alio nomine compilamenta seu collectanea rerum variarum appellari possunt[1] necnon et dicta quaedam methaphorica, eadem applicabilia ad uniuscuiusque sententiam. Prae gaudio igitur quo tum pridem affectus sum ex collatione iam dicta, pollicitus sum quidem, ut te adiirem paulo post, sed neque vacuus in conspectu tuo. [5] Quod nunc praesto annotatiuncula, quippe ha<n>c quam a pluribus mutuatus sum libris hancque ipsam in fasciculum ferme unum quo oblecteris nonnihil, cum lectitando ipsum pro tuo arbitratu, tum eundem monachis tuis ubi libuerit impartiendo.

---

[1] quae alio ... appellari possunt] This is added in the left margin, in the hand of the scribe.

... Chapter 29: On the *Symbolum nesianum*: where, too, the nature of the "symbol" is explained.

[Introduction] [1] As it happens, Giovanni Nesi participated in these events while they were going on. Nesi, the well-respected, exceedingly learned Florentine citizen, greatly enjoyed communal meals of this sort and approved of everything. He said: "Well I'm delighted with you, reverend father, that you take up these little gifts from your charges and friends. But I—that I might dine as an equal with them—want also to present my 'symbol'."

Father: "What is it?"

Nesi: "A kind of 'ordering' in which I have interpreted almost all of the apophthegms that Pythagoras proposed."

[2] Father: "Well, I would certainly like to join to those first two 'symbols' [i.e., of Marco and Luca] the Nesian Symbol, so that God may 'rejoice in an odd number.' Do you have it here?"

Nesi: "Not at all. I have it at home. I'll bring it the day after tomorrow."

Father: "Please do."

Nesi: "I'll get right to it."

[3] Prefatory letter to the Nesian Symbol.

Giovanni Nesi, Florentine, sends greetings to the reverend father, Prior of Santa Maria degli Angeli:

Three days ago, Reverend Father, when I was at your common dining hall, I rejoiced—and really with an exceeding joy—when I found Your Reverence in the midst of your monks, listening to them carefully and questioning them regarding their symbols. [4] Now symbols, as I see it, you take to mean those things which can be called, using another name, "compilings" or "collectings" of various things, and furthermore that they are certain metaphorical sayings applicable to the meaning of each. In view, then, of the joy which touched me back then at the aforesaid meal, I promised to come to you soon thereafter, but not empty-handed in your view. [5] And so now here is this little note, which I borrowed, naturally, from many different books and gathered into almost one fascicle which will delight you, not only in your own judgment when you read it, but also when you impart it to your monks, whenever, that is, it pleases you to do so.

[6] Sumus autem exposituri apophthegmata Pythagorae, dicta profecto quaedam, quibus Samius ipse vates ac si principiis quibusdam utebatur in schola sua, non tamen in scriptis, sed oraculo vivae vocis quae habet nescio quid latentis energiae, ut ait Hieronymus. [7] Has autem Diathecas appellari, ait Policianus noster in Epictetum; nos vero symbola nuncupamus, ad similitudinem militarem, ubi, neque doli surreptio fiat, symbolo districte unusquisque dux suis militibus tradit, quae latino signa vel indicia dici possunt, ut, si forte occurrerit quis de quo dubitetur, symbolum prodat, indicans hostis ne an socius existat. [8] Augustinus autem "Symbolum est," inquit, "consilium seu consultatio," quae quidem omnia referri quam optime possunt ad doctrinam nostram. [9] Haec autem pluribus in locis dispersa narrantur et a Policiano praedicto ridentur in praelectione Posteriorum atque id iniuria, cum intueor quanta cum reverentia de his agat divus Hieronymus ad Ruffinum in epistola quae incipit "Lectis litteris," capitulo 15. [10] Nos vero redegimus fere omnia in id unum nostrum quod tulimus Oraculum de novo secolo necnon et quaedam in dialogis nostris. Caeterum, tua causa et monachorum tuorum, resumpsimus singula in quandam //271// alphabeti seriem cum nonnullis interpretationibus suis, quibus ipse laetaberis utique tum quia philosophi illius praestantissimi haec monumenta sint, tum quoniam ex Hebreis laribus eadem mutuata fuisse pridem considerare possis. [11] Scribit autem ad Hireneum Ambrosius in epistola quadam, ideo Pythagorae documenta sacris letteris convenire, quod ipsarum autor ex Hebreis oriundus sit. Audi igitur tuaque illa qua in caeteros humanitate soles; inspice quae, pro nostro modulo, sumus coniectati in verbis eius.

Incipiunt Symbola Pythagorae cum interpretationibus suis.

1. [1] **Abstine a fabis.** Plutarchus, in libro De liberis educandis, per fabas comicia recipit a quibus abstinere debent philosophi sanctique et religiosi viri. Dicit enim Apostolus, "Nemo militans deo implicat se negociis secularibus." Fabis namque utuntur mag(ist)ratus omnes, ut patet in ista civitate. [2] Huic autem dogmati quemadmodum et socraticis monitis Aristippus adversans, regum aulas frequentabat, et

[6] Now then, we are about to expound the apophthegms of Pythagoras, which are indeed certain sayings which the Samian prophet employed as principles in his school, though not in writing, but rather as an oracle of living voice—a voice which had a sort of hidden energy, as Jerome says. [7] Our Poliziano in his Epictetus says that they were called *Diathecae*—covenants. But we call them symbols, in the military manner, where to avoid the creeping in of deceit every leader gives his soldiers strict instructions in the form of a symbol. These are instructions which in Latin can be called *signa* (signs) or *indicia* (clues), so that, should some suspicious person pop up, he might speak the symbol, to indicate whether he was friend or foe. [8] Now Augustine says "a symbol is a deliberation, or inquiry," all of which applies in the best of all possible manners to our instruction. [9] Moreover, these, quite widely dispersed, are recounted and ridiculed by the aforementioned Poliziano in his preface to Aristotle's *Posterior Analytics*—outrageously, when I see how reverently divine Jerome deals with them in the letter against Rufinus, which begins, "lectis litteris," at chapter fifteen. [10] In any case, I have collected almost all [of the symbols] into that one work I published, the *Oracle on the New Age*, as well as certain [symbols] in my dialogues. However, for your sake and that of your monks, I have brought every one into a kind of alphabetical order, along with certain of their interpretations. You yourself will rejoice in them, both because they are monuments of that most outstanding philosopher, and because you can consider that those same things had been borrowed long ago from the Jewish prophets. [11] Ambrose, moreover, writes in a certain letter to Irenaeus that the lessons of Pythagoras agree with sacred scripture because their very author was born among the Jews. Therefore, listen to those things of yours with the same friendliness that you are accustomed to offer others; take a look at the things which we, for our part, have conjectured concerning his words.

Here begin the Symbols of Pythagoras, along with their interpretations.

1. [1] **Abstain from beans.** Plutarch, in his book *On the Education of the Young*, takes "beans" to mean "banquets," from which philosophers and holy and religious men should abstain. Indeed, the Apostle says, "No one fighting in the cause of God mixes himself up in worldly affairs." For all of our magistracies make use of "beans," as is clear in this city. [2] Moreover, Aristippus, who withstood this

regibus utebatur, cum non pranderet holus patienter. [3] Ut Diogenes
ait, "Cum autem Dionisius, Siciliae tyrannus, interrogaret Aristippum
ipsum quid in causa foret ut ipse et alii quidam philosophi et eru-
diti homines regum aedes accederent, eorumque fores ac limina con-
tererent, divites autem et reges ad philosophos minime, 'quoniam
philosophi,' inquit, 'probe intelligunt quae regibus desint, et quibus
maxime egeant; reges autem et divites minime quae philosophis
opportuna sint.'" Dicacitas et astutia[2] fuit haec. Sed et Laertius permulta eiuscemodi retulit de eodem, quoad hic nequaquam a fabis,
idest, a mag⟨ist⟩ratibus, abstinuerit. [4] At M.Cicero in libro De divinatione primo dicit, "Jubet igitur Plato sic ad somnum[3] proficisci
corporibus affectis, nihil sit quod errorem animis perturbationemque
afferat. Ex quo etiam Pythagoricis interdictum putatur, ne faba vesce-
rentur, quae res habent inflationem magnam. Is cibus tranquillitatem
mentis quaerentibus constat esse contrarius." Haec Cicero. [5] Quibus
et temperatus, idest, non exquisitus victus et quae capiti obsint viten-
tur edulia studiosis viris, ut animis minus impeditis virtus inhaeserit.
Praetereundum autem minime videtur quod ponit Gellius in Noctibus
atticis libro quarto, capitulo undecimo, notabile quidem, Pythagoram
scilicet et eius discipulos et fabas commedisse et carnes (quas tamen
alii penitus de istis abnuant) sed et Pythagoram quasdam profecto
non omnes vetuisse carnes ad vescendum suis, pro fabis autem
intellexisse luxuriam, quare Empedocles, apophtegmate isto, non a
fabulo edendo sed a[4] rei venereae proluvio[5] homines deducere satage-
bat. Videatis latius Gellium in loco iam dicto. [6] Sed et id ipsum
astipulatur quam plurimum disciplinae nostrae, ut caste vivant omnes,
hique in primis qui sacris ministeriis debeant inservire. Huius igitur
symboli talis sit interpretatio: abstine a fabis, idest, fugito cibaria
quae tumorem in alvo et in capite vertiginem proferant. Abstine a
fabis, idest, caste vive.

---

[2] astutia] abstutia *cod.*
[3] somnum] summum *cod.*
[4] a] ad *cod.*
[5] proluvio] *corr. ad* profluvio *cod.*

dogma just as he withstood Socratic warnings, used to frequent the halls of kings and was friendly with kings (though he would not bear to lunch on vegetables). [3] As Diogenes Laertius says, "Moreover, when Dionysius, the tyrant of Sicily, asked Aristippus himself why he and certain other philosophers and learned men went to the quarters of kings and wiled away their time at the gates and borders but wealthy men and kings rarely came to philosophers, Aristippus said, 'because philosophers well understand what kings lack, and what they need; but kings and wealthy men don't have the least idea about the things fit for philosophers.'" This was adroitly satirical. But even Diogenes Laertius told quite a bit about the same man, up to the point that he did not at all abstain from beans, that is, from magistracies. [4] But Cicero in the first book of the *De divinatione* says, "Therefore, Plato orders that we go to sleep with our bodies in such a condition that there be nothing that might bring on uncertainty or disturbance to our spirits. This is the reason, too, it is thought, that the eating of beans was forbidden to Pythagoreans, since beans are things which lead to great flatulence. It is established that this is a food contrary to those seeking tranquility of mind." So far Cicero. [5] For those [scholarly men] it is the temperate, that is, non-exquisite foods [which are proper]; foodstuffs which tell against the head should be avoided by scholarly men, that virtue might inhere in less impeded spirits. Moreover, it seems that we must in no way pass over what Gellius discusses in the *Attic Nights*, book four, chapter eleven, certainly a notable thing. [He writes], namely, that Pythagoras and his disciples ate beans and meats (although others wholly disagree about this); that Pythagoras did not prohibit his followers completely from eating all meats; and moreover, that he thought that beans stood for luxury, which is why Empedocles, with that apophthegm, thought that [the intention of this saying] was not to lead men away from eating beans but to keep them from the caprices of sexuality. For more, see Gellius in the aforementioned place. [6] But this itself also agrees with our instruction, that all live chastely, and especially those who have to fulfil the demands of holy ministries. So let this be the interpretation of this symbol: abstain from beans, that is, flee from foods which bring swelling to your stomach and dizziness to your head. Abstain from beans, that is, live chastely.

2. [1] **Adversus solem ne mingito.** Plinius, libro 28, capitulo 6, trahit hoc dictum ad auguria seu ad magiam; ast Hesiodus longe melius sentire videtur, qui ait hoc pudorem et verecundiam indici, ut, iuxta Apostolum Paulum, ignobilioribus illis arctubus[6] tribuamus abundantiorem honorem. [2] Pythagoras enim ipse, teste Hieronymo, fuit vir pudicus et castus quique exhorruerit partes illas quas coopertas hoc suo voluisset edicto. Plutarchus etiam in Problemis dicit sacerdotes nil agere sub divo et hoc utique ob honorem dei, cuius est sol quasi exemplar in mundo. [3] Dominus autem dicit in Evangelio quod Pater noster caelestis "solem suum oriri facit super bonos et malos." Et in Malachia legimus esse quemdam iustitiae solem qui iustis et sanctis apparebit in gloria. [4] Adversus solem hunc ne mingamus, ne, scilicet, impudentes simus, ut quasi meretricis facies nobis infrunita[7] fiat sed erubescamus et domino cum Jeremia dicat unusquisque nostrum: "confusus sum et erubui, quia sustinui opprobrium adolescentiae meae." [5] Diogenes autem, licet cynicus, id tamen passim af//271v//firmare solebat: rubor est color virtutis. Juvene autem quodam deprehenso et erubescente ait: erubuit, salva res est. [6] Pro quo et in primo Officiorum dicit Ambrosius laudabilem esse admodum verecundiam iuvenibus; unus et per hanc ipse de quodam bene vaticinatus est, ut patet illic. [7] Qualem autem quantumve pudorem Essei illi apud Judeos servarint, videlicet, in ipsis naturae necessariis egerendis praegrandem, scilicet, ostendit De bello iudaico Josephus, libro secundo, dicens eos sub terram eiuscemodi rem facere et tegere ut penitus ignorentur. Quae quidem sunt omnia ad doctrinam nostram, qui caute ambulemus, providentes bona non tam coram deo sed etiam coram omnibus hominibus, ut, videlicet, sic in solem non mingamus, sed pudici passim et pudibundi vivamus in domino.

3. [1] **Adversus solem ne loquaris.** Magister meus venerabilis Dominus Marsilius Ficinus De sole opusculum edidit ad Petrum

---

[6] arctubus] i.e., artubus.
[7] infrunita] infrunitis *cod.*

2. [1] **Do not urinate into the sun.** Pliny, in book twenty-eight, chapter six, takes this saying to mean predictions, or magic, but Hesiod seems to understand it much better. He says it points to decency and shame, so that, according to the Apostle Paul, we attribute a richer honor to those members which are less noble. [2] Indeed Pythagoras himself, as Jerome testifies, was a decent and chaste man, and he shuddered at those parts which he wanted covered (as in this saying of his). Also, Plutarch, in his *Problems*, says that priests do nothing out in the open—this is certainly for the honor of God; the sun is almost His exemplar in the world. [3] The Lord also says in the Gospel that our heavenly Father "causes his sun to rise on the good and the evil." And in Malachi we have read that there is a certain sun of justice which will appear to the just and the holy. [4] Let us not urinate into this sun, lest, namely, we be impudent, and our face, almost like a prostitute's, become foolish; instead let us blush before the Lord and, with Jeremiah, let each and every one of us say, "I am confused and I blush, because I have borne the disgrace of my adolescence." [5] Moreover, Diogenes, although a cynic, nevertheless used to affirm this in passing: red is the color of virtue. And when a certain youth was caught red handed and blushing, he said: he has blushed, all is well. [6] On this account Ambrose in the first book of the *On Duties* says that modesty is thoroughly praiseworthy in youths; as is clear there, each and every [man mentioned by Ambrose], through [his] modesty, prophesied well concerning a certain one. [7] Moreover, Josephus shows in the second book of the *Jewish War* that the kind and the amount of shame those Essenes (among the Jews) maintained in discharging those things—namely, those necessary because of nature—was great; he says that they did this sort of thing underground and covered it up so that no one would know. All of these things certainly pertain to our instruction, so that we walk cautiously and look toward good things not only in the eyes of God but also in the eyes of all men, so that, namely, we thus do not urinate into the sun, but rather chastely and shamefacedly live in the Lord.

3. [1] **Do not speak against the sun.** My venerable teacher Marsilio Ficino wrote a book *On the Sun*, dedicating it to Piero de'Medici. [2] In it, in fact, in chapter six, he himself relates the praises of the ancients on the sun, and especially those of Orpheus, who says: the sun is "the eternal eye seeing all things, superceding

Medicen. [2] In eo autem, capitulo sexto, refert ipse antiquorum laudes in solem Orpheique in primis, qui ait: Sol est "oculus aeternus omnia videns, supereminens caeleste lumen, caelestia temperans et mundana, harmonicum mundi cursum ducens sive trahens, habens sigillum, omnia mundana figurans." [3] "Theologi veteres, Proculo teste, dicebant reginam omnium iustitiam e medio solis throno per cuncta procedere, omnia dirigentem—quasi sol ipse sit omnium moderator. Jamblichus De Egyptiorum <Mysteriis> sententiam dicit, 'quicquid habemus boni, habemus a sole.'" [4] "Physici veteres solem cor caeli nominaverunt, Heraclitus luminis caelestis fontem, plerique Platonici in sole mundi animam collocarunt." [5] Item, capitulo 9 eiusdem, Ficinus praedictus ait, mirabilia solis contemplans divinus Plato, "solem ipsius boni conspicuum filium nominavit; arbitratus quoque est solem esse perspicuam dei statuam, in hoc templo mundano ab ipso deo positam, intuentibus ubique prae caeteris[8] admirandam. Hunc veteres, ut Plotinus ait et Plato, venerabantur ut deum. In sole prisci gentium theologi omnia gentilium numina collocarunt. Quod quidem Jamblichus, Julianus, Macrobiusque testantur." [6] In sacris etiam libris idem reperimus quod Egyptii libabant reginae caeli, idest, lunae, ut est in Jeremia, et colebant "omnem militiam caeli," idest, solem et planetas omnes, quemadmodum in Actibus apostolorum Stephanus retulit. [7] E quibus tam multis concludere possumus istud: ipsum Pythagoricum dogma loqui posse de hoc materiali sole, in quem nonnulli antiquorum obloqui audebant, utpote Anaxagoras, qui exulavit Athenis obturpia in solem dicta. [8] Verum enimvero si cogitemus sole ipso omnia clarescere atque illustrari, censebimus ipsum pro veritate supponere, adversus quam deceat loqui neminem. Dicit enim Philosophus primo Ethicorum, "Platoni enim veritatem praeferimus, nam, duobus amicis existentibus, dignum est praestare veritatem et in primis colere." [9] Igitur adversus solem ne loqueris, idest, veritatis iura ne impugnes, sed neque Christum, qui est sol iustitiae, quique de se dicit, "Ego sum via, veritas, et vita," et rursus, "omnis qui est ex veritate audit meam vocem." Nemo insuper in spiritu sancto dicit anathema Hiesu, sed in hoc nomine omne genu flectatur caelestium, terrestrium, et infernorum.

---

[8] prae ceteris] praeceteris *cod.*

celestial light, tempering celestial and worldly things, leading or pulling along the harmonic course of the world, possessing a seal, representing all worldly things." [3] "The ancient theologians, with Proclus as witness, used to say that justice, the queen of all things, proceeds through all things from the middle of the throne of the sun—as if the sun itself were the moderator of all. Iamblichus, in the *Mysteries of the Egyptians*, expresses the sentiment that 'whatsoever we have that is good, we have from the sun.'" [4] "The ancient natural scientists called the sun the heart of heaven, Heraclitus called it the font of celestial light, and many Platonists have placed the soul of the world in the sun." [5] And again, in chapter nine of the same work, the aforesaid Ficino says that Plato, while contemplating the sun's marvels, "called the sun the visible son of the good; he also thought that the sun was the manifest statue of God, and was placed by that very God in this worldly temple, to be admired everywhere by observers beyond everything else. As Plotinus and Plato say, the ancients venerated the sun as if it were a god. The ancient pagan theologians placed all the gods of the gentiles in the sun. Certainly, Iamblichus, Julianus, and Macrobius bear witness to this." [6] In scripture we also find that the Egyptians used to give libations to the queen of heaven, that is, to the moon, as is written in Jeremia, and they worshipped the "whole army of heaven," that is, the sun and all the planets, just as Stephen related in the Acts of the Apostles. [7] From so many things we can conclude this: that the same Pythagorean dogma can speak about this material sun, which certain ancients dared to reproach, like Anaxagoras, who was exiled from Athens on account of the infamies he uttered against the sun. [8] So if we truly think that all things brighten and are illuminated with the aid of the sun itself, we shall be making a true supposition and one against which no one can decently speak. After all, the Philosopher says in the first book of the *Ethics*: "For we place the truth before Plato, since, if there are two friends, it is a worthy thing to put the truth first and honor it above all things." [9] Therefore, do not speak against the sun, that is, do not oppose the laws of truth, or even Christ, who is the sun of justice, and who says about Himself: "I am the way, the truth, and the light," and again, "everyone who is of the truth hears my voice." And besides, no one living in the holy spirit speaks an anathema against Jesus. Rather, in this name, let every knee—of the heavens, of earthly things, and of the underworld—be bent.

4. [1] **Ad finem ubi perveneris, ne velis reverti.** "Omnia in figuram contingebant" iudeis, ait Apostolus, "scripta sunt autem ad" doctrinam "nostram." Quod enim de uxore Loth "in statuam salis" versa dicitur. Illud, utique iuxta divi Hieronymi intelligentiam, edocet universos ut perseverent in via domini, ne vertantur retrorsum, ut erubescant. [2] Qui enim ponit "manum suam ad aratrum," si convertatur retro, non est "aptus regno" caelorum, ait dominus. Non enim qui receperit sed qui persevaverit usque in finem, hic salus erit, ut manifeste ponitur De poenitentia, distinctione 2, capitulo "Pennata," et in multis aliis capitulis. [3] Melius est enim non incipere, quam turpiter ab incepto desistere. Omnis vero laus in fine canenda est. Nam et magnus ipse Solon felicem nolebat appellare quemquem— sed neque ipsum ditissimum Croesum Lidorum regem—ni prius finem eius contemplaretur. [4] Nam ac Boetius dixit, "quod me felicem totiens iactastis amici? / qui cecidit stabili non erat ille gradu." Finis praeterea dici potest ipsa religio, iuxta //272// illud: "Omnis consu<m>mationis," idest, perfectionis et virtutis, "vidi finem," idest religionem, quod est "latum mandatum" dei "nimis," scilicet in latitudine charitatis. [5] Quisque ergo ad hunc finem pervenerit, permaneat et retrorsum non abeat, perinde ac "canis" rediens "ad suum vomitum," et quasi populus Israel vesanus qui, in deserto mansitans, corde redebat in Egyptum ubi olim sederant "super ollas carnium;" unde dicitur, ollas carnium,[9] peponum fercula, porros, caepas, pro manna, turba gulosa petit. [6] Illud ergo sapientiae dictum memoria repetamus. "Si spiritus potestatem habentis super te ascenderit, locum tuum ne dimiseris." Legitur autem in Jeremia, "Plangite eum qui egreditur, quoniam non revertetur ultra ad terram nativitatis suae." Item, iste "qui egressus est de loco isto, non revertetur huc amplius, sed in locum ad quem" translatus fuerit, "morietur," [7] quia vere deus ipse est finis omnium, qui dicit, "Ego sum alpha et omega, principium et finis." Profecto, quicumque ad eum per religionem venerit, non discedat ab ipso. Dicit enim Jeremia, "Domine, omnes qui te derelinquunt, confundentur, recedentes a te, in terra scribentur, quoniam dereliquerunt venam aquarum viventium, dominum." [8] His igitur consideratis, audiamus Samium vatem, qui ait, "Ad finem ubi perveneris, ne velis reverti," scilicet, quando te noscis ad dominum et ad eius semitam finalem pervenisse, persiste in ea, in ea usque ad mortem et ne velis reverti ad ea quae sprevisti in seculi vita. [9]

---

[9] ollas carnium] ollarum carnes *cod.*

4. [1] **Do not choose to turn back on the end you have reached.** "All things came to a figure" for the Jews, says the Apostle, and "moreover, they have been written according to our" instruction. For it is said about Lot's wife that she was turned "into a statue of salt." That, at least according to divine Jerome's opinion, teaches all to persevere in the way of the Lord, lest they turn back, causing them to blush. [2] For whoever puts "his hand to the plough," if he turns back, is not "apt to the reign" of heaven, says the Lord. For not he who has received, but he who perseveres to the end shall be saved, as is manifestly said in the *On Penance*, in the second distinction, at the chapter "Pennata," and in many other chapters. [3] For it is better not to begin than to pull back bitterly from a good start. But every praise should be sung at the end. After all, even the great Solon himself did not wish to call anyone happy—not even Croesus himself, the incredibly wealthy king of the Lydians—unless he first contemplates his end. [4] For Boethius also says, "why, friends, did you count me fortunate? Whoever has fallen was himself never in a stable state." Along these lines, religion itself can be said to be the end, according to that citation: "Of every beginning," that is, of perfection and virtue, "I have seen an end," that is, religion, which is the "exceedingly wide-ranging injunction of God,"— in the breadth, that is, of charity. [5] And so whoever reaches this end, let him remain and not go back like a "dog" returning "to his vomit," or like the frantic people of Israel who remained in the desert but returned in their hearts to Egypt, where once they had sat "on pots of meat," whence it is said that the gluttonous crowd pleads for pots of meat, dishes of melons, leeks, onions, and for manna. [6] Therefore let us repeat by memory that saying of wisdom. "If the spirit of the ruler rises up against you, do not leave your place." Moreover, it is read in Jeremia, "Weep for him who leaves, for he will not come back to the land of his birth." And again, it is written that he "who has left this place, will not come back, but will die in the place to which" he has moved, [7] because God himself truly is the end of all things, who says "I am the Alpha and the Omega, the beginning and the end." Certainly, whoever has come to him through religion may not forsake him. For Jeremia says, "Lord, all those who abandon you shall be confounded; as they recede from you, they shall be registered in the underworld, because they have left the Lord, the font of living waters." [8] Having considered these things, let us listen to the Samian prophet, who says,

Finis autem dicitur mors methaphorice, ex 5 Methaphisicorum. Cum ergo ad mortem veneris, negligas vitam, ne timeas illam quae vitae est ultima finis. Qui mortem metuit quod vivit perdit id ipsum, ait Sapiens. Non itaque multum de vita cures, sed ubi ad mortem veneris, libenter excipe ipsam, dicens, cupio "dissolui, et esse cum Christo."

5. [1] **Amicorum omnia communia.** Socrates ille magnus, qui a Pythio sapientissimus omnium est appellatus, id ipsum veluti pro adagio passim affirmabat, probabat autem et dilatabat sic: omnia bonorum sunt omnium non secus quam deorum; deorum autem sunt omnia. Boni viri sunt deorum amici, ergo et amicorum inter se communia sunt omnia quae et deorum et virorum bonorum. [2] Terentius in Adelphis ait—nam vetus quidem hoc proverbium est—amicorum inter se omnia esse communia. Plato autem nonne divinus in Republica sua talem tantamque pandit bonorum omnium communitatem ut, videlicet, mulieres ipsas velit esse communes? Sed in hoc is profecto deliquit, quod ipse forsitan non haberet uxorem. [3] Lactantius autem in tertio Divinarum institutionum libro hanc Platonis Rempublicam quam maxime damnat. Sed et divus Thomas identidem agit in libro De regimine principum ad regem Cipri. [4] Epicurei autem quandoque laudantur ob amicitiam custoditam atque ob hanc communitatem, nam et Torquatus (aput Ciceronem in primo De finibus) Epicureos dicit amicitiam in communione colere plusquam omnes gentes. [5] Sed, his obmissis, ad nostra pervenientes, Christum vere charitatis assertorem nonne scimus fecisse discipulis suis omnibus omnia communia, ubi et dividebatur unicuique prout opus erat, ut in Actibus legimus? Quare,[10] videlicet, Christiani ipsi—in primis vero monachi qui nihil habent proprii—si vere servent professionem suam in cenobiis contuberniis quoque communibus, vere Christiani et monachi iidemque Pythagorici amici esse videantur.

---

[10] Quare] Quoad *cod.*

"Do not choose to turn back on the end you have reached," that is, when you know that you have come to the Lord and to his final road, persist in it, persist in it up to death and do not choose to return to those things you spurned in the life of the world. [9] Metaphorically, the "end" also means death, as in the fifth book of the Metaphysics. When therefore you have come to death, leave life behind, lest you fear that which is the ultimate end of life. Whoever fears death loses whatever it is that lives, says the Wise Man. Therefore, do not care overmuch for life; when you have come to death, welcome it willingly and say: "I desire to be dissolved, and to be with Christ."

5. [1] **All things of friends are held in common.** Socrates, that great man whom Pythian Apollo called the most wise of all, always affirmed this *en passant*, as a kind of adage, and he approved of it and broadened it in this manner: all things belong to all good men just as if they belonged to the gods; and all things belong to the gods. Good men are friends of the gods, therefore all things of friends among themselves are things which are both of the gods and of good men. [2] Terence in the *Adelphoe* says—and this is certainly an old proverb—"of friends among themselves, all things are held in common." And doesn't divine Plato in his *Republic* stretch out the community of all goods to such a point, evidently, that he wants wives themselves to be held in common? But in this he certainly failed, perhaps because he himself did not have a wife. [3] Lactantius, moreover, condemns this *Republic* of Plato as forcefully as possible in the third book of his *Divine Institutions*. And so does divine Thomas in his book *On the Rule of Princes*, dedicated to the king of Cyprus. [4] The Epicureans, however, are often praised on account of their well-guarded friendship and on account of this community; and Torquatus as well (in the first book of Cicero's *De finibus*) says that the Epicureans honored friendship by holding things in common more than all others. [5] But putting these things aside and coming to our own tradition, don't we know that Christ, the proponent of true charity, made all things common for his disciples, where, as we read in Acts, each received according to his needs? So clearly, Christians themselves and especially monks who possess nothing of their own, if they really preserve their vow in common meals and common housing, are truly Christians and monks and at the same time Pythagorean friends.

6. [1] **Amicitia est aequalitas quae gradum nescit tam in animo quam in corpore.** Item: **amicus est alter ego.** Hoc idem sentit Ambrosius in sermone quodam, dicens, "amicitia gradum nescit." [2] Lex autem praecipit ut proximum tuum aeque ac te ipsum diligas, neque personam accipias in iudicio; sed dicit scriptura "diligite iustitiam, qui iudicatis terram," et rursus, "beati qui custodiunt iudicium et faciunt iustitiam in omni tempore." [3] Nihil enim est aequebilius iustitia, quae iura sua reddit unicuique, unde servari potest animorum quorumcumque concordia, quae vera est amicitia, qua nihil potest inveniri iucundius in hac vita. [4] Hanc autem Pythagoras describit in presenti dogmate, in quo //272v// nihil obscurum sed apertum omne; modo servetur id ipsum in humana conversatione, ubi permulta longe secus in dies factitari cernuntur.

7. [1] **Abstine ab his qui nigram habent caudam.** Plutarchus Chaeroneus, in eo quem De liberis educandis libellum inscripsit, caudas appellat actus et mores, qui, tamquam caudae quaedam, homines ipsos usque quaque sequuntur. [2] Quod et in Canonibus memini quandoque me legere ex. De hereticis (capitulo "Excommunicamus") qui diversas habent facies sed caudas habent ad invicem colligatas, quia de vanitate conveniunt in idipsum. Caudae ergo mores sunt et color ab alterutris distinguit eas. Albus enim color innocentiam, niger malitiam indicat. Cavere oportet nigras caudas, idest, mores malos, assequi vero et imitari caudas albas, idest, mores bonos. [3] Dicit namque Psalmigraphus, "cum sancto sanctus eris et cum perverso perverteris," et qui tetigerit picem inquinabitur ab ea et qui communicaverit superbo induet superbiam. [4] "Pares autem cum paribus veteri proverbio facillime congregantur," inquit ille Tullius, scilicet in Catone maiore. Hoc autem potest et pluribus affirmari rationibus quas omnes in praesentia reiicimus propter brevitatem. [5] Praeterea, dicterium istud de proditoribus potest intelligi, qui blandi sunt in principio et in novissimis mordent, ut colubri. Experimento erit Judas Scariothis qui obsculo tradidit Christum, dicens, "Ave, rabbi." De istiusmodi homuncionibus seu simiis vel simulatoribus permulta leguntur in sacris. [6] Illud nobis[11] apprime sapientia docet: "simulator ore decipit amicum suum; iusti autem liberabuntur scientia,"

---

[11] n(ostr)o *cod.*

6. [1] **Friendship is equality that knows no degree in spirit or in body.** Again: **a friend is an *alter ego*.** This is what Ambrose means in a certain sermon, when he says, "friendship knows no degree." [2] Moreover, the law orders that you love your neighbor as yourself, and that you not judge anyone; but scripture says, "love justice, you who judge the earth," and again, "blessed are those who watch over justice and practice justice all the time." [3] For there is nothing fairer than justice, which grants its laws to everyone. From it, concord of all different sorts of spirits can be preserved; this is true friendship, and nothing more joyful than this can be found in this life. [4] And this is what Pythagoras is describing in the present opinion. In it nothing is secret and everything is open; may this be itself preserved in human interaction, where very many things seem to be done over and over, both in the long term and from day to day.

7. [1] **Abstain from those things with a black tail.** Plutarch of Chaeronea, in the little book he called *On the Education of Children*, takes "tails" to mean "behavior and character," which follow men all over the place, as if they were tails. [2] This is also in the Canons; and I remember having read at some point in the *Decretals of Gregory IX*, in the section *On Heretics* (in the chapter "Excommunicamus"), that there are those who have diverse faces but have tails which are tied to one another, since they come together when it comes to vanity. Tails, therefore, are morals, and color distinguishes them from each other. For the color white indicates innocence, black, malice. One must beware black tails, or bad morals, and follow and imitate white tails, or good morals. [3] For the Psalmist says, with the holy "you will be holy and with the perverse you will be perverted;" and he who has touched pitch will be polluted by it and he who interacts with the proud will wear the mantle of pride. [4] "Moreover, equals are gathered together most easily with equals, according to the ancient proverb," as Tullius says, namely in his *Cato*. And this can be affirmed by any number of arguments, all of which we have passed over for now on account of brevity. [5] Beyond all this, this saying can be understood to refer to those traitors who are gentle in the beginning and bite at the end, like serpents. Judas Iscariot will serve as an example: he betrayed Christ with a kiss, saying, "Ave, Rabbi." About horrible little men of this sort, or rather monkeys, or about hypocrites, one can read quite a bit in scripture. [6]

quandoquidem maliciam sapientia vincat. Cantor etiam dicit, "Molliti sunt sermones eius super oleum et ipsi sunt iacula." Autor autem hic monet ut his moribus homines caveamus, ac si scorpiones qui nos blando ore ambiunt, ledunt autem cauda nigra, fallaci scilicet ac mortali quorum utique infinitus est numerus.

8. [1] **Anulum arctum non habeto.** Divus Hieronymus ait hoc significari ne vixeris anxie, neve te ipsum alienae servituti subiicias aut eiusmodi instituto a quo te eximere nequeas. Qui enim anulum angustum gestat, is sibi vincula ferme parat et servat. [2] Id autem ad matrimonium referri potest, cuius anulus insigne est, ut tecum reputes illud Nasonis in Deianira: "si qua voles apte nubere, nube pari." "Quam male inequales veniunt ad aratra iuvenci," tam premitur magno coniuge nupta minor et econverso. Qui enim nubunt more alieno vivant necesse est. [3] Legi autem in Decretis 17, questione 2, capitulo "Nos novimus," "navigasti, idest, uxorem duxisti." Appellat enim navigare uxorem ducere, ubi dicit glosa, "hanc merito comparationem fieri. Nam sicut navigans subiicit se variis periculis nec proprio motu regitur sed a ventis, sic habens uxorem." Haec Glosa. [4] Is ergo est anulus quo stringitur viri animus ad subeundos alterius mores et ad servandam fidem. Is autem non sit arctus et nimis strictus, ne superioris conditionis iugum subeas, sed paris vel inferioris. [5] Potest etiam id transferri ad animam cuius sponsus et dominus aut Mammona aut Deus est. Illius iugum inexorabile et durum est, huius vero "suave" et "honus" eius "leve;" iuxta illud Esaiae: Virgam oneris "eius, et sceptrum exactoris eius superasti" et illud "ambulavimus vias difficiles." "Non" enim "est pax impiis, dicit dominus," nam et cor impii, velut mare aestuans, quod quiescere non potest. Econtra vero ait ille, "quaenam summa boni? Quae mens sibi conscia recti." [6] Habet enim mens beneficorum gaudium intimum, inextimabilemque laetitiam; anima enim nostra ad dicenda cuipiam altius, scilicet, non enim duobus dominis servire potest. [7] Anulum dei, idest, religionem et virtutem subeat leviorem, nec induat peccati servitium, ac si anulum arctum quem eumdem merito contemnet et merito odio habebit. Id ergo praecepti assequuntur monachi omnes et religiosi viri qui ambulant in latitudine charitatis et anulum peccatorum servilem usque quaque contemnunt.

Wisdom teaches us this best of all: "the hypocrite deceives his friend; but the just shall be freed by wisdom," since wisdom will conquer malice. And the Cantor says, "Gentle are his words on oil and they themselves are darts." The author warns us, then, to beware men of this character, as if they were scorpions who embrace us with a sweet mouth and then kill us with a black—that is, a treacherous and deadly—tail, whose number is everywhere and infinite.

8. [1] **Do not wear a tight ring.** Divine Jerome says this should be taken to mean that you should not live anxiously, or that you should not subject yourself to servitude to another or to any kind of arrangement from which you cannot extricate yourself. After all, whoever wears a narrow ring practically prepares and maintains fetters for himself. [2] One can, moreover, relate this symbol to matrimony, for it is symbolized by the ring; so you might want to think over that line of Naso in the *Heroides*: "if you wish to marry aptly, marry an equal." "How sad it is that those not equal become yoked to the plow," as the lesser partner is oppressed by the greater and vice versa. After all, those who marry necessarily live in a different way. [3] Moreover, I have read in the *Decretals of Gregory IX*, 17, question 2, chapter "Nos novimus:" "you have navigated, that is, married." For "navigate" means "marry," to which the Gloss says, "This is a deserved comparison. For just as, when navigating, one subjects oneself to various dangers and is not ruled by one's own motion but by the winds, so also is the man who has a wife." Thus says the Gloss. [4] This, then, is the ring by which a man's spirit is constrained to bear the morals of another and to keep promises. Let it not be narrow and too restrictive, lest you suffer the yoke of a [wife of a] superior condition; rather, [take a wife] of an equal or lesser one. [5] One can also transfer this symbol to the soul, whose spouse and lord is either Mammon or God. The yoke of the former is inexorable and harsh, but that of the latter is "sweet" and his "burden" is "light;" according to that passage in Isaiah: "You have surmounted" the rod "of his" burden, "and the dominion of his executor," and the passage, "we have walked difficult roads." For "there is no peace for the impious, says the Lord," for the heart of an impious man is like the swelling sea, which cannot rest. But on the other hand that man says, "What then is the highest good? The mind conscious of its own rightness." [6] For the mind has a deep delight and an inestimable happiness in its own kindnesses; after all,

9. [1] **Bonum cibum in matellam ne reponas.** Plutarchus
Chaeroneus isthuc ipsum apophthegma edisserens ait, "Urbanum
bonumque sermonem in animum viri mali ne ingeras." Epictetus itidem, aput //273// Gellium, etiam atque etiam inquit, videndum est
in cuiusmodi animam sermonem mictas. [2] Dicit autem dominus,
"Nolite sanctum dare canibus" et "margaritas vestras ne proiicia-
tis ante porcos." "Nam syncerum est, nisi vas quodcumque infundit
arescit," ait Flaccus. [3] Cibum autem dici sermonem et praedi-
cationem verbi dei, satis patet aput the<o>logos et sanctos viros
Cassianum, Augustinum, Ambrosium, Hieronymum, et omnes alios
iuxta illud Salvatoris in Evangelio: "non in solo pane vivit homo,
sed in omni verbo quod procedit de ore dei." [4] Legimus insuper
ex. De officio ordinarii, capitulo "Inter cetera:" "[Inter cetera] quae
ad salutem spectant populi christiani pabulum verbi dei quam maxime
sibi noscitur esse necessarium, quia sicut corpus materiali, sic anima
spirituali cibo nutritur, eo quod 'non in solo pane vivit homo, sed
in omni verbo'" sanctae exhortationis. Haec ibi. [5] Uti vero Divus
Gregorius praecipit et habetur distinctione 43, capitulo "Sic rector,"
sal opus est medico spirituali et predicatori ut discrete, scilicet, iuxta
audientium facultatem, loquatur. [6] Quod ipsum hoc symbolo dicitur, ne bona malis forsitan propinentur; quod et Plato per saepe
abnuit tum alibi, tum ad amicos scribens in epistolis suis, ne fortas-
sis in matellam cibus bonus infundi videatur. Hinc arguitur ut con-
sideremus quibus cum loquimur, ne sermonem placidum et benignum
viris proferamus ingratis, quique verbum dei bonum ostentui habeant
et idipsum usque quaque contemnant.

our soul [exists] for the purpose, namely, of communicating to someone higher [i.e., God], for it cannot serve two masters. [7] May it
submit to the ring of God, that is, to religion and to a gentler kind
of virtue, and may it not vest itself in the servitude of sin, as if that
were the "narrow ring," and the very ring it deservedly condemns
and hates. Accordingly, all monks and religious men who are so
instructed and walk in the wide embrace of charity appreciate this
notion and despise on all occasions the sinners' servile ring.

9. [1] **Do not place good food in a chamber-pot.** In explaining this very apophthegm, Plutarch of Chaeronea says, "Do not force
elegant and good speech into the spirit of a bad man." Epictetus in
like manner (in Gellius) says over and over again that you must see
that you piss away your conversation on a soul of that sort. [2] And
the Lord says "do not give what is holy to dogs" and "do not cast
your pearls before swine." "For it is sound, unless the vessel dries
up whatever one pours in," says Flaccus. [3] Moreover, that "food"
means speech and the praeching of the word of God is clear enough
from [the writings of] the theologians and the holy men Cassian,
Augustine, Ambrose, Jerome, and all the others; according to that
passage of the Savior in the Gospel: "man does not live by bread
alone, but in every word that proceeds from the mouth of God."
[4] In addition we have read in the *Decretals of Gregory IX*, in the
book *On the Duty of the Regular Clergy*, in the chapter "Inter Cetera:"
"Among other things which pertain to the health of the Christian
people, it is thoroughly well-known that the nourishment of God's
word is necessary, since, just as the body is nourished by material
food, so the soul is nourished by spiritual food, because 'man does
not live by bread alone, but in every word'" of holy exhortation.
So much for that. [5] And as divine Gregory also instructs, and as
we have it in distinction 43, chapter "Sic rector," the spiritual doctor and preacher needs "salt" so that he can speak discretely, namely,
according to the perceptual abilities of the listeners. [6] This is itself
said in this symbol so that, perhaps, good things not be yielded up
to bad men, something Plato also shuns in a number of places and
especially when he writes his letters to his friends, lest perhaps good
food seem to be poured into a chamber-pot. So it is argued that we
consider the people to whom we speak, lest we offer a placid and
kind speech to ungrateful men, men who have the good word of
God shown to them yet despise it everywhere.

10. [1] **Choenici ne insideas.** Hieronymus pro hoc dicto loquens ait, Ne nimis praesentia cures, differasque edulia, ne vel[12] sis sollicitus usque in diem crastinum. Est autem Choenix, seu Cohenica mensurae nomen, quotiens, scilicet, sextarius, quatenus assummitur, sive est mensura escae diurnae. [2] Quatenus super choenica non sederimus, si de cibo in crastinum solliciti non simus, quoniam autem non debeamus cogitare de crastino [ad amandum] divus Hieronymus sapientissime docet in suis quaestionibus.

11. [1] **Cor ne edito.** Thomas Aquinas doctor angelicus De regimine principum libro 4, capitulo 22, hoc adducit elogium quo signatur, ne curis nimis atteramus et quasi consumamus corda nostra. [2] Nam cor non commedendum, idest, animus non est vanis saeculi sollicitudinibus affligendus. Cura autem dicitur quia cor urat. [3] Dicit autem sapiens, "sicut tinea vestimento et tarmes[13] ligno, sic tristia viri nocet cordi;" iuxta illud: "O, Tite, siquid ego adiuto curam ve levasse quae nunc te coquit et versat sub pectore fixa," et quae deprimeris. [4] Econtra autem cum psalmo cantandum sit: "Cor meum etiam caro mea" exhilarat "in deum vivum." Item, "Pax multa diligentibus" nomen tuum "et non est illis scandilum." [5] Peccatum autem urit cor et quasi vermis quidam inextinguibilis ve ignis excruciat ipsum, virtus vero exhilarat laetificatque. Vitetur itaque illud, conqueratur ista et fiet quod innuitur in isto praecepto.

12. [1] **Coronam ne carpito.** Divus Hieronymus arbitratur hoc indici urbium leges observandas esse, non violandas aut arguendas; bona et enim lex est corona civitatis, qua melius ipsa regitur quam a rege bono, ut dicit philosophus tertio Politicorum. [2] Non enim potest seduci lex ut rex, quamvis Antonius Corsettus in libro De regia potestate, quaestione 32, oppositum sentiat. Ait enim "Princeps bonus est iustitia animata, lex autem bona est iustitia inanimata." Unde et melius per bonum regem quam per bonam legem gubernantur

---

[12] Vel] ve *cod.*
[13] tarmus *cod.*

10. [1] **Do not sit on the "choenix" (bushel).** Discussing this saying, Jerome says, "Do not care overmuch about the present, nor fuss about food, nor even be anxious about tomorrow." Now the "Choenix" or "Cohenica" is the name of a measure whose quantity is that of a "sextarius;" or rather, it is a measure of daily food intake. [2] So we don't "sit on the bushel," in so far as we are not worried about tomorrow's food, because, moreover, divine Jerome teaches us most wisely in his questions that we ought not think about tomorrow.

11. [1] **Don't eat your heart.** In Book four of his *On the Rule of Princes*, the Angelic Doctor Thomas Aquinas brings this elegaic saying into his discussion. It means that we should not wear ourselves down with excessive cares and almost consume our hearts. [2] For the heart must not be eaten, that is, the spirit must not be afflicted with the vain worries of the world. Moreover, [St. Thomas] uses the word "cura" ("care") because the heart ("cor") burns ("urat"). [3] Now the wise man says, "just as a maggot is harmful to cloth and a woodworm to wood, so, too, do gloomy thoughts wound a man's heart." Close upon this there is that saying: "Titus, if in some way I help even to have lightened the care which now cooks you and, embedded, turns over and over in your breast, and which depresses you. . . ." [4] On the contrary, then, let us sing, along with the psalm: "My heart and flesh" exult "in the living God." And again, "there is much peace for those who love your name "and there is no scandal upon them." [5] Now sin burns the heart and, like a kind of worm or inextinguishable fire, torments it, but virtue exhilarates and gladdens the heart. Therefore, let sin be avoided, let virtue deplore sin, and may what is taught in this precept actually happen.

12. [1] **Snipe not at the crown.** Divine Jerome thinks that this means that the laws of cities must be observed, not violated or criticized. After all, good law is the city's crown, by which it is better ruled than by a good king, as the Philosopher says in the third book of his *Politics*. [2] For law cannot be seduced as can a king, even if Antonio Corsetti in his book *On Royal Power* maintains the opposite. For he says, "a good prince is justice animate, a good law, justice inanimate." And so [in his view] cities are better governed by a good king than by good law; in addition, one lives in a holier fashion where a good king governs without law. But in any case it is not our job to settle such controversies.

urbes; ibique sanctius vivitur, ubi rex bonus sine lege gubernat. Sed
non est utique nostrum inter eos tantas componere lites.

[3] Id dumtaxat in praesentia dicimus, civitatum coronam vel regem
esse vel legem, quam eamdem minime carpendam asserimus, neque
verbo, neque facto; sed in monasteriis desistant monachi coronam
carpere, idest, praelatos suis murmurationibus ledere. [4] Sunt namque
praelati, velut signum ad sagiptam, ut omnes impetant eos et lace-
rent detrahendo, ut assolet fieri inter eos, qui vel postquam fuerint
impinguati, incrassati, et dilatati, calcitrant in autores suos; seu etiam
si non fuerint saturati, murmurabunt; [5] iidemque, ut a multis audivi,
saepe censent ac si secundum praestantiam¹⁴ ipsam esse murmura-
tionem; et hi quidem melius saperent, si Pythagorici essent, qui coronam non carperent, sed suis praepositis equanimiter oboedirent, non
tantum bonis et modestis sed etiam discolis, quia sic est voluntas dei,
ut omnis anima potestatibus sublimioribus subdita sit. [6] "Non est
enim potestas, //273v// nisi a deo," ut dicit Apostolus, "quae autem
a deo sunt, ordinatae sunt; itaque et qui potestati resistit dei ordi-
nationi resistit." Corona igitur cuiuscumque universitatis est lex seu
praepositus eius. Coronam igitur ne carpas, et principi populi tui ne
maledixeris. [7] Omnia autem quae dicunt vobis servate et facite,
secundum vero opera eorum ne faciatis, neque carpatis praelatos
vestros. Poenituit enim Davit cum fimbriam Saul in caverna tulisset.
Quae quidem scripta sunt ad doctrinam nostram, ut sciamus coronam
ipsam nequaquam esse carpendam, sed neque per ambitum a quo-
vis iniuste rapiendam, ut tyranni faciunt, et ambitiosi.

13. [1] **Deponentibus ne adiicito.** Hieronymus hinc iubet: "ad
virtutem incedentibus" tradenda esse praecepta, ociosos autem
desidesque seu etiam recusantes esse relinquendos. [2] Debemus enim,
apum instar, aut dona accipere venientium aut agmine factos ignavos
desidesque reiicere ac tepidos evomere, ut sacra testantur eloquia.
[3] Dicit enim Oratius in Poetica: "Quintilio siquid recitares ... si
defendere delictum quam vertere malles; nullum ultra verbum aut
operam summebat inanem." Hoc autem generale est dictum pro

---

¹⁴ praestantiam] pitantiam *cod.*

[3] At any rate, for the moment we say that the crown of cities is either king or law, and we declare that one must in no way snipe at it, in either word or deed; but in monasteries let the monks resist sniping at the crown, that is, let them resist wounding the prelates with their murmurings. [4] Now then, there are prelates who are like a call to arms, so that all attack and wound them by disparaging them, just as usually happens among those who—even after they have been fattened, thickened, and puffed up—are refractory against their authors; and there are also those who, even if they were not sated, will gossip; [5] and the same, as I have heard from many, often think that gossip is in keeping with excellence itself. And they would certainly know better if they were Pythagoreans, who do not snipe at the crown, but rather obey their betters with equanimity— and not just the good and modest ones, but the morose ones as well, because the will of God is such that every soul is subject to loftier powers. [6] "For there is no power that does not come from God," as the Apostle says; "moreover, those powers that are from God are ordained; therefore, whoever resists power also resists God's authority." Thus the crown of everything whatsoever is law, or rather, the representative of law. So snipe not at the crown, and do not speak ill of the prince of your people. [7] So: obey and carry out whatever they tell you, but do not do it according to their works [that is, according to what they do], and do not snipe at your prelates. For David repented after he had cut off Saul's hem in the cavern. Certainly these things were written to teach us, so that we know not to snipe at the crown and also that no one must corruptly and unjustly steal it, as tyrants and ambitious men do.

13. [1] **Do not associate with the careless.** Hence Jerome orders that precepts should be handed down to those "moving toward virtue," and that the leisurely and slothful who protest should be left behind. [2] For we must, in the manner of bees, either accept the gifts of those who come, or reject completely those who have made themselves into slothful knaves; we must vomit out the tepid, as the sacred pronouncements testify. [3] For Horace says in his *Poetics*: "If you would recite something with Quintilian, . . . if you would rather defend than commit a crime; he used to take nothing beyond an inane word or work." Now this is a general saying for the learning

doctrina mundi proque his omnibus quae ad salutem necessaria non sint. [4] Secus namque pro aliis in Esaia legimus, "Clama, ne cesses, quasi tuba, exalta vocem tuam et annuncia populo meo scelera eorum, et domui Jacob peccata eorum." Et rursus alius quidam pro istis dicit, "Cum moveas aliquem, nec se velit ipse moveri; si tibi sit carus, noli desistere ceptis."

14. [1] **Dextram nemini cito tradas.** Solonis est dictum celebre, amicos nec cito approbandos, nec cito respuendos. Aristoteles autem salis modium inquit commedamus oportet, antequam nobis amicum fidum quempiam censeamus. [2] Sed et amicum ita habeas fieri, ut posse hunc inimicum putes; aiebant et Bias Pirenneus et Seneca. Ideoque neminem inconsulto amicum accipias, nec temere quemcumque in familiaritatem summas. [3] Probare autem oportet spiritus, utrum sit ex deo, ait Apostolus. Quidam enim veniunt sub pellibus ovium, intrinsecus autem sunt lupi rapaces. Sed nisi cito dexteram porrigamus eis, si convivamus eis aliquantisper, a fructibus eorum cognoscemus eos. [4] Qui autem cito credit, levis est corde. "Manus autem nemini cito imposueris," ait Apostolus. "Pravum enim est cor hominis et inscrutabile, et quis cognoscet illud?" ait Jeremia. Nulla autem est deterior pestis quam animus fictus, qui est familiaris inimicus et latro domesticus. [5] Quilibet igitur alicubi probandus est, priusquam dicatur amicus ut ei dextera detur, quid est amicitiae signum, ut per saepe in sacris legimus.

15. [1] **Ex vitibus amputatis ne libaveris.** Moisi praecepit dominus, ut altare sibi strueret de lapidibus quos ferrum non tetigisset. Salomonis etiam templum, toti orbi venerandum atque mirabile, absque tinnitu et absque malleorum ictibus constructum est. [2] Quae enim ferro tanguntur, dura sunt et aspra crudelitate confecta. Deus autem dicit, "misericordiam volo et non sacrificium." [3] Id ipsum utique censuit hic noster Samius, qui vel in brutis animalibus atque etiam in plantis pietatem clementiamque colebat. [4] Quandoquidem vulgo fertur aput Laertium quod is a carnibus abstinebat omnigenis, imo et aviculas pisciculosve emebat et passim dimictebat, quasi pietate ductus; maluit insuper mori, aiunt, quam fabas ledere. [5] Ex his

of the world and for all those things which are not necessary to health. [4] Now on the other hand we read otherwise in Isaiah: "Shout, do not cease; like a tuba, raise your voice and announce to my people their crimes, and to the house of Jacob their sins." And back again, someone else says on those matters: "Though you would move someone, [you cannot do so if] he himself doesn't wish to be moved; if he is dear to you, do not hold back from your plans."

14. [1] **Do not swiftly shake hands with a man.** It is Solon's famous saying that friends should be neither swiftly accepted nor swiftly rejected. And Aristotle claims that we have to eat a measure of salt before we consider anyone a faithful friend. [2] But you should also hold a friend in such regard that you think it might happen that he could someday become your enemy; that is what Bias of Pirene and Seneca used to say. And so accept no one as a friend without due consideration, and do not take anyone rashly into familiarity. [3] Moreover, it is the spirit that has to be able to tell whether one is from God, says the Apostle. For certain men approach in the guise of sheep, but within are rapacious wolves. But if we do not offer them our right hand right away, if we live with them for a while, then by their fruits shall we know them. [4] Now whoever believes swiftly is light of heart. "Moreover offer the hand swiftly to no one," says the Apostle. "For the heart of man is corrupt and inscrutable, and who will know it?" says Jeremiah. Now there is no worse plague than a false spirit, which is a familiar enemy, like a robber in the house. [5] Therefore, anyone anywhere must be proven before he is called a friend and offered the right hand, which, as we always read in sacred scripture, is a sign of friendship.

15. [1] **Do not offer libations from vines which have been cut.** The Lord ordered Moses to construct an altar for Him from stones which iron had not touched. And Solomon's temple—a marvel, respected and venerated by the whole world—was constructed without noise and without the blows of hammers. [2] After all, things touched by iron are harsh, bitter, and made with cruelty; moreover, God said "I want mercy, not sacrifice." [3] Without any doubt this Samian of ours thought that very thing, he who worshipped piety and clemency in brute animals and even in plants. [4] And everywhere in his work Diogenes Laertius commonly says that Pythagoras used to abstain from all types of meats—and not only that: he would

autem id nobis documento sit, ut deo omnia cum charitate sistamus quatenus ei acceptabile fiat sacrificium nostrum. Nam nihil placitum sine pace deo. Quidni praecipit ipse, "si . . . offers munus tuum ad altare et" recorderis quod "frater tuus habet" aliquod "adversum te, . . . vade prius reconciliari fratri tuo."

16. [1] **Exsurgens lectu stragulas complicato: seu corporis vestigium confundito.** Davit in psalmo penitentiae canit, "lavabo per singulas noctes lectum meum lachrimis meis, stratum meum rigabo," quibus in verbis delictorum paenitudo concluditur. [2] "Qui enim dormiunt, nocte dormiunt," ait Apostolus. Noctis vero nomine peccatum significatur in sacris. [3] Paenitentia autem est //274// mala praeterita plangere ac veluti somni stragulas complicare et iacentis corporis vestigium demoliri; est quasi plangenda iterum non committere. [4] Iacere namque hominum est torpore desidiave occupari immergique criminibus. Reviviscere autem atque expergisci est a peccato surgere. [5] Tollere autem vestigium est omnem erroris labem ac speciem omnino deponere, ut nulla appareat macula, sed neque indicium quidpiam ubi pridem in nobis fuerint ac si vulnera quaedam nonnulla delicta. [6] Omnis autem errantium dispositio sic immutetur, ut proprius affectus in habitum contrarium converti videatur, 26, q. 7, capitulo, "affectum."

17. [1] **Echon invoca flantibus ventis.** Alexander medicus qui a[15] nonnullis dicitur Afrodisicus in suis problemis per multa de echo disputat. Hanc autem censet ipse aeris refractionem esse et vanam vocem ad nutum cuiuspiam loquentis, seu percutientis effectam. [2] Speusippus autem in libro de diffinitionibus Platonis ait: Ventus est agitatio aeris circa terram. De ventis autem perbelle Phavorinus aput Gellium disserit, libro 2, capitulo 22. [3] In libro autem 16, capitulo 11, Psyllos, ait Gellius, fuisse quosdam in terra Africa et eos "re aquaria defectos" ob quandam ventorum vim "eam iniuriam graviter

---

[15] medicus qui a] medicus qui a non ullis medicus *canc. cod.*

also buy little birds and fish and, as if led by piety, everywhere set them free; and above all, they say, he preferred to die rather than wound beans. [5] So let these considerations cause this precept to be an inducement to us to hand all things over, charitably, to God, in so far as our sacrifice is acceptable to him. For nothing pleases God without peace. Did he not himself order that "if you bring your offering to the altar and remember that your brother has something against you, go, first, and reconcile yourself to your brother?"

16. [1] **Upon getting out of bed, fold the sheets: or rather, erase the trace of the body.** In the psalm of penitence David sings: "Every night shall I wash my bed with my tears, and drench my sheets;" in those words you detect regret for sins. [2] "For those who sleep, sleep by night," says the Apostle. Now in scripture the noun "night" signifies sin. [3] Moreover, "penitence" means to weep for past evils and, for example, "to fold the sheets" of a dream and demolish the trace of the body which lies down; it is almost as if one must weep not to commit [the sin] again. [4] Now, "to lie down," when used of men, means to be preoccupied by the torpor and sloth of the body and to be immersed in crime. Moreover, to come to life again and to awaken is to rise up from sin. [5] But to erase the trace means to put away every disgrace of error, so that no stain appears; it also means that there should be no trace whatsoever where formerly there were in us a number of crimes, which existed as if they were wounds, of a sort. [6] Moreover, let every disposition of sinners be changed in such a way that his very emotional state seems to be converted into its contrary (26, question 7, in the chapter, "affectum").

17. [1] **When the winds blow, call upon Echo.** In his *Problems*, Alexander the doctor, who is by some called Aphrodisias, talks a lot about Echo. Now he thinks that it is a refraction of the air and the insubstantial created voice of the one speaking, or rather striking. [2] But in his book *On the Definitions of Plato*, Speusippus says: the wind is the agitation of the air about the earth. Moreover Favorinus speaks very beautifully about the winds in Gellius, at book two, chapter twenty-two. [3] Moreover in book sixteen, chapter eleven, the Psylli, Gellius says, were certain men in Africa that "were lacking water," thanks to a certain power of the winds [and that] "gravely incensed at that injury caused by the South Wind, they decided to

austro succensuisse decretumque fecisse ut armis sumptis ad austrum
perinde quasi ad hostem iure belli res petitum[16] proficiscerentur. [4]
Atque ita profectis ventum austrum magno spiritus agmine venisse
obviam eosque universos cum omnibus copiis armisque, cumulis mon-
tibusque harenarum superiectis, opperuisse. Eo facto Psyllos ad unum
omnis interisse." Haec Gellius. [5] Ast hi profecto non dum resciver-
ant hoc Pythagorae dictum, ne armis, scilicet, sed echo invocata con-
tenderent in ventorum vim. [6] Sed haec fabulosa abeant et cetera
quae de Psillorum venenis referri solent, in aliud autem prorsus
meditemur in nostro autore, ut vana vanis metiamur et paribus paria
semper tribuamus. [7] Ventus enim res vana est et momentanea.
Echo et persimilis eius. [8] Cum ergo veniunt fluvia et flant venti,
non cedant illis aedes nostrae, qui firmi sumus in Christi petra, sed
inclamemus: "Vanitas vanitatum et omnia vanitas," quia nimirum
universa vanitas omnis homo vivens qui frustra conturbatur, cum
omnia quae sunt in mundo debeat ipse pro nihilo reputare.

18. [1] **Farinam sacrificiis apponito.** Valerius Maximus, libro
quinto, apprime laudat humanitatem et animi moderationem. Hic
autem noster morum mansuetudinem hoc in loco commendat, ut per
angustias attriti mitescere velimus, non autem in superbiae fervorem
excandescere. [2] "Deus" enim "superbis resistit, humilibus autem dat
gratiam." Mansuetorum quoque et humilium semper sibi placuit dep-
recatio. Est autem inter iram et stuporem mansuetudo media, ut in
secundo Ethicorum et quarto dicit Aristoteles; ne igitur irascamur,
ira enim viri iustitiam dei non operat. Nam impedit ira animi, ne
possit cernere verum, et furor iraque mentem praecipitant. [3] Sed
neque stupidi et quasi attoniti sine intellectu simus, tales enim et
ignavi et tepidi evomuntur ex ore dei. [4] At mites simus, mansueti
et humiles, quatenus hac virtutis mediocritate amicti et quasi inter
utramque molam attriti imolemus deo sacrificium laudis et reddamus
altissimo vota nostra, farinam apponentes albam et attritam inter
utrumque lapidem, quae fiet agina[17] in dei libamine, ubi erit pax,

---

[16] petitum] potitum *cod.*
[17] agina] agima *cod.*

take up arms and march against the South Wind, as if they were
going against an enemy to demand restitution according to the law
of war. [4] And once they had marched out, the South wind came
upon them in a great group with a huge blast of air and, having
scattered them with heaps and mountains of sand, buried them all,
along with all their forces and arms. And in that way all the Psylli
without exception were killed." So much for Gellius. [5] But they
certainly never got to know this saying of Pythagoras, so that they
should have fought the force of the winds not with arms but by
invoking echo. [6] But away with these fantastic tales and with other
such customarily reported things concerning the poisons of the Psylli;
moreover, let us immediately ponder something else in our author,
so that we measure vain things by means of vain things and always
attribute equal to equals. [7] For the wind is a vain and fleeting
thing. Echo is greatly similar to it. [8] When, therefore, the waters
come and the winds blow, may our homes not yield to them—we
who are firm in the rock of Christ—rather, let us cry out: "Vanity
of vanities, and all things vanity," because surely every living man
who is perturbed in vain *is* a universal vanity, when he himself ought
to disdain as nothing all the things which are in the world.

18. [1] **Add flour to your sacrifices.** Valerius Maximus, in book
five, praises humanity and moderation of spirit in the highest degree.
Now this man of ours [Pythagoras] here recommends mildness of
character, so that, even if we have been worn out through the narrow straits in which we have been placed, we wish to become milder
in character and not flare up in the fervor of pride. [2] For "God
resists the proud and gives grace to the humble." In addition, the
entreaty of the mild and humble has always pleased him. Now mildness is a mean between anger and torpor, as Aristotle says in the
second and fourth books of the *Ethics*; therefore let us not become
angry, for a man's anger does not serve God's justice. For the anger
of the soul gets in the way, so that one cannot discern what is true,
and rage and anger destroy the mind. [3] But let us also not be
stupid—stunned, almost and without intellect—for such types, slothful and tepid, are vomited from the mouth of God. [4] Let us rather
be mild, gentle and humble, in so far as we are draped in this mean
of virtue and worn down between both of the two millstones, as it
were; let us offer the sacrifice of praise to God and turn our prayers
to the Most High, as we add white flour which has been smoothed

benignitas, charitas, "quod est vinculum perfectionis," ut dicit Apostolus. [5] Virtutum namque quidam sunt nexus, quibus panis angelorum fiat, aptus ad sacrificium dei in sanctitate et iustitia coram ipso, ubi, prae caeteris, humilitas et mansuetudo annumeratae sint.

19. [1] **Gladium acutum declinato.** Democlis felicitatem improbat hic noster autor, illi enim impendere Dionisius tyrannus gladium peracutum fecit in caput, cum ipse videretur epulis accumbere divum. [2] Hoc autem doli atque insidiae designantur a quibus debet unusquisque cavere, ne invadatur aut opprimatur. Est etiam acutus gladius sermo regius. Dicit enim scriptura: ne loquaris contra verbum principis, ne nitaris contra ictum fulminis vel fluminis. [3] Gladius quoque anceps et peracutus est in ore dei, ut patet in Apocalipsi, quo innuitur indignatio eius, de qua in psalmo, "cum exarserit //274v// in brevi ira eius." [4] Et Johannes: "Quis" vos, inquit, docuit "fugere a ventura ira?" Atque idipsum est facere fructus dignos poenitentiae perque eosdem acutum dei gladium declinare.

20. [1] **Gladio ignem ne fodias.** Hieronymus, hoc interpretatus, ait, ira percitum ne lacessas, quin magis aquiescere illi et concedere convenit, et placidis verbis eius animum placare. Nam responsio mollis frangit iram; sermo durus suscitat furorem. [2] Lucianus in veris narrationibus ait se Rhadamantum monuisse tria, scilicet, ne gladio ignem diverberaret, ne lupinis vesceretur, tertium autem non licet homini loqui, nam bestiale est. [3] Diogenes Laertius, hoc ipsum edisserens, ait, "potentium et ferocium iracundiam non esse convitiis exagitandam." Dicit enim Ovidius, "Dum furor est in cursu, currenti cede furori. Difficiles aditus impetus omnis habet." Quo enim flamma plus agitatur, eo ipsa magis invalescit, [4] quoniam nitimur in vetitum semper cupimusque negata, ac si privatio ipsa appetitum moveat, fastidium copia. Plato autem de legibus libro vi. ait dissecare ignem eos, qui frustra aliquid moliuntur. [5] Basilius quoque alludit ad hoc nepotibus scribens ut iidem sibi nolint ignem gladio

between each of the two stones, and which will become the "tongue of the balance" in God's offering, where there shall be peace and charity "which is the bond of perfection," as the Apostle says. [5] For there are certain interconnections of the virtues which bring about the bread of angels, a bread suited to God's sacrifice in sanctity and justice before Him, where humility and mildness are counted before everything else.

19. [1] **Avoid the sharp sword.** This author of ours disapproves of Damocles' happiness, for the tyrant Dionysius made an exceedingly sharp sword hang over his head, even though he seemed to be taking his place at table at the banquets of the Gods. [2] Now this denotes tricks and traps of which every man ought to beware, lest he be assaulted or overpowered. In addition, the "sharp sword" also means royal speech. For scripture says: Do not speak against the prince's word; do not strive against the blow of thunder or a river. [3] As is clear in the Apocalypse, the sword is also double-edged and extremely sharp in the mouth of God, the sword to which his indignation beckons; we read about this in the psalm: "since His anger is quickly kindled." [4] And John: "Who" taught you, he says, "to flee from the anger about to come?" And this means the same as making fruits worthy of penitence and through those same fruits avoiding God's sharp sword.

20. [1] **Do not poke fire with a sword.** In interpreting this Jerome says it means you should not provoke a turbulent man to anger; rather, it is fitting to acquiesce and yield to him and with calming words placate his anger. For a mild response mitigates anger; harsh speech calls forth rage. [2] In his *True Stories* Lucian says that Rhadamanthus warned himself of three things, namely not to strike fire with a sword, not to eat lupins, and third, that a man is not permitted to speak because it is bestial. [3] Diogenes Laertius explains this very saying by averring that "the irascibility of the powerful and ferocious must not be stirred up by mockery." For Ovid says, "While rage rushes forth, yield to the coursing rage. Every impulse has difficult points of access." For the more the flame is agitated, the stronger it grows, [4] because we are drawn to the forbidden and always desire what is denied, in the same way that privation itself stimulates the appetite and abundance stimulates a lack thereof. Now

dissecare et cribro haurire[18] aquam. Uterque autem sensus est bonus et unicuique tenendus pro suo arbitratu.

21. [1] **Figuram et aram in primis honorato.** Maronis prae-ceptum in Georgicis datur: "Imprimis venerare deos atque annua magnae / Sacra refer Cereri." Et sapiens ille ait, "Si deus est ani-mus, nobis ut carmina dicunt / hic tibi praecipue sit, pura mente colendus." [2] Hoc autem religio ipsa praecipitur, ea enim est hominis propria atque veridica, ut aperte demonstrat Marsilius noster in libro De christiana religione. [3] Sed et Lactantius ipse mirifice ostendit in libro De ira dei, quod homo ipse non risu quidem sed religione a caeteris animalibus differt; risus enim quidam et in brutis reperi-tur, religio autem in solo homine. [4] Haec vero et in affectu et in effectu[19] ponitur, ut mente et manu deus ipse colatur; figura enim ad animum, ara ad manum spectat, ut, scilicet, deum corde timea-mus, et vacui non appareamus in conspectu eius, uti et Moises prae-cepit in Deuteronomio. Figura autem dei solo corde concipitur, ara vero in sacris habetur. [5] Nolebant iudei figuram quamvis in tem-plo, ut per in lege Moisi et in Josepho De bello iudaico libro ii, ubi Pilatus Caesaris imagines vel coopertas et velatas Jerosolemis tenere non potuit; et auream Herodis aquilam sophistae illi tulere de tem-plo, ut dicit idem Josephus in primo libro.

22. [1] **Gallis albis parcito.** Proculus in libro De sacrificio ait: Leones et galli sunt numinis solaris participes; plus tamen gallus qui leonem fugat, et canit cum redit nobis[20] aurora solemque reducit. [2] Non numquam etiam sunt visi daemones solares leonina fronte qui, obiectis gallis, aufugerunt imagini deferentes digniori. Haec ille.

---

[18] haurire] aurire *cod.*
[19] in effectu] Possibly cancelled in *cod.*
[20] nobis] a nobis *cod.*

Plato in book six of *The Laws* says that fire tears apart those who labor in vain. [5] And Basil alludes to this when he writes to his nephews that they not wish for themselves to tear apart the fire with a sword and to draw water from a sieve. Now each of the two senses is good and should be maintained by each man according to his own judgment.

21. [1] **First and foremost honor figure and the altar.** In the *Georgics* Vergil's precept is given: "First and foremost worship the gods and give annual tribute to great Ceres." And that wise man says, "if God is our soul, as the poems say, let it be especially important to you that He be worshipped with a pure mind." [2] Now religion itself is taught by this precept, for it is properly and truly characteristic of man, as our Marsilio demonstrates in his book *On the Christian Religion.* [3] But Lactantius too, in his book *On the Anger of God,* marvellously shows that man himself differs from the other animals not because of laughter, to be sure, but because of religion; for a certain laughter is found even in brutes, but religion is found only in man. [4] But religion is reckoned both in the inner habit and in outward performance, so that God might be worshipped with both mind and hand; for "figure" pertains to the soul, "altar" to the hand, so that, namely, we fear God in our heart and do not appear empty-handed in his view, as Moses also teaches in Deuteronomy. Now the "figure" of God is conceived in the heart alone, but the "altar" is believed to consist in sacred ceremonies. [5] The Jews did not want any "figure" in the temple, as one reads in the Law of Moses and in Josephus' *On the Jewish War,* book two, where Pilate could not have the images of Caesar in Jerusalem, not even the covered, veiled ones. And those sophists took away Herod's golden eagle from the temple, as the same Josephus says in the first book.

22. [1] **Spare white cocks.** In his book *On Sacrifice* Proclus says: Lions and cocks partake of the solar deity; still, it is more the cock who causes the lion to flee, and he sings when dawn returns and leads the sun back to us. [2] In addition, solar demons of leonine countenance have sometimes been seen who flee if cocks are placed in their way, and defer to the more worthy image. So much for Proclus. [3] But our Pico in a certain oration of his calls white cocks the messengers of truth and preachers of the word of God, for "truth gives birth to hatred," and those who speak the truth are from time

[3] Sed Picus noster in quadam sua oratione gallos albos appellat veritatis nuncios, et verbi dei praedicatores, quia vero "veritas odium parit," et qui veritatem dicunt quandoque disperduntur, ut prophetae domini propter verbum dei lapidati sunt, secti sunt, temptati sunt, in occisione gladii mortui sunt! [4] Sed et olim exularunt philosophi ab urbe sub Nerone et Domiciano, ut aput Philostratum de Apolonio legimus, quod ipsum et Gellius libro 15. capitulo 11. affirmat, quod philosophi, Domiciano imperante, senatusconsulto eiecti atque Urbe et Italia, interdicti sunt; qua tempestate Epictetus quoque philosophus, propter id senatusconsultum, Nicopolim Roma decessit. [5] Id vero quoniam et aput antiquos erat, ut veritatis assertores abiicerentur, iccirco Samius noster vates non vult gallos albos laedi, non utique contentus, ut tamen sint galli, idest, lucis nuncii; iuxta illud, "ales diei nuncius," et rursus, "praeco diei iam sonet, noctis profundae pervigilat," etc. "Gallo canente, spes redit," etc. [6] Sed et addidit "albis," ut lucem intellectualem ominemur in eis. Ideoque eiusmodi nunciis, daemonum inimicis, deique et angelorum sodalibus applaudamus oportet et gaudeamus eisdem, ne dum ipsos quoquomodo laedamus. //275// [7] Sunt insuper galli albi praepositi boni, qui nos arguunt, obsecrunt, et increpant in omni patientia et doctrina, quibus parcere debemus, ut nullubi laedamus eos, at ipsis omnino passim obsequamur.

23. [1] **Hyrundinem domi non habeto.** Divus Hieronymus, Aristotelis auctoritatem sequutus, interpretatur hoc, ut abstineamus a commercio garrulorum et susurronum. [2] Id ipsum tamen potest et secus intelligi pro eo quod in Rhetoricis ad Herennium dicitur: in fide amicitiae similitudo ab hyrundinibus, quae, vere ineunte, praesto sunt, hyeme, absunt. Amici enim ficti opes non virtutes consectantur. [3] Plutarchus etiam in symposiacis decade octava, ideo abiciendas esse hyrundines autumat per Pythagoram, quoniam illae ex rapto vivant et in domibus nostris absque omni utilitate versentur. [4] Perindeque nullam referant gratiam communicati hospitii, et insuper, una cum muscis, animalia domestica cum sint, numquam mansuescant, hoc etsi Albertus Magnus abnuit, qui hyrundinem mansuetam et domesticam viderit. [5] Tamen id perraro, si forte fuerit, ut ferme semper mali quippiam suspicentur, quam ob causam doceantur numquam, et numquam cicurescant. [6] Hoc igitur Pythagorico decreto iubemur convictorem ingratum parumque firmum et usque adeo nobis

to time brought to ruin, so that the Lord's prophets have been
stoned, cut to pieces, attacked, and killed by the blow of the sword!
[4] But formerly, too, philosophers were exiled from the City under
Nero and Domitian, as we read in Philostratus *On Apollonius*; this
itself Gellius too affirms in book fifteen, chapter eleven, i.e., that the
philosophers were thrown out from both Rome and Italy by a *senatusconsultum* when Domitian ruled and were placed under interdict;
in this time and thanks to this *senatusconsultum* Epictetus, also a philosopher, left Rome for Nicopolis. [5] But it was also the case among
the ancients that those who asserted the truth were rejected, on
account of which our Samian prophet, not entirely satisfied, does
not want white cocks to be harmed, so that there still are "cocks,"
that is, messengers of the light, according to those sayings, "winged
messenger of the day" and again "the herald of the day now sounds,
he is watchful of the profound night," etc., "with the cock singing,
hope returns," etc. [6] Now he also added "white," so that we might
interpret the intellectual light that is in them. So it is necessary that
we applaud messengers of this sort, enemies of demons, allies of God
and the angels, and let us rejoice with them as well, lest we harm
them in some fashion in the meantime. [7] Besides, those aforesaid
white cocks are good; in everything, they censure, scold, and implore
us with patience and learning. We must spare them, so that we never
injure them, so that, rather, we always and everywhere obey them.

23. [1] **Have no swallow in your house.** Divine Jerome, having followed the authority of Aristotle, interprets this to mean that
we ought to abstain from commerce with garrulous and gossiping
men. [2] Still, this itself can also be understood differently, as referring to what is discussed in the *Rhetoric to Herennius*: in faithfulness
there is a similarity to friendship which can be shown from swallows, since swallows are at hand when spring comes but are absent
in winter. For false friends follow wealth, not the virtues. [3] In addition Plutarch in his *Table Talk*, 8, avers that swallows, in Pythagoras'
view, should be thrown out because they live from plunder and are
domiciled in our houses without any utility whatsoever. [4] In like
manner they offer no thanks for the hospitality bestowed, and above
all, even though they are domestic animals, just like flies are never
trained, even if Albert the Great does negate this idea, since he saw
the swallow as mild and domestic. [5] Still, this happens exceedingly
rarely, if ever, so that they are almost always suspected of something

diffidentem ablegare; his de causis utique quibus addire loquacitas, instabilitas, varietas, rapacitas, hyrundines nobis reddunt odiosas.

24. [1] **In templum praeter propositum minime ingreditor.** Valerius libro primo De servata religione ait: "Sulpicio inter sacrificandum e capite apex prolapsus eidem sacerdotium abstulit, et occentus soricis auditus, Fabio Maximo dictaturam et C. Flaminio[21] magisterium equitum deponendi causam praebuit." [2] "Vestalis etiam virgo, quia quadam nocte parum diligens, aeterni illius ignis custos fuisset, digna visa est quae flagro admoveretur," et verberibus cederetur. [3] Item libro 3. capitulo 3. "Regi Alexandro nobilissimi pueri praesto erant sacrifica<n>ti. E quibus unus thuribulo accepto ante ipsum astitit. In cuius brachio carbo ardens dilapsus est. Quo etsi ita urebatur ut adusti corporis eius nidor ad nares circumstantium perveniret, tamen dolorem silentio pressit brachiumque immobile tenuit, ne sacrificium Alexandro aut excusso thuribulo impediret aut edito gemitu aures regias aspergeret. [4] Rex quoque patientia pueri magis delectatus, hoc certius perseverantiae experimentum sumere voluit. Consulto[22] enim sacrificavit diutius, ne hac re eum approposito repulit. [5] Si huic miraculo Darius inseruisset oculos, scisset eius stirpis milites vinci non posse cuius infimam aetatem tanto robore praeditam animadvertisset." [6] Id ipsum exempli refert divus Ambrosius in principio ferme tertii libri De virginibus. At quorsum haec? Nempe, ut intelligatur quanta fuerit sollicitudo aput antiquos quantaque curiositas ad divinum cultum. [7] Cuius in hoc edicto Pythagoras meminit, qui tantam vult esse diligentiam nobis ad facienda divina ut ad ea accedere nequaquam debeamus praeter propositum, idest, incauti et quasi casu quodam sed firma intentione et animo praeparato, utpote ituri ad thronum gratiae dei, et ad illum in quem desiderant angeli prospicere. [8] Si enim, cum volumus alloqui principem quempiam et magnum virum non utique de improviso, sed apparati et praemeditati accedimus ad eum, quanto magis id

---

[21] Flaminio] flamanio *cod.*
[22] consulto] consueto *cod.*

evil, thanks to which they are never trained and never domesticated. [6] By this Pythagorean decree, then, we are ordered to banish an ungrateful and disloyal housemate, and one who is, regarding us, distrustful; for these reasons—to which one can certainly add loquacity, instability, fickleness, and rapacity—swallows are made hateful to us.

24. [1] **Do not go into the temple beyond measure.** Valerius, in his first book *On Preserved Religion*, says: "In Sulpicius' case, the fact that his crown fell from his head while he was sacrificing lost him the priesthood; and the perception of the cry of a little mouse became the cause of deposition for Fabius Maximus and Caius Flaminius, the one from the post of dictator, the other from master of the cavalry." [2] "In addition, the Vestal Virgin, because on a certain night she was not diligent while she was supposed to be guarding that eternal flame, seemed deserving of a whipping" and yielded to blows. [3] Again, in book three, chapter three, "the noblest boys were near to King Alexander while he was sacrificing. One of them took an incense-burner and stood by him. But a burning piece of coal fell on his arm. However, even though he was burned to such an extent that the smell of his burned body reached the noses of the bystanders, he still bore the pain in silence and held his arm immobile, so as not to impede Alexander's sacrifice by dropping the incense holder, or by issuing a groan which might sully the royal ears. [4] The king was delighted by the boy's patience, and wanted to take up this experiment of perseverance in a more certain fashion. So he intentionally prolonged the sacrifice for a time so that the boy not be thrust aside from his goal. [5] Had this miracle taken place before the eyes of Darius, he would have known that soldiers of that stock could not be conquered and he would have noticed that even from a young age they were endowed with a prodigious strength." [6] Divine Ambrose refers to that very example close to the beginning of the third book of his *On Virgins*. But why these examples? Of course: so that it might be understood how much concern and curiosity there was among the ancients when it came to divine worship. [7] Pythagoras reminds us of this in this edict; he wants us to be so diligent when it comes to practicing religion that we must in no way approach religion "beyond measure," that is, incautiously and almost by chance; rather we ought to approach religion with unwavering concentration and with our souls prepared,

debemus accedentes ad illum qui est rex regum et dominus dominantium, in cuius manu sunt omnium potestates et omnium iura regnorum, ut ponit divus Benedictus in regula vestra.

25. [1] **Iuxta sacrificium ungues ne incidito.** Hoc ipsum cum superiori concordat elogio, ut ante deum stantes non simus corde vagantes. Quia, si cor non orat, in vanum lingua laborat. [2] Iuxta illud Esaiae dictum: "Populus" hic "labiis"[23] me honorat, "cor autem eius longe est a me." Homo enim aspicit ea, quae foris patent, deus autem intuetur cor. [3] Possunt autem occulta hominum et interiora nonnihil per aperta haec atque exteriora deprehendi, ut patet in capitulo "Clericus" distinctione 41. [4] Cum ergo viderimus quempiam vel in choro vel ad altare, ungues sibi incidere, digitulos complicare, mordere, et nares frequenter immictere, caput sibi ad manum reclinare, idipsumque sculpere //275v// uno digito, hunc utique vagabundum corde censemus, et non indignum illa divi Benedicti virga, quae ipse percussit monachum illum vagum et sanavit eum. [5] Est tamen et altius quiddam hoc enigmate interclusum, si recte cogitemus. Unguium enim partes illae quas solemus incidere, non sunt de hominis essentia, neque requiruntur neccessario ad naturam eius. Sunt profecto parvulae quidem et nullius roboris vel momenti. [6] Cum autem ad tribunal divinae maiestatis accedimus, non nitamur a nobis minima haec eiicere, quasi venialia delicta, sed maiora crimina, quae qui agunt, regnum dei non consequentur. [7] Ipocritae namque discutiunt culicem et deglutiunt camelos; decimant quippe "mentam et anetum," lavant quod est exterius "calicis et parapsidis." De manuum lotione curant, quae autem sunt legis graviora dimictunt. [8] Non igitur pharisei illius iactantis se ipsum et quasi ungues incidentis, sed publicani imitemur exemplum, ne dominentur nos[24] scelera nostra, sed emundemur a delicto maximo.

---

[23] labiis] labiit *cod.*
[24] nos] nostri *cod.*

given that we are about to approach the throne of God's grace, and Him upon whom angels desire to look. [8] For if, when we wish to speak to some prince or great man, we certainly do not do it unprepared but rather approach him well-equipped and having thought things through, how much more ought we to do this when we approach Him who is the king of kings and lord of lords, in whose hand are the powers over all things and laws over all kingdoms, as divine Benedict sets forth in your *Rule*.

25. [1] **Do not pare your nails during sacrifice.** This one accords well with the above precept, i.e., that we ought not wander in our heart when standing before God. Because, if the heart does not pray, in vain does the tongue bray. [2] According to that saying of Isaiah: This "people" honors me "with its lips but its heart is far from me." For man looks upon those things which are clear from without, but God sees within the heart. [3] Now the hidden and interior parts of man to a certain extent do depend on those open and exterior things, as is clear in the chapter "Clericus," distinction forty-one. [4] When therefore we shall have seen someone either in the choir or at the altar cutting his nails, fiddling with his little fingers, biting them, plunging his fingers over and over into his nose, reclining his head on his hand, scratching it with one finger— this man we certainly deem inconstant of heart, and not unworthy of that rod of divine Benedict with which he beats that inconstant monk and brings him to reason. [5] Still, there is also something higher hidden within this enigma, if we think rightly on it. For those parts of the fingernails which we are accustomed to pare are not part of man's essence, nor are they necessarily requisite to his nature. To be sure: they are certainly quite small and of no strength or moment. [6] Now when we approach the tribunal of divine majesty, we do not struggle to expel from ourselves these minutiae, almost as if they were venal crimes; rather, we try to expel the major crimes—the crimes that, whoever commit them, do not gain the kingdom of God. [7] Now hypocrites argue over a flea and swallow camels; certainly they "tithe mint" and "anise," and "wash" what is the outside of the "cup and platter." They care about washing their hands but dismiss those more serious matters of the law. [8] And so let us not imitate the example of the that pharisee, showing off and thus almost "pairing his fingernails;" rather, let us imitate the

26. [1] **In via ne scindito.** "Cum consuetudinis ususque longaevi
non parva sit auctoritas, et discordiam persaepe patiant novitates,"
ex. De consuetudine, capitulo "cum consuetudinis;" consuetum autem
quod sit, quasi pervium est, quod vero praeter usum, quasi invium
censeri potest. [2] Consuetudo igitur servari debet et secundum usum
suum omnia regi, ut dicitur scilicet decretalibus in multis capitulis.
Nam sicut consuevimus, ita dignum est dici, inquit Aristoteles. Hoc
igitur edicto cavetur, ne quid insolitum seu praeter usum fiat, quod
invii nomine censeri posset. [3] Moises autem in lege dixit non "transgrediaris terminos quos posuerunt tibi parentes tui." Salomon quoque
dicit: "Ne innitaris prudentiae tuae." [4] Ille autem, secundum divinum Hieronymum, innititur prudentiae suae, qui quod sibi censendum
viditur patrum sententiis anteponit. [5] Usus autem vertitur in naturam, dicit philosophus, propterea qui usui obsistit, viditur quasi
gigantum more bellare cum diis, quid non est aliud, ut ait Cicero,
quam repugnare naturae, idest, inclinationi naturali. Vertere autem
naturam gratia nulla potest.

27. [1] **Iugum ne transcendito.** Aulus Gellius dicit in Noctibus
atticis libro undecimo, capitulo duodecimo: "Chrysippus ait omne
verbum ambiguum natura esse, quoniam ex eodem duo vel plura
accipi possunt. Diodorus autem, cui Crono cognomen fuit, 'Nullum',
inquit, 'verbum ambiguum est, nec quisquam ambiguum dicit aut
sentit'." [2] Nos aut inpraesentiarum Chrysippo adhaeserimus,
dum nomen ambiguum duoque significans prae manibus habemus.
Iugum enim et praesidis designat impervium et montis verticem. [3]
Dicit enim dominus in evangelio, "Iugum enim meum suave est."
Maro autem dicit, "Dum iuga montis aper, fluvios dum piscis amabit."
[4] Iuga autem boum et animalium et campos seu iugera et ligna
illa demonstrant. "Quingenta" enim "iuga boum" habebat Job et
"iuga boum emi quinque," ait ille. [5] In Numeris autem 19 dicitur de vacca ruffa, quae nondum portaverit iugum. Illud vero apprime
nobis in praesentia quadrat quod in praepositos Psalmista ait: "Dirumpamus vincula eius et proiiciamus a nobis iugum ipsorum."

example of the tax-gatherer, lest our evil deeds dominate us; and let us clean ourselves thoroughly of the greatest crime.

26. [1] **Do not part on the way.** "Since the authority of custom and long-established usage is not small, and since novelties quite often allow of discord. . . ." (see extrav., *De consuetudine*, in the chapter "cum consuetudinis"). Now what is customary is almost passible, but what is beyond usage can almost be thought to be impassible. [2] Therefore custom must be preserved and everything ruled according to its usage, as is said, namely, in the decretals in many chapters. For just as we have been accustomed, so it is worthy to be said, says Aristotle. Therefore by this edict one is warned lest something unusual or beyond common usage happens, for it could be judged with the name of impassible. [3] But Moses in the law said, "do not go beyond the limits which your parents have set for you." And Solomon says: "put no faith in your own prudence." [4] Now he who puts faith in his own prudence, according to divine Jerome, is one who places what seems best to himself before the opinions of his elders. [5] Moreover, common usage turns into nature, says the Philosopher, because he who stands in the way of common usage seems—almost in the manner of the Giants—to war with the gods, which, as Cicero says, is nothing other than to fight against nature, that is, against natural inclination. And there is no grace that can subvert nature.

27. [1] **Do not transcend the yoke.** In the eleventh book of the *Attic Nights*, in the twelfth chapter, Aulus Gellius says: "Chrysippus says that every word is by nature ambiguous, since two or more meanings can be taken from that same word. But Diodorus, sur-named Cronus, says 'there is no ambiguous word, nor does anyone speak or think an ambiguous word.'" [2] Now we, under present circumstances, shall have adhered to Chrysippus, since we have before us an ambiguous noun signifying two things. For a yoke designates both the imperviousness of a guard and the high point of a mountain. [3] For the Lord says in the Gospel, "For my yoke is sweet." But Vergil says, "as long as the wild boar will love the tops of the mountain, so will the fish love the rivers." [4] But the yokes of oxen and animals signify also the fields or rather acres and those woods. For "Fifty yokes of oxen" had Job and "I bought five yokes of oxen," says he. [5] Now in *Numbers*, 19, the "reddish cow" is spoken of, which does not yet wear a yoke. But that really does square very

[6] Iugum autem servitutem designat. "Bonum erit" homini, in Trenis dicitur, "cum portaverit iugum ab adolescentia sua prima." Ad Thimotheum 6 dicitur "Quicumque sunt sub iugo, servi dominos suos omni honore dignos arbitrentur." Alibi autem dicit Apostolus: "Nolite iugum ducere cum infidelibus." [7] Est enim iugum bonum, iugum malum, servitus, scilicet, salutis et perditionis; illa dei, haec diaboli. Sunt enim duo domini, quibus nemo potest pariter servire. [8] Viri autem religiosi, ac si religati sub iugo et servitute dei in voto oboedientiae cui imposuit deus homines super caput eius ipsius, utique, servire regnare est, et homini propter deum obsequi supprema dignitas est; abnegare se ipsum propter deum—haec est tota perfectio. [9] Quicumque igitur hanc professus est viam, illi hic dicit noster vates: iugum ne transgredito, idest, serva mandata omnia et qua<s>libet oboedientiae vires, est enim oboedientia melior cunctis holo//276//caustomatibus, ut dixit Samuel.

[10] Iugum autem, idest, montis verticem transcendit nemo. Nam hic vertex nobis, ne nobis altiora quaeramus et fortiora minime scrutemur, qui enim scrutator fuerit maiestatis opprimetur a gloria. [11] Psalmigraphus autem dicit: "Non ambulavi in magnis neque in mirabilibus super me." Sunt vero summitates nobis quas transcendere non valemus aut in moralibus aut in intellectualibus. [12] In moralibus degalogum Moisi habemus constitutiones quoque leges et praecepta; maioribus[25] oboedire et servare debemus ad metam. [13] In intellectualibus dantur nobis principia et regulae pro scientia quamvis et pro fide articuli ipsi atque ecclesiae sanctiones quibus mundus omnis gubernatur et regitur. Eisque subest universus terrarum orbis. [14] Nullus igitur ista iuga transcendit, dicitur enim ex. De constitutionibus, "Canonum statuta ab omnibus custodiantur et nemo in actionibus vel iudiciis ecclesiasticis suo sensu sed eorum auctoritate ducatur." Id ipsum iugum sit ab omnibus christicolis usque quaque servetur.

---

[25] maioribus] maiorum *cod.*

well right now for us with what the Psalmist says against those in power: "Let us break his chains and throw their yoke away from us."

[6] Now the yoke also designates servitude. "It will be good" for man, it is said in the *Lamentations*, "should he bear a yoke from first adolescence." In the letter to Timothy, 6, it is said "whosoever are under the yoke, may they as servants think their lords worthy of every honor." And elsewhere the Apostle says: "Do not harness yourself with unbelievers." [7] For there is a good yoke and a bad one, the servitude, namely, of well-being and of perdition; the former is of God, the latter, of the devil. For there are two lords, whom no one can serve equally. [8] Now it is characteristic of a religious man, certainly, that to serve is to rule—and this is so even if he has been bound under the yoke and servitude of God in a vow of obedience to which God has attached men directly; for man, the highest dignity is to submit for the sake of God. To deny oneself on account of God—this is total perfection. [9] Therefore whosoever has professed this life, to him our prophet says: "Do not transcend the yoke," that is, pay heed to all orders and to any powers of obedience, for obedience is better than all holocausts, as Samuel said.

[10] Now the yoke, that is the vertex of a mountain, no one transcends. For let this be the vertex for us, that we do not seek for ourselves higher things nor look for more powerful things, for whoever would seek majesty is oppressed by glory. [11] Now the Psalmist says: "I have not taken part in great things nor in wonders beyond my scope." But there are heights for us that we cannot transcend either in moral or in intellectual matters. [12] In moral matters, we have the principles of Moses' *Decalogue* as well as laws and precepts; we must obey and heed our elders to the end of our life. [13] In intellectual matters, we are given principles and rules for all sorts of knowledge, and when it comes to faith we are given the very articles and sanctions of the church by which the whole world is governed and ruled. And the whole world is subject to them. [14] Therefore no one transcends those yokes, for it is said in the ex. *De constitutionibus*, "The statutes of the canons are protected by all and let no one in actions or in ecclesiastical judgments be led by his own sense but rather by their authority." Let this itself be the yoke preserved by all worshippers of Christ everywhere.

28. [1] **Lira utitor canendo.** Basilius Magnus ad nepotes scribit: "Thimoteus quotiens libuisset animos hominum et vehementi accendebat harmonia et rursus molli ac placida delinibat. [2] Quippe cum aliquando in Alexandri convivio eum cantum quem Phrygium appellant modularetur, usque adeo regem excitasse dicitur, ut ad arma capienda prosiliret atque ad comessationes epulasque reduxisse, modulatione mutata, tantas vires habet in musicis gymnicisque certaminibus ad finem suum directa excitatio. [3] Pythagoras etiam cum iuvenibus quibusdam vitio sertis saltuque per civitatem lascivientibus obviat, iussisse dicitur ei qui modos tibia faciebat, ut mutata armonia doricum personaret. [4] Quod ubi factum est bachantes illos adeo resipuisse ferunt ut serta abiicerent et rubore vultus verecundiam confessi domum abirent; tantum interest corrupta an salubri musica implere. Qua usus David propheta sacrorum carminum regem ferunt ab insania liberavit." Haec Basilius. [5] Sic igitur musica et lira bona vel mala; illa utamur, hanc abiiciamus. Solebant autem— ut per Platonem constat—viri²⁶ in gymnasticis quam plurimum <musica> occupari, quod et in Politicis philosophus non improbavit. [6] Hic autem noster apprime laudavit exercitum musices et exercitationem lirae, qua uti, secundum ipsum, debeat unusquisque canendo.

²⁷[7] Est autem memorabile quiddam in ea re, quod ipsum Magnus Laurentius Medices alumnus et patronus noster immo et patriae nostrae pater, ubique concelebrat,²⁸ inquiens, "omnes homines dum loquuntur habent suam liram." [8] Appellat autem liram quemdam pausandi modum quo utuntur qui loquuntur et, non desistentes, adhuc quid loqui debeant meditantur illorum instar qui lira canentes donec succurrant quae dicantur lira personant. [9] Sic pariter loquentes homines faciunt, gerunt enim quaedam verba communia quae frequentent, dum aliquid excogitant, utpote "in effectu," "tandem," "tantum est," "in summa," "finaliter," et "huiusmodi." [10] Hae dicuntur lirae a domino meo. Lyra autem bene sonora sit, et concentus

---

²⁶ viri *add. interlineariter cod.*
²⁷ Here a red paragraph divider but no new number.
²⁸ concelebrat] concelebrant *cod*; should we read this as *concelebravit?*

28. [1] **Utilize the lyre in singing.** Basil the Great writes to his nephews: "To a great extent did Timothy please the souls of men and he used to light them on fire with sharp harmony and then mollify them with mild and placid harmony. [2] Certainly, when once, at one of Alexander's dinner parties, he played his song in the Phrygian mode, they say that he had excited the king to such a point that he leapt forward to take up arms; but then, when Timothy changed his playing, the king returned to the feasts and banquets—so much force does vigor directed towards its proper end have in musical and gymnastic exercises. [3] In addition they say that Pythagoras, coming upon certain lascivious youths, festooned with vice and jumping about the city, ordered the one playing the modes on the tibia to change the harmony and play the doric mode. [4] Once this was done, they say that those bacchants recovered their reason to such an extent that they tossed off their wreaths and with redness of face went home, having confessed their shame—so much difference does it make whether one is filled with corrupt or wholesome music. They say that using music, David the prophet liberated the king [Saul] from insanity." So much for Basil. [5] Thus there is a good music or "lyre" and a bad; let us use the former and toss off the latter. Now men—as is established in Plato—used to pay great attention to music in their gymnastic exercises, which even Aristotle in his *Politics* does not disapprove of. [6] But this prophet of ours praised in the highest practicing music and playing the lyre, which each must engage in, according to this precept, by singing.

[7] As far as this material goes, there is something worthy of note which the great Lorenzo de' Medici, our fellow Florentine and patron—and really, the father of our homeland—everywhere celebrates when he says, "all men have their own lyre when they speak." [8] Now what he means by "lyre" is a certain manner of hesitating which speakers employ when they do not cease thinking about what they are talking about, to the point where they have to say something; they are like those who, singing with the aid of a lyre, play the words with their lyre until the words come to mind. [9] And so, men behave similarly when they speak, since they employ certain common, frequently used words while they are thinking something through, words like "in effect," "after all," "such that," "in short," "finally," and "of this sort." [10] These are the "lyres" my lord [Lorenzo] speaks of. Now let the lyre be beautifully sonorous, making sweet sounds, and thus let its musical intervals also be

suaves agat, sic et moduli isti sint rationabiles, qui decorum servent
in loquente et audientis animam minime fastidiant. Hac igitur lira
uti nos iubet hic noster vates bene quippe disposita et personis locisque
cunctis usque quaque concordi.

29. [1] **Lumine carens, de lumine ne tractes.** Marsilius noster
De sole et lumine quam multa perbelle agit, dicens: "Res nulla magis
quam lumen refert naturam boni. [29]Primo, quidem lumen in genere
sensibili purissimum eminentissimumque apparet. [2] [30]Secundo, facillime omnium et amplissime momentoque dilatatur. [31]Tertio, innoxium
occurrit omnibus atque penetrat et lenissimum atque blandissimum est.
[32]Quarto, calorem secum fert almum omnia foventem, generantem,
atque moventem. [33]Quinto, dum adest inestque cunctis, a nullo
inficitur, nulli miscetur. [3] Similiter ipsum bonum totum rerum
ordinem supereminet, amplissime dilatatur, mulcet et allicit omnia,
nil cogit, amorem //276v// quasi calorem habet ubique comitem
quo singula passim inescantur bonumque libenter asciscunt. [4]
Denique, sicut ipsum bonum inestimabile est, atque ineffabile, ita
ferme et lumen. Quamobrem Iamblicus Platonicus huc postremo
confugit, ut lumen actum quemdam et imaginem perspicuam divinae
intelligentiae nominaret." Haec Ficinus. [5] Quibus lumen, ac si divinum quiddam censeri potest, ut per hoc et Psalmistae oratio doceatur;
"in lumine," inquit, "tuo videbimus lumen," et rursus, signatum est
"super nos lumen vultus tui, domine." [6] Deus etiam dicitur lumen,
iuxta illud: "Deum de deo lumen de lumine," et rursus: "Erat lux
vera quae illuminat omnem hominem venientem in hunc mundum."
Dimissis igitur caeteris, De lumine, idest, de deo, sine lumine, idest,
sine deo, agat nemo, per dogma istud. [7] Quod et Plato ille divinus in Cratylo de recta nominum ratione sentit, cum ait, Cavendum
est ne de Deo sine Deo loquamur, et ne pro natura nostra metiri
velimus inmensum. Cum autem de Deo loquimur, non ut homines
loquimur, sed ut tubae dei. [8] Lumen etiam censeri potest et habi-
tus quique intellectualis, quo nimirum perficitur et illustratur animus
noster ad aliquid cognoscendum. [9] Sicuti igitur caecum natum

---

[29] Here red paragraph divider in cod.
[30] Here red paragraph divider in cod.
[31] Here red paragraph divider in cod.
[32] Here red paragraph divider in cod.
[33] Here red paragraph divider in cod.

reasonable, so that men may preserve decorum in speaking and not bore the listener's soul. Therefore, this prophet of ours orders us to use a well-tempered "lyre" and to harmonize with everyone, everywhere.

29. [1] **Lacking light, do not treat of light.** Our Marsilio treats especially well of many things *Concerning the Sun* and concerning light when he says: "Nothing more than light brings home the nature of the good. In the first place, light certainly appears as the purest and most eminent in the genus of sensible things. [2] Second, it spreads out most easily and widely of all, and it does so in a moment. Third, it presents itself and makes its way to all in an unharmful fashion and is both exceedingly gentle and tranquil. Fourth, it brings with itself a nourishing heat which incubates, generates, and moves all things. Fifth, while it is present and in all things, it is tainted by nothing, is mixed with nothing. [3] Similarly, the good itself stands above every grade of thing, is most widely spread out, soothes and wins over all things, forces nothing, and has love, just like heat, everywhere as its ally—love, with which individual things everywhere are filled and because of which they willingly take on the good. [4] Finally, just as the good itself is inestimable and ineffable, so too, practically, is light. Wherefore Iamblichus the Platonist has recourse to this, calling light a certain act and the self-evident image of the divine intelligence." Thus far Ficino. [5] With the aid of these things light can be thought of as something divine, so that through this precept even the oration of the Psalmist might be taught: "in the good," he says, "shall we see your light," and again, "Above us has been signed the light of your face, Lord." [6] In addition God is called light, according to that passage: "God from God, light from light," and again, "There was a true light illuminating every man who comes into this world." Therefore, all else aside, "from light" means "from God," and this tenet means that no one acts "without light," that is, "without God." [7] Divine Plato also believes this in the *Cratylus, On the right reason of names*, when he says, "One must beware lest we talk about God without God, and lest we wish to measure what is immeasurable with the aid of our own nature." Now when we speak of God, we speak not as men, but rather as God's trumpets. [8] Light can also be considered as a kind of intellectual habit by which our soul is without doubt perfected and illuminated for the purpose of recognizing something. [9] Therefore,

dedecet de coloribus iudicare, ita et inscium quemque de quavis scientia, cuius ipse principia, progressus et leges nihil recognoscat. [10]
Is ergo de tali lumine, idest, scientia sine lumine, idest, sine peritia
ipsius non loquatur; quod nonnulli impudentes audent qui garruli-
tatem auctoritatem putant (Distinctio 46, in principio).

30. [1] **Malacen herbam seu malvuum transferas, sed minime
commedas.** Mirum profecto esset, si putaremus de herbae illius
commestione agere autorem nostrum in hoc edicto. Eius autem consuetudo fuit ut symbolice loqueretur, et in parabolis[34] os suum aperiret.
[2] Enygmatice igitur agens, malace utitur herba, quae corpori deter-
gendo solet esse proficua, si tamen per posticum non autem per os
ingeratur. [3] Hinc illud animadvertamus, quod quamvis nihil sit ocio-
sum in natura, omnia tamen in usum debitum sunt assumenda sicuti
namque omnia bona in tempore suo, ita et bona sunt omnia ad ea
quae a natura ipsa pridem fuerint procreata, ut probe narrat Aurelius
in 2. De moribus ecclesiae catholicae, capitulo 8., per exempla quam
plurima. [4] Transferre igitur malvuam debemus ad profluvium ven-
tremque ciendum, ad commedendum minime, ut omnibus utamur
natura duce quaecumque usui nostro aperta videantur.

31. [1] **Nudis pedibus rem divinam facito.** Aristoteles in Problemis
particula 4. problemate v., quaerit "cur nuditas pedum obesse in re
venerea potest," et dicit, "quoniam corpus quod concubiturum sit
calidum intus atque humidum esse debet, quale per somnum potius
esse quam per vigiliam solet. [2] Ex quo etiam celeriter ac sine corporis agitatione semen dormientibus profluit, vigilantibus vero non
sine labore prodit. [3] Similiter autem fit ut et reliquum corpus tale
existat, et pedes humidiores sint atque calidiores, indicium[35] quod,
cum dormimus, pedes obtepescere solent, ut qui una cum internis
partibus ita afficiantur. [4] At nuditas pedum econtrario agit; siccat
enim atque refrigerat itaque sive impossibilis sive difficilis sit, ut res

---

[34] in parabolis] imparabolis *cod.* Cf. 33.1.
[35] indicium] iudicium *cod.*

just as it is unseemly for a man born blind to make judgments about colors, so to is it unseemly for anyone without knowledge to make judgments about any branch of knowledge whatsoever of whose principles, developments, and laws he knows nothing. [10] Therefore let him not speak about such a light, that is, such a branch of knowledge, without light, that is, without knowledge about it, as some impudent men dare to do who think garrulousness is authority (distinction 46, at the beginning).

30. [1] **Transfer the herb mallow, but do not eat it.** It would be a wonder indeed, were we to imagine that our author were speaking only about the eating of this particular herb in this edict. Now it was his custom to speak symbolically, opening his mouth in parabolas. [2] And so, proceeding in an enigmatic fashion, he uses the herb mallow, which is usually well known for cleaning out the body, even if it is taken through the back door, and not the mouth. [3] Hence we notice this: that even though there is nothing in vain in nature, still, all things must be taken for their proper use, for just as all things are good in their own time, so also are all things good for those things born of nature herself long ago, as Augustine rightly discusses in the second book of *On the Character of the Catholic Church*, in chapter eight, with many examples. [4] Therefore, we have to employ mallow to move the bowels and the stomach, but not to eat, so that we employ all things which seem open to our use with nature as our guide.

31. [1] **With naked feet practice religion.** In his *Problems*, Aristotle (part four, problem five) asks "why nudity of the feet can be a hindrance in sex," and he says "because the body which is about to lie down has to be hot within and wet, such as usually happens more in sleep than wakefulness. [2] This also causes the semen to flow swiftly and without bodily agitation from those who are asleep, but it comes not without labor from those who are awake. [3] Similarly, moreover, it happens that even the remainder of the body is that way, and the feet are wetter and hotter, a clue that when we are asleep the feet usually become warm, so that they are affected together with the internal parts. [4] But nudity of the feet works in the contrary fashion; for it dries and cools to such an extent that it is either impossible or at least difficult to have sex without hot feet." [5] This is literally what the Philosopher says, from which it is as

agatur venerea sine pedibus calidis." [5] Haec philosophus ad verbum, e quibus colligi quam facillime potest castitatem ipsam pedum
nuditate signari, nam casta placent superis, propterea iubet hic noster autor ut nudis pedibus, idest, castis animorum affectibus, rem
divinam faciamus. [6] Pedes insuper affectuum nominant qualitatem,
affectibus namque anima incedit, ut corpora pedibus. Cum autem
oramus, reiiciamus appetitum nostrum et iactemus cogitatum omnem,
dicentes ei, "Fiat voluntas tua." [7] Sit ergo nudus animus ab omni
destinatione et nihil certum in oratione perquirat, nisi quod velit
deus, omnem sollicitudinem nostram reiiciens[36] in deum, quia ipsi
cura est de nobis. [8] Nam et Pythagoras hic et Apollonius orantes
dicebant, "Dii date nobis quae bona sunt." Quod et Plato apprime
de Lacedemoniis laudat in Etyfronte, cum agit de sanctitate. [9]
Valerius autem libro septimo De sapienter dictis et factis ait, "Socrates,
humanae sapientiae quasi terrestre oraculum, nihil ultra pe//277//ten-
dum a diis immortalibus arbitrabatur quam ut bona tribuerent, quia
hi demum scirent quid unicuique esset utile. [10] Nos autem plerumque
id votis expetere<mus> quod non impetrasse melius foret. Etenim,
densissimis tenebris involuta mortalium mens, in quas late patentem
errorem caecas precationes tuas spargis? Divitias appetis quae multis exitio fuerunt; honores concupiscis qui complures pessundederunt;
regna tecum ipse voluis, quorum exitus saepe numero miserabiles
cernuntur; splendidis coniugiis inicis manus, et haec ut aliquando
illustrant, ita non numquam funditus domos evertunt! [11] Desine
igitur stulta futuris malorum tuorum causis quasi felicissimis rebus
inhiare! Teque totum caelestium arbitrio permicte, quia qui tribuere
bona ex facili solent, etiam eligere aptissime possunt." [12] Haec
Valerius Maximus ubi s(cilicet) quibus itidem ferme agitur atque di-
cent cum vate nostro, "Nudis pedibus rem divinam facito," idest, ne
alliges animum tuum ad hanc seu ad illam cupiditatem, at vacuus,
nudus, et liber accede ad altare dei et roga quae ad pacem sunt;
et quae tibi sint bona in conspectu dei.

---

[36] reiiciens] reiicentes *cod.*

easy as possible to gather that chastity itself is what is meant by nudity of the feet, for chaste things please the gods, on account of which our author orders that with "naked feet," that is, with chaste emotions in our souls, we practice religion. [6] Besides, feet designate the quality of the emotions, for the soul arises upon the emotions as bodies arise upon feet. Now when we pray, let us reject our desire and toss away every thought, saying to Him, "Thy will be done." [7] Therefore the naked soul from its every determination seeks everywhere in prayer nothing certain, except what God wishes, handing over to God our every care, for His care is for us. [8] For both Pythagoras here and Apollonius when praying used to say, "Gods give us the things which are good." In this respect Plato, too, praises the Spartans in the highest degree in the *Euthyphro*, when he treats of sanctity. [9] But Valerius in the seventh book *On Things Wisely Said and Done* says, "Socrates, almost a terrestrial oracle of human wisdom, used to think that there was nothing to be sought from the immortal Gods other than that they give good things, because they know, finally, what is useful for each person. [10] So we would seek with prayers what it would have been better for the most part not to have obtained. O mortal mind, concealed in the densest darkness, over what blind entreaties do you not widely spatter clear error? You desire riches which for many were their destruction; you covet honors which have sunk many a man; you want for yourself kingdoms, whose outcomes are seen so often to be wretched; you lay hands on showy wives, wives who have on any number of occasions thoroughly overturned homes just as they have sometimes illuminated them! [11] Cease, then, casting your eyes on foolishness; these things, seemingly the happiest, are the future causes of your ills! Give yourself completely to the judgment of the heavens, for those who are accustomed to grant good things easily also have the capacity to choose most ably." [12] Thus Valerius Maximus, where, namely, with those words he means just about the same as our prophet and says: "With naked feet practice religion," that is, do not tie your soul to this or that desire, but rather go empty, naked, and free to God's altar, asking for those things which pertain to peace; and may they be things which are good for you in God's view.

32. [1] **Ollae vestigium in cinere deturbato.** Plutarchus in symposiacis id ipsum interpretatur nullum evidens iracundiae vestigium
oportere relinqui, sed simul ut deferbuerit atque resederit animi
tumor, omnem praeteritorum malorum memoriam penitus tollendam
esse. [2] Studeamus igitur opus, ne irascamus, ira enim viri iustitiam
dei non operatur. Quod si irascamus, saltem non peccemus et sol non
occidat super iracundiam nostram. [3] Pulcherrime id ipsum monuit
Basilius nepotes per exempla philosophorum, dicens: "Potissimum
esset nullo modo irasci. Sin id fieri non potest at rationis freno mode-
randum est nec permictendum longius efferi. [4] Sed reducamus ora-
tionem nostram ad clarorum virorum exempla. Pulsavit quispiam
Socratem Sophronisti filium, faciem eius petulantissime cedens. Socrates
vero non repugnavit, sed illius irae ac petulantiae se permisit, donec
ei vultus undique tuber fieret. [5] Verum ubi ira illius saciata est,
Socrates quidem nihil aliud egit, nisi quam fronti suae inscripsit per-
cussoris nomen, quemadmodum statius fieri solet. Ille, inquit, hoc
opus effecit, nec ulterius ulcisci porrexit. [6] Haec, quae nostris simi-
lia sunt, perdigna esse imitatione duco; hoc enim Socraticum illi
nostro convenit, quod monet ut percutienti maxillam unam, alteram
porrigamus, tantum abest ut ulciscamur. [7] Id autem Periclis aut
Euclidis simile est illi quo monemur persequentes expectare et benigne
iras illorum tollerare, et inimicis bona precari, non autem maledicere.
[8] Nam qui erit in illis pereruditus,[37] is postea praeceptis nostris
acquiescet, nec quasi impossibilia sint aspernabitur." Haec ille. [9]
Quibus isthuc ipsum paradigma nostrum excuditur, ut ollae vestigium
deturbemus in cinere, qui, scilicet, nullam exardentis irae imaginem
relinquamus, at penitus demittamus debita debitoribus nostris, et una
cum Caio Cesare iniuriarum tamen obliviosi simus, reliqua reminis-
camur, donantes proximis offensas omnes de cordibus nostris.

---

[37] pereruditus] preeruditus *cod.*

32. [1] **Erase the mark of the pot in the ashes.** In his *Table Talk* Plutarch interprets this very precept to mean that one must leave behind no evident vestige of anger, but also that the inflamed state of the soul should calm down and subside, and that every memory of past woes be thoroughly taken away. [2] So let us strive after this achievement: not to become angry, since the anger of a man does not serve God's justice. But if we do get angry let us at least not sin, and let the sun not set on our anger. [3] Most beautifully does Basil recommend just this to his nephews through the use of examples of philosophers, when he says: "It would be best not to become angry at all. But if this cannot occur, it must at least be moderated by the brake of reason, nor must it be permitted to go on too long. [4] But let us redirect our speech to examples of famous men. Someone hit Socrates, son of Sophronistus, striking his face most petulantly. Socrates, however, did not hit back but rather surrendered himself to the offender's anger and petulance, until his face everywhere became swollen. [5] But once the offender's anger was satisfied, Socrates did nothing, other than inscribing on his forehead the name of the one who struck him, as if it was accustomed to happen on a rather regular basis. 'That man,' he said, 'did this work,' and he didn't strike out for any more revenge than that. [6] These things are similar to our [i.e., Christian] concerns and seem to me quite worthy of imitation, for this Socratic warning seems especially to agree with ours, which advises us to turn the other cheek to the one who has struck us on the cheek—far be it from us to seek vengeance. [7] And the example of Pericles or Euclides is akin to that precept which advises us to bear those who persecute us and benignly tolerate their anger, even to the extent of wishing good things for our enemies, and not cursing them. [8] For whoever will be thoroughly learned in these matters, he will hereafter acquiesce to our precepts and will not spurn them as if they were impossible." So far St. Basil. [9] With these words is our paradigm forged, to such a point that we "erase the mark of the pot in the ashes," we who, namely, do not leave behind the image of one burning in anger, but rather settle our debts with our debtors and together with Caius Caesar be nonetheless oblivious to injuries; let us remember the rest, waiving from our hearts any offenses our neighbors do to us.

33. [1] **Oleo sedem ne tergito.** Aperuit in parabolis os suum hic noster vates, illius forsitan non ignarus: "oleum peccatoris non impinguet caput meum." [2] Ea autem adulatione super quam nihil sedeamus, cui non inhereamus, quam nullubi prorsus admictamus, ne forsan seducamur. [3] Uti namque insidentis cuiuslibet super oleosam sellam inquinaretur vestimentum, sic et qui innititur adulatoriis gestis dilabitur et inficitur. [4] Adulator enim ore decipit amicum suum, sapiens autem cavebit ipsum ut truculentissimam bestiam; nihil namque deterius est quam familiaris inimicus, ne cui igitur dextram cito exhibeamus, nec oleo inungamus nostra sedilia, ut dictum est. [5] Monet praeterea Aurelius in Cresconium grammaticum scribens, libro quarto, ne oleum peccatoris inpinguet nos, ne, scilicet, aliorum errores sequi aut tueri ullo pacto velimus. Qui enim alienos defendit errore incidit in suos.

34. [1] **Panem ne frangito.** M. Tullii et divi Augustini et aliorum quorundum est celebre dictum: Amicitias dissuendas esse, non rescindendas. Nomine autem panis amicitia venit, uti namque e multis gra//277v//nis tritici fit unus panis, sic e multis votis fit una voluntas. [2] Eadem autem velle, atque eadem nolle firma est amicitia, inquit[38] Ambrosius. Unum vero corpus et unus spiritus multi sumus omnes qui de uno pane et de uno calice participamus, ut vulgo fertur in misterio Eucharistiae nostrae. [3] Non igitur de cibario triticeoque pane agit hic noster autor, sed de amicitia, est enim amicitia homini ad vivendum necessaria haud secus ac[39] panis. Nam nemo eligeret vivere sine amicis, octavo Ethicorum dicit Aristoteles. [4] Cum itaque inveneris amicum, putato te invenisse thesaurum et preciosam margaritam, quam utique non frangas, sed vendas omnia tua ut emas illam.

35. [1] **Pedem dextrum priorem calciato, pedem sinistrum priorem lavato.** Pedibus designare affectus humanos exploratum fit, ut persaepe annotatur in sacris, quod diximus supra. [2] Pes ergo

---

[38] inquit] inquia *cod.*
[39] ac] ve *cod.*

33. [1] **Do not wipe off the seat with oil.** This prophet of ours opens his mouth in parabolas, not ignorant, perhaps, of this one: "the oil of the sinner will not soil my head." [2] Now when it comes to flattery, let us set nothing upon it, let us not adhere to it, let us nowhere admit it, lest perhaps we be seduced by it. [3] For just as the vestment of anyone whatsoever who sits upon an oily seat is soiled, so also whoever supports himself by flattering gestures goes to pieces and is tainted. [4] For the flatterer deceives his friend with his mouth, but the wise man will beware the flatterer as he would a truculent beast; for there is nothing worse than a familiar enemy (to whom we should not quickly offer our right hand); and let us not anoint our seats with oil, as has been said. [5] Beyond this, in writing against Cresconius the grammarian, Augustine warns (in book four) lest the "oil of a sinner soil us," lest, namely, we should wish to follow or in any way to condone the errors of others. For whoever defends others who are in error falls into his own.

34. [1] **Do not break bread.** There is a famous saying of Cicero, Augustine, and any number of others: friendships should be gently severed, not cut off. Now friendship takes the name of bread here, seeing that just as one loaf of bread comes about from many grains of wheat, so too does one will come about from many wishes. [2] Now firm friendship, says Ambrose, means both to want and be adverse to the same things. But all of us are one body and one spirit, we who participate in one bread and one cup, as is said commonly in the mystery of our Eucharist. [3] Therefore, this author of ours is not talking about food or bread made of wheat, but rather friendship; after all, man needs friendship to live, just as he needs bread. For no one would choose to live without friends, as Aristotle says in the eighth book of the *Ethics*. [4] So once you have found a friend, understand that you have found a treasure and a precious pearl; not only should you not break it, but you should rather sell all your possessions to buy it.

35. [1] **Put your right shoe on first, wash first your left foot.** That by the feet the human emotions are meant has been explored, as is quite often noted in holy writ; we discussed this above. [2] Now: the right foot is the part of the soul that desires, the left the part that becomes angry; for with the former we allow favorable matters, with the latter we refuse adverse matters. Let us, therefore,

dexter est concupiscibilis, sinister irascibilis animae pars; illa enim admictimus prospera, hac recusamus adversa. Nos igitur adversis abstergamus prius mundemusque, posterius oportuna quaeramus. [3] Item pede sinistro terram, dextro caelum pervagamus, quia nos "in multis offendimus omnes." A levioribus incohantes terrena purgemus, antea subinde altiora caelestiaque investigemus. [4] Cum autem munire nos induereque velimus, quaeramus ante omnia regnum dei et iustitiam eius, qua nos calciemus dextrum pedem in praeparationem evangelii pacis et caetera cuncta adiicientur nobis, ut dicit dominus in evangelio; sic enim Vatis huius nostri edictum praesens opere complebimus.

36. [1] **Pisces ne commedito.** Narratur quod Pythagoras hic noster empto retio iactu pisces captos dimiserit, persoluto illorum nomine pretio piscatoribus. [2] Dicit autem Plutarchus in quaestionibus convivialibus esum piscium Pythagoram vetuisse, quia iniustum videtur persequi et occidere et manducare animal quod hominem ipsum nec laedat nec laedere possit unquam. [3] Et ea propter Homerus non solum Graecos sed et Pheaces et Poenelopes procos—alioqui helvones et turpes viros—a piscibus ait abstinuisse et pepercisse. Neque socii Ulixis unquam aut hamo aut retibus usi sunt, donec farina suppeteret. Verum omni commeatu assumpto, paulo priusquam sacros soli boves devorarent, piscari coeperunt, non obsonii[40] causa, sed ob famem depellendam. [4] Non desunt insuper qui a Samio pisces ablegatos fuisse dicant, quia muti et minime loquentes sint. Alii dicunt eo pisces post habendas quod mare colant, ubi saeculi mores vitaque dignoscitur, a quibus removere se debeant saeculi amatores. [5] Nos igitur, qui litteram non sequimur, occidentes[41] dentibus et ventri pisces praebeamus et quasi Ictiophagi simus in observantia regulari, ubi pro carnibus pisces deliciose commedimus. [6] Quicquid vero male designatur ex istis, semper improbemus; cibos tamen summamus omnes ad arcendam esuriem, non ad voluptatem. Id vero mali dumtaxat ominamur prohibitum hoc in edicto, ne cui noceamus qui nobis nocere nec velit nec possit, qui vere aliena prorsus et non nostratia perscrutetur.

---

[40] obsonii] ob sonii *cod.*
[41] occidentes] occidentem *cod.*

rid ourselves first of adverse things and clean them away, then thereafter seek what is advantageous. [3] Again, it is with the left foot that we wander the earth, with the right, heaven, for "in many things we offend all." As we begin with lighter things, let us purge ourselves of what is earthly before we thence seek out higher, celestial matters. [4] Now when we wish to defend and to array ourselves well, before everything else we seek God's kingdom and His justice; let us first shoe our right foot [with His justice] in preparation for the gospel of peace, and may everything else be given to us as well, as the Lord says in the gospel. For thus shall we fulfill with work the present edict of this prophet of ours.

36. [1] **Do not eat fish.** It is told that this Pythagoras of ours bought a net [full of fish] only to throw away the fish that had been caught, after he had paid what they were worth to the fishermen. [2] And Plutarch in his *Table Talk* says that Pythagoras forbade the eating of fish, since it seems unjust to capture, kill, and eat an animal which does not and could never injure man himself. [3] And on account of these things Homer says that not only the Greeks but also the Phaeacians and the suitors of Penelope—who were otherwise gluttonous, horrible men—abstained from and even spared fish. Nor did the allies of Ulysses ever use either a hook or nets, as long as flour was at hand. But once they had run out of all food, shortly before they devoured the bulls who were sacred to the sun, they began to fish, not for provisions but to drive away their hunger. [4] Besides, not absent are those who say that the Samian stayed away from fish because they are mute and do not speak. Others say that in his view fish should be regarded as inferior because they inhabit the sea, where the ethics and life of the world are discerned, from which the lovers of the world must remove themselves. [5] Now we do not follow the letter of the words, so let us allow fish in our stomach, as we kill them with our teeth, and let us be almost Ichthyophagues in regular observance, whereby we eat fish instead of meat—with great delight! [6] But whatsoever of those things is designated as evil, let us always condemn; and in any case, any foods which we eat let us take for the purpose of keeping our hunger at bay, not for pleasure. But strictly speaking this is the evil we can interpret as prohibited in this edict: that we not injure anyone who would not or cannot injure us, anyone, in short, who investigates matters which are truly foreign and not our own.

37. [1] **Peregre profectus ne redito.** Perfecta hominis cognitio versatur in eo ut se ipsum ad altiora natum recognoscat, ideoque se hospitem et peregrinum esse in hoc terrarum orbe. [2] Id ipsum vero monachi dumtaxat et viri religiosi secum censent, qui non habeant hic civitatem manentem, sed sint "hospites et advenae" abstinentes se "a carnalibus desideriis, quae militant adversus animam, conversationem suam inter gentes habentes bonam," ut dicit Apostolus. [3] Quicumque autem sic fuerint peregre dei gratia disponente profecti, hi nequaquam redeant ad vomitum, sed perseverent usque in finem et legitime certent sufferentes temptationem, ut accipiant coronam vitae, quam repromisit deus diligentibus se. //278//

38. [1] **Quae ceciderunt ne accipito.** Stare virtutis, cadere delicti est. Quae ceciderunt a sapiente, neglecta, ne accipias. Quae studiosis placent, ardua et acclivia, sume. Si casum quaeres, invenies, nam qui diligit periculum incidit in eum, ut sacra testantur eloquia. Quod aliis bene sapientibus non placuerit, ipse respuito. [2] Quae autem aristas colligit dilabentes, Ruth, et Cananea, quae colligit micas cadentes de mensa dominorum canis instar, haud quaquam[42] improbatur, non enim haec in deliciis et per contentum fiebant. [3] Sed illa Israel virgo quae cecidit et lucifer ille qui mane oriebatur contemnantur et non accipiantur a nobis, ne una cum illis dilabamur in foveam quam ipsi fecerunt. Quae igitur ceciderint peccata demonstrant. Ea ne accipito, at odi peccatum virtutis amore.

39. [1] **Rubeum aliquid ne suscipito.** In Esaia legimus, "Quare ergo rubrum est indumentum tuum et vestimenta tua sicut calcantium intorculari," et infra, "et aspersus est sanguis eorum super vestimenta mea, et omnia indumenta mea coinquinavi." [2] Quod ergo rubeum seu rubrum fit asperitatem, sanguinem, crimenve designat; "libera me de sanguinibus," idest, de peccatis, "deus deus salutis meae," etc. [3] Et rursus Esaie primo, "Si fuerint peccata vestra sicut

---

[42] quaquam] quamque *cod.*

37. [1] **Having gone far, do not turn back.** Man's completed knowledge turns on this: that he recognize that he himself was born to higher things, and therefore that he is a guest and pilgrim in this world. [2] But precisely this is what monks and religious men believe about themselves, since they have no permanent city here, but are rather "guests and strangers" who "abstain from carnal desires which militate against the soul, who have their conversation honest among the gentiles," as the Apostle says. [3] Now whoever has travelled far with God's ordering grace, may they in no way return to what has been vomited up, but rather, may they persevere to the end and legitimately combat those who suffer temptation, so that they might accept the crown of life which God has promised to those loving him.

38. [1] **Do not pick up what has fallen.** To stand is characteristic of virtue, to fall of crime. Do not take up those things which the wise man has allowed, neglected, to fall. But do take in hand the things that please the studious, the daunting things, high upon a hill. If you are looking for trouble, you will find it, since whoever loves danger tumbles into it, as the eloquence of holy writ shows. Should something not please other men who are well-deemed wise, you yourself spit it out. [2] Now Ruth, the one who gleaned the wheat, as well as the woman from Canaa, who, like a dog, collected crumbs falling from the table of the lords, is not to be blamed, for these deeds did not happen to be done for pleasure or satisfaction. [3] But let us condemn and not accept that virgin of Israel who fell and that Lucifer who arose early in the morning, lest together with them we fall into the pit which they themselves made. Therefore "those things which have fallen" mean sins. Do not accept them, but rather, in the love of virtue, hate sin.

39. [1] **Do not take up anything red.** In Isaiah we read, "Why therefore are your garments red and your clothes like those of men treading the winepress?" and further on, "and their blood was sprinkled on my clothes and I have stained all my garments." [2] Therefore, what becomes "ruby" or red means harshness, blood, or crime. "Free me from blood," that is from sins, "God, God of my salvation," etc. [3] And again in the first chapter of Isaiah, "Though your sins be as scarlet, they shall be made as white as snow, though they be red as crimson, they shall be like white wool." [4] So: what is signified

coccinum, quasi nix dealbabuntur, et si fuerint rubra, sicut vermiculus, quasi lana alba erunt." [4] Rubeo itaque colore et panno
menstruatae peccatum significatur, quid abiici a nobis debet in hoc
nostro praecepto.

40. [1] **Recurvis unguibus aves ne alito.** Aeschilus etiam dixit
"catulum leonis non esse alendum." Id utique contra Pisistratum passim affirmabat Solon, insectans ubique tyrannicos conatus eius. Aves
enim quae super caetera animantia volitant, reges sunt. [2] Hi vero
unguibus lenibus nemini obsunt, recurvis autem ex rapto vivunt et
praeda facta semper utique in praeiudicium aliorum, ne sit hospes
ab hospite tutus, non socer a genero, fratrum quoque gratia rara sit.
[3] Qui ergo isthaec peragant haud utique alendi sunt neque in eis
usque quaque fidendum, quia volucres sunt et cito hunc aut alium
sibi servulum sortiuntur. [4] Exemplo erit illud quod in Apophthegmis
Plutharchus scribit, inquiens: "Orontes regis Artaxerxis gener, cum
ob iram in ignominiam excidisset contemptuique esset, ait, quemadmodum computatorum digiti nunc decies millenarios numeros, nunc
unarios queunt imponere, eodem quoque more, regum amicos posse
quandoque totum, quandoque minimum." [5] Hinc psalmista: "Nolite,"
inquit, "confidere in principibus et in filiis hominum, quibus non est
salus." Jeremias autem dicit eos qui confidunt in homine maledictos
esse ac veluti miricas in deserto fore. [6] Non ergo alendi sunt
eiusmodi principes, qui numquam in eodem statu permanent, et
sicut Hieron dicit aput Xenophontem, alienis laboribus vivunt absque
retributione.

41. [1] **Salem apponito.** Hoc enygmate sapientiam indici, nulli
dubium est, ut sermo noster sit sale conditus, idest, sapientia et dis-
cretione firmatus. [2] Gregorius autem in Pastoralibus et habetur,
distinctione 43, in capitulo "Sit rector." "Sacerdos ergo," ait, ". . .
veritas dicit" in Marco: "'. . . Salem in vobis et pacem habete inter
vos.' Per salem quippe verbi sapientia designatur. Qui ergo loqui
sapienter nititur, magnopere metuat ne eius eloquio audientium unitas confundatur; hinc Paulus ait ad Romanos, 'Non plus sapere quam
oporteat sapere, sed sapere ad sobrietatem.'" Haec ibi. [3] Quae
et ex. De haereticis, capitulo, "Cum ex iniuncto." Id ipsum vero

by the red color and by the cloth of a woman who has menstruated is sin, which in this precept of ours must be cast away.

40. [1] **Do not nourish birds with crooked claws.** Aeschylus, too, says that "a lion's cub mustn't be nourished." In any case Solon used to affirm this everywhere against Pisistratus, always inveighing against his tyrannical undertakings. For birds which fly above the other animals are kings. [2] Now the ones with mild claws injure no one, but those with crooked claws live by plunder and always unfailingly take their prey to the detriment of others, so that a guest is not safe from his host, a father-in-law from his son-in-law, and even the mutual love between brothers is rare. [3] Therefore whoever carries these things out must certainly not be "nourished" and in fact they should not even be trusted. After all, they are birds and quickly choose this one or that one as their little servant. [4] For example, Plutarch writes in his *Apophthegms* and says: "Orontes, the son-in-law of Artaxerxes, since on account of his anger he had fallen into contempt and was held in scorn, says that just as the fingers of mathematicians can deal with tens of thousands of numbers at one time, and at another time only units, so too have the friends of kings at one moment total power, at another almost none." [5] Hence the Psalmist: "Do not confide," he says, "in princes and in sons of men, in whom there is no safety." And Jeremiah says that those who confide in man are cursed and will be just like tamarisks in the desert. [6] So, princes of this sort, who never remain in the same state, must not be "nourished;" just as Hiero says in Xenophon, they live by the work of others and offer no restitution.

41. [1] **Serve salt.** No one can doubt that this enigma points to wisdom, as our conversation should be spiced with salt, that is, strengthened by wisdom and discretion. [2] Now we also keep in mind Gregory, in the *Pastorals* (in distinction forty-three, in the chapter "Sic rector"). "Therefore a priest," he says, "speaks as the truth," in Mark: "'possess salt in yourselves and peace among you.' Certainly for salt the wisdom of the Word is meant. So whoever makes the effort to speak wisely greatly dreads lest the unity of his listeners be confused by his eloquence; hence Paul to the Romans, 'Do not know beyond what you need to know, rather, know up to the point of

quemadmodum de se pateat, quid, scilicet, salis nomine censeatur, non alterius exponatur, nisi cum exhortatione quapiam ad amorem sapientiae, de qua grandis nobis restat sermo et interpretabilis ad docendum. Sed de his alias peramplius et perfectius.

42. [1] **Sanguinem saxis operito.** Et sanguinis et saxii nomine crudelitatem dici, nulli sit dubium, ut crudelia crudelibus, dura duris, aspera asperis agitemus, conteramus, obruamus. [2] Nam amor laesus debet irasci, ait Bernardus; et furor fit[43] laesa saepius patientia, aiunt et Publilius[44] et Se//278v//neca. [3] Valerius autem libro tertio, capitulo tertio, Zeno eleates, inquit, cum a Phalaride tyranno in foro torqueretur ut socio seditionis proderet, ipse quidem neminem "eorum nominavit, at proximum quemque ac fidelissimum tyranno suspectum reddidit increpitansque Agrigentinis ignaviam et timiditatem effecit, ut subito mentis impulsu concitati, Phalarim lapidibus prosternerent." [4] Hi ergo, quasi Pythagorici effecti, saevitiam tyranni saxis operuerunt; eiusdem autem nominis philosophus alter a Clearcho tyranno captus et afflictus ut conscios maleficii panderet, ostendit "quod secreto eum audire admodum expediret laxatoque equleo postquam insidiis oportunum tempus animadvertit, aurem eius morsu corripuit nec ante dimisit quam et ipse vita et ille corporis parte privaretur." [5] Paria quoque paribus reddenda sunt, sed haec pro christianis spectant ad eos qui gladium ferunt pro admnistranda iustitia, quique sciant "parcere subiectis et debellare superbos." [6] Qui autem in minoribus degunt, sciant humo, idest, humilitate sanguinem, idest, crudelitatem tegere, quoad percussi in una maxilla, praebeant et alteram, et auferenti tunicam sinant et pallium iuxta doctrinam domini in evangelio, et prout ponitur 23., quaestio prima, capitulo "Paratus."

---

[43] fit] sit *cod.*
[44] Publilius] Publius *cod.*

moderation.'" So much for that quotation. This is also in the ex. *On heretics*, in the chapter "Cum ex iniuncto." Now let what is meant by the name of salt be something clear in itself and may it not be expounded elsewhere, unless it is done with a certain exhortation to a love of wisdom; there remains to us an abundant sermon on this topic, and it is one which can be interpreted for the purpose of instruction. But concerning these things we shall speak elsewhere more widely and completely.

42. [1] **Cover up blood with stones.** Let no one doubt that the name of both blood and stone means cruelty, so that we insist upon, employ, and cover over cruel things with cruel things, harsh with harsh, and bitter with bitter. [2] For injured love must get angry, says Bernard, and rage has been wounded more often than patience, as both Publilius and Seneca say. [3] Now Valerius in his third book, chapter three, says Zeno of Elea, when he was tortured in the forum by the tyrant Phalaris to make him give up his ally on a charge of sedition, himself named none "of them, but rather offered as a suspect a very well trusted neighbor of the tyrant; chiding the idleness and timidity of the Agrigentines, he swiftly incited their minds to action and brought it about that they struck down Phalaris with stones." [4] These men almost became Pythagoreans: they covered up the severity of a tyrant with stones. Now another philosopher of the same name was captured and tortured by the tyrant Clearchus, in the hope that he might reveal those whom he knew to be guilty of evildoing; he said "that Clearchus should release him so that he could hear him in secret; but once the torture had been loosened, he noticed an opportune time to betray Clearchus, and he attacked the tyrant by biting him on the ear, not letting go until he himself lost his life and the tyrant lost a body part." [5] Now one must pay back in equal measure what one receives, but with respect to these things Christians look toward those who bear the sword for administering justice, and who know how "to spare the conquered and war down the proud." [6] Now those who spend time in the lower stations know how to cover over "blood," that is, cruelty, with "earth," that is, humility, even to the point that, if they have been struck on one cheek they offer also the other, and if someone wants their tunic they give him their cloak, according to the doctrine of the Lord in the Gospel, and just as it is set out in twenty-three, first question, in the chapter "Paratus."

43. [1] **Semitam ingreditor.**[45] Hoc utique verbo Vates indicat arc-
tam viam quae ducit ad vitam et paucos qui ingrediuntur per eam;
lata autem est illa quae ducit ad mortem. [2] Hic igitur ostenditur
quasi bivium Pythagoricae litterae, si tamen Pythagoras eiusce fuerit
autor, an Palamedes, qui .V. litteram a gruibus rite volantibus sump-
sit, ut nonnulli putant. [3] Nos autem a Samio mutuemur eam litteram quae surgentem dextro monstravit limite callem. [4] Libet
autem huc adducere, De Hercule illo magno, quod Basilius scripserit
ad nepotes ad hanc de qua agimus, semitam cognoscendam. Ait
enim, Prodico autore, "Hercules, cum adolescens esset, diu secum
multumque dubitavit utram viam caperet, cum duas vident, unam
voluptatis, alteram virtutis." [5] Ait autem, inter ambigendum "duas
accessisse matronas, has vero esse et virtutem et malitiam. Statim
quidem igitur et si illae silerent manifestam fuisse diversitatem illarum.
[6] Videri enim alteram accuratissime ornatam fluentem deliciis, et
omnium voluptatum examen post se trahentem. Hanc itaque ostent-
tantem et multo etiam plura pollicentem secum trahere Herculem
temptavisse. [7] Alteram vero asperam et duram severeque intuentem
talia econtra dixisse polliceri se, nec voluptatem aliquam nec qui-
etem, sed labores pericula sudoresque infinitos terra marique tolleran-
dos. Praemium autem illorum fore, ut ille aiebat, Deum fieri. [8] Et
hanc demum Herculem sequutum fuisse dicit. Et fere omnes qui
modo aliquid in philosophia[46] scripsere, ut quisque maxime potuit,
virtutem laudarunt." Haec Basilius. [9] Quibus innotescit ipsa virtutis semita quam ingrediamur non autem communem et publicam
aliorum viam, de qua nonnulla in inferioribus.

44. [1] **Stateram ne transilias.** Hac utique sententia indicitur animi
moderatio. Est autem moderatio naturarum, cupiditatum quaedam
quasi refrenatrix, quae solutius evagari non sinit affectus, sed tamquam
caeterarum virtutum auriga hominis animum ita componit ut quicquid fecerit aut dixerit, omnino reprehensione careat. [2] Hac autem

---

[45] ingreditor] ingredior *cod.*
[46] philosophia] philosophie *cod.*

43. [1] **Go along the narrow path.** To be sure, with this phrase the Prophet indicates the narrow way which leads to life and the few who travel upon it; for the road which leads to death is wide. [2] So here is shown something like the "bivium" of the Pyrthagorean letter, if, still, Pythagoras was its author, or perhaps it was Palamedes, who according to religious custom took the letter "V" from cranes flying in formation, as some think. [3] But let us borrow from the Samian this letter, which showed a mountain-pass rising from the right border. [4] Now, it might be permitted here to tell what Basil wrote on our theme concerning the great Hercules, to his nephews, so that they might get to know this road. For Basil says, with Prodicus as his authority, that "Hercules, when young, was often in great doubt as to which of the two roads he would take, since he saw two, one of pleasure, the other of virtue." [5] Now he says that, while Hercules was in doubt "two women approached: virtue and vice. Straightaway, despite their silence, their difference was clear. [6] The one seemed to be decked out with the greatest of care—charm practically flowed from her and she trailed behind her a multitude of pleasures. So, since she showed as much as she did and promised even more, she tried to draw Hercules with her. [7] But the other was bitter and harsh and she looked severe; she said that she offered exactly the opposite: neither pleasure nor rest of any sort, but rather labors, dangers, and infinite toil, all of which were to be carried out on land and sea. But the reward of these things would be, as Prodicus said, 'to become a god.' [8] And Basil says that, in the end, she was the one that Hercules followed. And just about anyone who has written anything on philosophy has praised virtue as the greatest thing one can attain to." This is what Basil has to say. [9] This is how the way of virtue becomes known. Let us travel the way of virtue and not the common, public way of others. But we shall have more to say about this below.

44. [1] **Do not leap over the scale.** Certainly this sentiment points toward moderation of soul. Now there is a moderation of natures, a certain restraint of desires, which does not allow the emotions to roam too freely, but rather like a chariot-driver for the other virtues, composes man's spirit in such a way that whatever he should do or say wholly lacks censure. [2] Now, instructed in this, Architas of Taranto, after he had been trained for a long time and with great labor and industry in Pythagorean studies, returned to his homeland

instructus, Architas Tarentinus, cum a Pythagoricis studiis in quibus multo tempore fuerat cum summo labore et industria versatus in patriam reversus esset et praedia sua, villici negligentia, squalida et inculta offendisset. Ira commotus maluit impunitum villicum dimictere, quam per iram excedere punitionis modum. "Intuensque male meritum sumpsissem," inquit, "a te supplicium, ni tibi iratus essem," ut narrat M. Tullius Tusculorum libro quarto et divus Ambrosius Officiorum primo. [3] Sed neque praetereundum puto Dionis[47] illud. "Is" enim, "cum a Dionysio tyranno pulsus exularet Megaris et eius urbis Theodorum principem domi convenire vellet, nec admicteretur, multum diuque ante fores retentus comite suo; 'patienter hoc ferendum est,' ait, 'forsitan enim et //279// cum in gradu dignitatis essemus, aliquid tale fecimus.'" [4] Hanc igitur animi moderationem staterae nomine latam assummamus nobis, qui sciamus id apprime in vita esse utile, ut "nequid nimis" et sola ipsa mediocritate et animi quiete contenti simus. [5] Dicitur insuper, "Omnis qui iuste iudicat, stateram in manu gestat," ut iusticiam cum misericordia temperet, distinctio 45, capitulo "Omnis qui" et distinctio 50, capitulo "Ponderet." [6] Hinc Psalmista ait: "Iuste iudicate, filii hominum," quasi cum Vate isto diceret, Stateram ne transilias.

45. [1] **Temporum duorum curam habeto.** Aristotele teste in Naturalibus libro tertio: de tempore non habemus nisi nunc, sed quoniam istum nunc est instans et quasi inperceptibile, propterea tempus praesens. [2] Vate nostro dimictitur, quo ad futurum tantum vel praeteriti temporis cura habeatur, quod utique est viri prudentis officium. [3] Dicit enim Cicero Officiorum libro primo, "Sed inter hominem et belluam hoc maxime interest, quod haec tantum, quantum sensu movetur, ad id solum quod adest quodque praesens est se accomodat, paulum admodum sentiens praeteritum aut futurum. [4] Homo autem, qui rationis est particeps, per quam consequentia cernit, causas rerum videt earumque progressus et quasi antecessiones non ignorat, similitudines comparat, rebusque praesentibus adiungit atque adnectit futuras, facile totius vitae cursum

---

[47] Dionis] Dionisium *cod.*

and his estates, which he found squalid and uncultivated thanks to his groundskeeper's negligence. Moved by anger, he preferred to dismiss the unpunished groundskeeper, rather than letting his anger cause him to exceed proper punishment. "Seeing this evil," he said, "I would have extracted a deserved punishment from you, had I not been angry with you," as Tully tells in the fourth book of the *Tusculan Disputations* and as divine Ambrose tells in the first book of his *On Duties*. [3] But I do not think we should pass over that comment of Dion. For "after he was expelled by the tyrant Dionysius he went to Megara, desiring to meet Theodorus, this city's prince, at his house; but he was not admitted and was made to wait at the door for quite some time along with his friend. He said, 'this must be borne patiently; after all, perhaps if we too had ranked so highly, we might have done something similar.'" [4] So: let us take up for ourselves this moderation of soul which is meant by the name "scale"; let us know that this is useful in life to the highest degree, so that— "nothing too much"—we are happy simply with a middling status and with psychological repose. [5] It is said, moreover, "anyone who judges justly, bears a scale in his hand," so that justice is tempered with pity, as in distinction forty-five, in the chapter "Omnis qui" and in distinction 50, in the chapter "Ponderet." [6] Hence does the Psalmist say: "Judge justly, sons of men," as if he were saying, along with this Prophet, "Do not leap over the scale."

45. [1] **Care for two times.** Aristotle testifies in the third book of the *Naturalia*: "Concerning time, we have nothing except now, but since this now is an instant and is almost imperceptible, on that account there is present time." [2] Our prophet dismisses this, so that even our worries about the past look toward the future, as is certainly the duty of a prudent man. [3] For Cicero says in the first book of the *De officiis*, "But between man and beast this is the greatest difference: the beast accomodates itself, in so far as it is moved by sense, to what is there, what is present, and understands little whatsoever of the past or future. [4] But man, who partakes of reason and who through reason discerns consequences, sees the causes of things as well as their progressions and antecedents, draws comparisons, and connects and associates the present and the future, easily sees the course of an entire life and prepares what is necessary to carry it out." This is what Cicero has to say. [5] By these words it is made clearer than light what "caring for two times" means. This is

videt ad eamque degendam praeparat res neccessarias." Haec M. Tullius. [5] Quibus nimirum luce clarius innotescit, quae sit duorum temporum cura capienda. Sic enim Janus bifrons pingitur, qui tali prorsus cura invigilet. [6] Quod et Augustinus de Romanorum diis agens, Janum, inquit, ipsum bifrontem et quadrifrontem etiam tamquam geminum fecerunt; et quoniam multi "dii selecti erubescenda perpetrando frontem amiserant, quanto iste innocentior esset, tanto et frontosior appareret." [7] "Manasses quoque hebreorum rex," ut tradit Crinitus noster, "cum statuam sibi poneret, eam quincuplici facie ornatam voluit, quo maior in eo prudentia et maiestas, ut puto, signaretur." [8] Sed his post habitis ad nostra redeuntes, dicimus duo tempora curanda esse, praeteritum, scilicet, et futurum; unum, scilicet, et quo et terminum utrumque nostrum, vel semper ut cogitemus novissima nostra et in aeternum non peccabimus.

46. [1] **Vulvam animalium ne edito.** In quarto Regum libro, capitulo sexto, legimus quod Benadab, Rex Syriae, congregavit universum exercitum suum et ascendit et obsedit Samariam. [2] Factaque est fames magna in Samaria, et tandiu obsessa est ut venundaretur caput asini octoginta argenteis, et quarta pars cabi[48] stercoris columbarum quinque argenteis. [3] Ezechielis autem quarto dicitur, "Quasi subcinericium ordeaceum commedes, et stercore quod egredietur de homine, operietur illud in oculis eorum," et infra, "Ecce dedi tibi fimum boum pro stercore hominum, et facies panem tuum in eo." [4] Haec autem propter egestatem fiunt. Mulieres autem commedisse filios suos aput iudeos prae fame non semel legimus. Nam duris in rebus urget egestas. [5] Tempore autem necessitatis nulla lex viget, sed omnia sunt communia, nam necessitas non habet leges, ut Canones dicunt, ex. De regulis juris, capitulo, "Quod non est licitum in lege, necessitas facit licitum." [6] "Nam et sabbatum custodiri praeceptum est, Machabei tamen, sine culpa sua, sabbato pugnant, sic et hodie, si quis ieiunium fregerit aegrotus, reus iuris non habetur." Haec ibi. [7] Si quis igitur immundas animalium vulvas commedat nulla necessitate compulsus, delinquet in Vatem nostrum. [8] At dicet fortasse quispiam, "si carnes Pythagorici respuunt, cur hic in specie de hac particula agitur a magistro? Nam et vulva animalium caro est." [9] Hic forsan adduci poterit quod divus Benedictus in regula prohibuit quadrupedum carnibus vesci monachos, qui sciant hinc sibi

---

[48] cabi] cibi *cod.*

why Janus, who watches indeed with such care, is painted with two faces. [6] Augustine also notices this when he speaks about the gods of the Romans. He says that they made Janus with two faces as well as with four, as a twin, so to speak; and because many of "the select gods lost face by committing shameful acts, since Janus was more innocent, he should appear to have more faces." [7] "In addition, Manasses, king of the Hebrews," as our Crinito relates, "when he erected a statue to himself, wanted it ornamented with a quintuple face, so that, it seems to me, his prudence and majesty would be signalled all the more." [8] But having taken a look at these things let us return to our own, and say that two times must be cared for, namely, the past and the future; the one, namely, is the time "from which" and both of the two are end-points for us, so that we will always be thinking of the last things and shall never sin into eternity.

46. [1] **Do not eat the vulva of animals.** In the fourth book of Kings, chapter six, we read that Benedab, king of Syria, gathered together his entire army, and ascended and besieged Samaria. [2] It happened that there was a great famine in Samaria, and it was besieged such a long time that the head of an ass was sold for eighty pieces of silver, and the fourth part of a kab of dove's excrement for five. [3] Now it is said in Ezechiel in the fourth chapter, "You are to consume this in the form of a barley cake, baked where they can see you, on human excrement," and below, "Lo, I have given you the dung of oxen for the excrement of men: make your bread on that." [4] Now these things happen on account of indigence. Moreover, we read more than once that women among the Jews, faced with hunger, ate their sons. For when times are hard indigence presses upon one. [5] Now in time of necessity no law is in force, but rather all things are held in common, for necessity has no laws, as the Canons say, in ex. *On the Rules of Law*, in the chapter, "What is not licit in law, necessity makes so." [6] "For even though is was ordered to guard the sabbath, still, the Machabees, without fault of their own, wounded it. And even today if someone who is ill violates a fast-day, he is not held to be under charges by the law." Thus Canon law. [7] So if someone eats the unclean vulvas of animals and was not forced to do so by some necessity, he transgresses against our prophet. [8] But perhaps someone might say, "if the Pythagoreans spit out meats, why does the master treat this little matter specifically? For the vulva of animals, too, is meat."

et carnes volatilium inhiberi, quia, si de quo minus videtur inesse,
et inest, ergo et de quo magis. Si enim quadrupedia prohibentur,
ergo et volatilia, quae sunt lautiora. [10] Sic igitur in proposito, si
vetuit vulvas animantium commedi immundas et turpes, hic noster
Samius, ergo et reliquas animantium partes quae sunt gratiores et
delitiosiores. [11] Seu etiam hic agitur enygmatice, ut vulva immunda
abiiciatur, quatenus propellatur immunditia omnis, omne scelus et
omnis turpitudo. [12] Dicit enim Thomas, De regimine principum,
libro quarto, capitulis 21 et 22, quod //279v// omnis policia Pythagorae tendebat ad purgationem animorum; his namque bene dis-
positis, corporalia facillime omnia diriguntur. [13] "Laudabat autem
is cotidie virtutem et vitia reprimebat, casumque civitatum hac peste
perditarum enumerabat. Tantumque studium ad frugalitatem perdis-
cendam multitudini persuasit ut aliquos ex eis luxuriosos fuisse incredi-
bile videtur." Haec Thomas. Quibus utique et vulvae turpitudinem[49]
ad vitiorum repulsam dici, manifestum est.

47. [1] **Virgam in via ne ferto.** Salvator dixit discipulis suis: "nihil
tuleritis in via neque virga neque peram," etc. Alibi autem dicit:
"nihil tuleritis, nisi virgam tantum." Virga igitur concessa, ut a virga
prohibita differat, necesse est. [2] Nam et 20., quaestio tertia, in
capitulo "Praesens," dicitur, "Iccirco dominus non ferendam in via
virgam, per quam violentia ulli inferatur, praecepit. [3] Quapropter
consultius agitur, si piis suasionibus contemptum mundi et amorem
dei praedicando, quam violentiam inferendo ad caelestem amorem
accenderimus." [4] Non ergo virga terrore, scilicet, ut de Antisthene
fertur, qui discipulos et terrore pulsabat et virga, sed amore et charitate uti debemus in via hac qua ambulamus. [5] Homines enim verbis, bestiae verberibus agendae sunt, nisi homines mali sint, qui bestiis
deteriores dicunt (septimo Ethicorum). [6] Dicit enim Salomon: "Qui
parcit virgae, odit filium suum, qui autem diligit, instanter erudit."

---

[49] turpitudinem] turpitudo *cod.*

[9] Here one could bring forward the idea that divine Benedict in the *Rule* prohibited monks from eating the flesh of quadrupeds, so that they might know for themselves from this to refrain also from the meat of birds, because, if something lesser on a scale of evils is prohibited, so too is something greater. For if quadrupeds are prohibited, so also are birds, which are even more luxurious. [10] Thus the same follows in the case at hand: if this Samian of ours has forbidden the eating of the vulvas of animals as unclean and filthy, so also are the rest of the animals' parts forbidden which are more pleasing and delightful. [11] Or we might also consider this in an enigmatic fashion, that is, that the unclean vulva is cast away in so far as all uncleanness, evil, and foulness are driven away. [12] For in the *On the Rule of Princes*, book four, chapters twenty-one and twenty-two, Thomas says that every policy of Pythagoras tended toward the purgation of souls; for if souls are well-disposed, all matters dealing with the body are most easily arranged. [13] "Moreover, every day he used to praise virtue and hold vice in check, and he reckoned that the decline of fallen cities was due to this plague [of vice]. And he urged upon the crowd such zeal to learn frugality that it seems unbelievable that some of them were inclined toward luxury." This is what Thomas has to say. These things certainly make it clear that the foulness of the vulva means to lead us toward the denial of vices.

47. [1] **Do not take a rod on the journey.** The Savior said to his disciples, "take nothing for the journey, neither the rod nor the wallet," etc. And elsewhere he says: "take nothing except a rod." So it is necessary that the rod which is allowed differs from the rod which is prohibited. [2] For also in Case Twenty, third question, in the chapter "Praesens," is it said, "Therefore the lord has ordered that the rod through which violence is brought on anyone must not be brought on the journey. [3] So it is done in a more considered fashion, if by pious persuasion we kindle heavenly love by preaching contempt for the world and love of God rather than by using violence." [4] Therefore, on this journey we are on, we must use the rod not with terror—as is told, namely, about Anstisthenes, who used to beat his disciples with terror and a rod—but with love and charity. [5] For men are to be handled with words, beasts with blows, unless the men are evil, in which case they are said to be worse than beasts (see the seventh book of the *Ethics*). [6] For Solomon

[7] Dicit namque Ambrosius et habetur quinta quaestione, quinto capitulo: "Non obsculatur semper pater filium, sed aliquando castigat. Ergo, quando castigatur qui diligitur, tunc circa eum pietas exercetur. [8] Habet enim et amor plagas suas, quae dulciores sunt, cum amarissime inferuntur. Dulcior enim est religiosa castigatio quam blanda remissio, unde ait scriptura: Dulciora sunt vulnera amici quam voluntaria obscula inimici." Haec ille.

[9] Virga ergo quandoque tenenda dicitur, ut frater cum charitate corrigatur, abiicenda autem ut saevitia exulet. "Nam iudicium sine misericordia erit illi qui non fecerit misericordiam," ut sacra testantur eloquia. [10] Et Salomon ait: "Noli esse iustus multum seu nimis" (23. quaestione quarta, capitulo "Non potest"). Propterea "misericordiam volo," ait dominus, "et non sacrificium." [11] Et hoc ipsum Samius agit in isto paradigmate, ne quis sit nimis durus et quasi bestialis utens virga. Non tamen renuet, hic interrogatus, ut virga teneatur pro correctione fraterna.

<48>. [1] **Viam publicam declinato.** Hieronymus ait hoc indici ne vulgi sequamur errores, nunquam enim tam bene cum rebus humanis actum est, ut optima plurimis placuerint. Paucis autem placet via ardua et quasi privata quae ducit ad vitam. [2] Hinc Bias ait, "Plures mali quam boni" et Poeta ille inquit, "Pauci quos aequus amavit Iuppiter / aut ardens evexit ad aethera virtus." [3] Declinare itaque debemus communem multorum viam et semitam tenere cariorem non in vulgo quidem et in plateis, sed in solitudine, quod monachi ipsi per professionem gerunt, ut solitarii vivant. [4] Monachus namque solitarius dicitur, quia sedet solitarius et quiescit, levans se super se, ut dicitur 16, quaestio prima, capitulo "Placuit." [5] Hi ergo viam publicam hac in vita declinant, ut numerentur in paucis de terra ut sint in labore hominum et cum hominibus flagellantur ad salutem animarum suarum quae erit in aeterna requie, ad quam nos perducat deus, qui est benedictus in saecula saeculorum. Amen. Finis.

says "Whoever spares the rod, hates his son, but whoever is free with correction loves him." [7] For Ambrose says this and it is maintained in the fifth question, fifth chapter: "A father does not always kiss his son, but occasionally castigates him. Therefore, when one who is loved is castigated, piety is shown toward him. [8] For love also has its wounds, which are sweeter when most harshly inflicted. For religious castigation is sweeter than a mild submissiveness, whence scripture says: Sweeter are the wounds of a friend than the willing kisses of an enemy." This is what he has to say.

[9] Therefore, it is said that one must, sometimes, take firm hold of the rod, in order to correct the brother monk with charity, but one must sometimes cast the rod away, in order to banish savageness. "For whoever acts without mercy will be judged without mercy," as sacred eloquence testifies. [10] And Solomon says: "Do not be just to excess" (see Twenty-three, fourth question, chapter "Non potest"). Therefore, "I want mercy," says the Lord, "and not sacrifice." [11] And this is just what the Samian is doing in this paradigm, lest anyone be too harsh and almost bestial in his use of the rod. Still, if we questioned Pythagoras more deeply, he would not oppose the notion that the rod can be employed for the correction of brother monks.

<48>. [1] **Refuse the public road.** Jerome says that this means we should not follow the errors of the crowd, for human affairs have never turned out so well that the best things have pleased the most people. And few like the arduous and almost private journey which leads to [eternal] life. [2] Hence Bias says, "There are more bad men than good," and Vergil avers, "Few has equitable Jupiter loved, and few has fiery virtue carried to the heavens." [3] Therefore we have to refuse the common way of the many and believe that that path is more valuable which is certainly not that of the crowd and busy streets, but is instead a solitary one; monks themselves do this as a profession, so that they live alone. [4] For a monk is said to be alone, because he sits and rests alone, raising himself above himself, as is said in Sixteen, first question, in the chapter "Placuit." [5] So: in this life monks refuse the public road, that they might number among the few on earth, that they labor for the sake of men and with men are beaten for the salvation of their souls, the salvation that will lead to eternal repose, toward which God is leading us, God who is forever blessed. Amen. The end.

Epilogus.[50] [1] Hoc sit tibi monachisque tuis, Reverende Pater, Symbolum Nesianum super Pythagorae dictis singulariter editum. Potuissent utique in eis et latiora dici et graviora. Sed hoc tam brevi tempore haud quaquam valui plura congerere. [2] Sed et ne debui quidem, qui alloquar eos qui et doctissimi sint monachi tui, et ad dogmata omnia usque quaque promptissimi. [3] Habeto igitur libellum istum triduo hoc prae tua in me benignitate confectum; quod vero debuissem ego ipse, saltem <tu>, qui mihi es amantissimus pater, nonum servabis in annum, membranis intus positis, //280// ut delere quandoque liceat, quod non edideris. [4] Commendo itaque unice ipsum Reverendae paternitati tuae, cui me ipsum per omnia dedo et eam cupio diu bene valere. Florentiae, die decimo Januarii 1499 [*i.e., 1500*].

Praesentatio libelli.

[5] Venit igitur condicta die Johannes Nesius, attulit Symbolum. Accepit pater, tradidit Raphaeli monacho, qui ipsum coram omnibus alta voce perlegit. [6] Placuit autem cunctis, qui eum apprime laudarunt et praetulerunt longe et Luciano et Marciano praemissis, admirantes, quomodo vir laicus et qui iugiter versetur in saeculo tam vegetus et uber sit in literis sacris, ut ipsis inpinguet nedum aspergat et ornet omnia dicta eius.

[7] Libellum igitur ipsum Pater accipiens, mihi subinde praebuit transcribendum et ait, "Tu semper auditor es, Paule, nunquam ne repones? Edes et ipse aliquid?"

"Erubesco," dixi. "Nondum transegi quinquennale silentium."

[8] "At quid, cotidie lectitas," ait Pater, "nonne et scribis?"

"Scribo equidem," aio.

"Quod ni?"

---

[50] Here in the text there is a number, 49, which I have left out, in order to preserve the numeration of the list of symbols.

Epilogue. [1] For you and your monks, Reverend Father, let this be the *Nesian Symbol* on the sayings of Pythagoras, each individually treated. Would that they had been spoken of both with more breadth and more seriously. But in such a short time there was no way that I could get together more material. [2] But I also really didn't have to, since I am addressing those men who are also your most learned monks, who are extremely quick to learn everywhere all the learned opinions. [3] Therefore take this little book, a work of three days time, which I put together because of your kindness toward me; what I should have done, you shall do, my dearest father, who will preserve it nine years with the pages that are in it, so that you might delete whatever you do not want published. [4] So I commend this especially to your Reverend Paternity, you to whom I surrender my very self in all things and who I hope stays healthy for a long time to come. Florence, tenth day of January, 1499 [*i.e., 1500*].

Presentation of the little book.

[5] On the aforesaid day, then, Giovanni Nesi came and brought his *Symbol*. Upon accepting it the father handed it to the monk Raphael, who read through it in front of everybody in a loud voice. [6] And it pleased everyone: they praised it in the highest degree and preferred it by far to the already set out *Symbols* of Luca and Marco. They admired the manner in which a layman was versed in such a fruitful way in the world and at the same time was also abundantly learned in sacred scripture, so that he did not harm scripture; far from sprinkling it about, rather, he ornamented everything he said with it.

[7] And so the father, upon accepting the little book, gave it to me to be transcribed forthwith and said, "Oh Paolo, are you always a listener, do you never give anything back? Do you yourself publish nothing?"

"I am ashamed," I said. "But I haven't yet completed the five-year period of [Pythagorean] silence."

[8] "But do you read something every day," says the father, "and not write anything?"

"I certainly do write," I say.

"What then?"

[9] "Quaecumque perlegeri ex eis decerno, quippiam semper pro arbitrio, ut memoriae meae dilabenti quoquo modo succurram."

"Affer quae annotavisti."

[10] Attuli ergo stridoneos sales, dicens, "Hos ego te autore conscripsi, abs te exponendos prae tua in me dilectione et humanitate. Dix<is>ti enim ut ipsos inpugillari reponerem, quos mihi subinde una omnes interpreter.⁵¹ En eos accipe, ut abs te declaratos audiamus cuncti, qui divi Hieronymi servitores sumus." [11] Accepit illos Pater alio in tempore coram omnibus recensendos, et dixit mihique praecipiendo mandavit, ut aliquid omnino afferrem in medium, quasi per contionem. [12] Voluit enim hic ut concionarer et dei verbum quandoque populis in ecclesia praedicarem, quod et deinceps persaepe feci, eius iussui parens utcunque potui. [13] Ea propter dimissi omnes sumus hilares quidem et periucundi Symbolo Nesiano effecti, et ad cellulas nostras cuncti remigravimus. [14] Ego vero anxius nonnihil mihi recessi, quod deberem et ipse proferre in medium aliquid et non dum scirem quid essem facturus.

Explicit.

---

⁵¹ interpreter] interpretere *cod.*

[9] "Whatever I can grasp from those things that are read through [at mealtime], so that I might through my better judgment somehow aid my ailing mind."

"Bring forward what you have noted down."

[10] And so I brought forth the strident witticisms, and said, "These have I written down, with you as the author; because of your love and humanity toward me, you should explain them. After all, you did say that I might put them back on the table so we could argue about them, so that I might promptly interpret them all together. Here, take them, so that all of us servants of divine Jerome might hear you declaim over them." [11] The father accepted them to be reviewed at another time in front of everyone, and he said and in fact ordered me by giving me the command to bring something forward myself, almost as if I had to address a public meeting. [12] For he wanted me to deliver a public speech and then at some time preach the word of God to the people in church, which thereafter I did quite often, following his order in so far as I have been able. [13] Because of all these things we certainly were sent away happy, especially since we had been made so agreeable due to the Nesian *Symbol*; and then we all went back to our little cells. [14] But I withdrew, a little bit anxious with myself, since I had to come out with something myself and still did not know what I was going to do.

The end.

COMMENTARY

Introductio.1: inquit] I.e., to Prior Guido da Settimo.

Introductio.1: syntagma] The somewhat rare word *syntagma* was also used by Orlandini in an earlier chapter of the *Gymnastica monachorum*, in this manuscript (i.e., Florence BN II.I.158), at f.259v.

Introductio.2: numero . . . gaudeat] cf. Verg., *Ecl.* 8.75: numero deus impare gaudet. The eighth *Eclogue* deals with spells, in part. Perhaps Nesi is implying that the Pythagorean symbols are imbued with just such a magical power. Undoubtedly he is also echoing his teacher Ficino, who in chap. 10 of his *Comm. in Epist. Pauli* writes (*Op.* 1.425–72, 443): "Quapropter iure dictum, 'numero Deus impare gaudet,' id est, ternario, tum in recipiendo, tum in dando." Also cited in Allen, *Nuptial*, 85 n.8 (the page number in *Op.* is there mistakenly given as 445). Ficino also cites this Vergilian line in his *De amore* (ed. Marcel) 2.1. Earlier in this manuscript (i.e., MS Florence BN II.I.158), in the treatise on virtue, Orlandini had written (f.37): "Hoc enim numero deus impare gaudet, quem et Pythagoras ipse plurimum commendare solebat. . . ."

Introductio.5: annotatiuncula] Perhaps use of this word, "little note," reflects a Polizianesque Gellian tendency; it is used by Gellius at *NA* 17.21.50 and 19.7.12 though in both places in the plural.

Introductio.7: Has autem . . . in Epictetum] cf. Poliziano's preface (dedicated to Lorenzo) to his translation of the *Epicteti enchiridion* in the (unpaginated) 1498 Aldine *Opera Omnia*. Poliziano suggests that the language of the *Enchiridion* is "wholly efficacious and full of energy;" he avers that the style of the *Enchiridion* is one that "shares secret knowledge [*conscius*], is pellucid, and spurns any rhetorical ornament;" in that respect, it is "wholly similar to the precepts of the Pythagoreans:" "Sermo autem in eo omnino efficax est atque energiae plenus; et in quo mira sit ad permovendum vis. Suos enim quivis affectus in eo agnoscit. Adque eos emendandos, ceu quodam aculeo excitatur. Omnia vero ordinem inter sese mirum habent, omnibusque veluti lineis, quamvis in plura id opus capita sit distinctum, ad excitandum rationalem animum, quasi ad ipsum centrum

contendunt, ut is et suae dignitatis curam habeat et propriis actionibus secundum naturam utatur. Stilus autem qualem res postularet,
conscius est, dilucidus, quique omnem respuat ornatum, Pythagoreorumque praeceptis, quas illi Diathecas vocant, quam simillimus. Hoc
ego opus cum latinum facere eggrederer, ut indulti a te nobis huius
tam suavis ocii rationem aliquam redderem, in duo omnino mendosissima exemplaria incidi, pluribusque locis magna ex parte mutilata. . . ."

Introductio.9: Haec autem . . . id iniuria] cf. Poliziano, *Lamia* 4.

Introductio.9: Hieronymus ad Ruffinum . . . capitulo 15] cf. Hier.,
Ep. Ruf. 39–40.

Introductio.10: Nos vero . . . novo seculo] cf. Nesi, *ONS*, a^{ix-x}. See
also Weinstein, *Savonarola* 195.

Introductio.11: Scribit . . . sit] Ambrose, *Ep.* 28 (Migne, *PL* 16, cols.
1095–1098).

Introductio.11: sumus coniectati] for the unusual deponent use of
coniectare see *LLL* s.v.

1. *Abstine a fabis*

1.1: Plutarchus . . . viri] ps.Plut., *De lib. ed.* 12f.

1.1: "Nemo militans deo implicat se negociis secularibus."] 2 Tim.
2.4; most modern editors omit "deo." This phrase was the basis for
an attack on Savonarola by Giovanni Caroli in the pamphlet war
of 1495. The disputation occurred on 18 January 1495 and Caroli
used the Pauline phrase as the basis of a two-pronged attack against
both Savonarola's prophesying and his propensity to get involved in
Florentine politics (Polizzotto, 61).

1.2: Huic . . . adversans] On Aristippus of Cyrene's (somewhat anti-
Socratic) character see Xen., *Mem.* 2.1 and 3.8, and Diog. Laert.
2.8.65–6.

1.3: Diogenes . . . sint] cf. Diog. Laert. 2.8.69.

1.4: Jubet . . . magnam] Cic., *Div.* 1.62 *apud* Gell., *NA* 4.11.

1.5: Praetereundum . . . dicto] cf. Gell., *NA* 4.11.

1.5: apophtegmate isto] Here I believe Nesi refers not to the present
symbol but to the saying of Empedocles reported in Greek in Gell.,

NA 4.11.9 (= DK 31 B 141): Δειλοί, πάνδελοι, κυάμων ἄπο χεῖρας ἔχεσθαι, i.e., "Wretches, utter wretches, from beans withhold your hands." (Tr. J.C. Rolfe)

2. *Adversus solem ne mingito*

2.1: Plinius libro... ad magiam] cf. Pliny, *HN* 28.69: "Magi vetant eius [i.e., urinae] causa contra solem lunamque nudari aut umbram cuiusquam ab ipso respergi. Hesiodus iuxta obstantia reddi suadet, ne deum aliquem nudatio offendat." For the divinity of the sun in Pliny, see *HN* 2.12–13.

2.1: ast Hesiodus... verecundiam indici] cf. Hesiod, *Works and Days*, edited with prolegomena and commentary by M.L. West (Oxford: Clarendon, 1978) 727–759; see also the erudite comments of West, at 727, 730, and 733f.

2.1: Apostolum... honorem] cf. 1 Cor. 12.12–31, esp. 23–25: "et, quae putamus ignobiliora membra esse corporis, his honorem abundantiorem circumdamus et, quae inhonesta sunt nostra, abundantiorem honestatem habent, honesta autem nostra nullius egent. Sed Deus temperavit corpus, ei, cui deerat, abundantiorem tribuendo honorem, ut non sit schisma in corpore, sed idipsum pro invicem sollicita sint membra."

2.2: Pythagoras... teste Hieronymo] I do not know where Nesi finds this attribution to Jerome regarding Pythagoras' chaste personality.

2.2: Plutarchus... mundo] cf. Plut., *Quaest. Rom.* 40 (*Moralia* 274).

2.3: Dominus... malos] cf. Mt. 5.43–48, esp. 44–45: "Ego autem dico vobis: Diligite inimicos vestros et orate pro persequentibus vos, ut sitis filii Patris vestri, qui in caelis est, quia solem suum oriri facit super malos et bonos et pluit super iustos et iniustos."

2.3: Malachia... gloria] cf. Mal. 4, esp. 4.2–3: "'et orietur vobis timentibus nomen meum sol iustitiae et sanitas in pinnis eius et egrediemini et salietis sicut vituli de armento et calcabitis impios cum fuerint cinis sub planta pedum vestrorum in die qua ego facio,' dicit Dominus exercituum." Some editors do not divide Malachi into four books, so in some editions the above passage is not Mal. 4.2–3 but Mal. 3.20–1.

2.4: confusus... meae] Ier. 31.19; quia] quoniam *Ier.*

2.5: Diogenes . . . virtutis] cf. Diog. Laert. 6.54.

2.6: Pro . . . iuvenibus] Ambr., *De officiis ministrorum.* 1.17.65: "Est igitur bonorum adulescentium timorem dei habere, deferre parentibus, honorem habere senioribus, castitatem tueri, non aspernari humilitatem, diligere clementiam ac verecundiam, quae ornamento sunt minori aetati. Ut enim in senibus gravitas, in iuvenibus alacritas, ita in adulescentibus verecundia velut quadam dote commendatur naturae." Ambrose discusses *verecundia* in *De officiis ministrorum* 1.18, as well as in 1.20.

2.6: unus . . . illic] In *De officiis ministrorum* 1.17.66, Ambrose mentions various Old Testament figures who on account of their modesty were entrusted by the Lord to prophesy great things.

2.7: Qualem autem . . . penitus ignorentur.] cf. Joseph., *BJ* 2.148.

3. *Adversus solem ne loquaris*

3.1: Marsilius Ficinus De sole] See Ficino, *De sole et lumine* (*Op.*, 1.965–975).

3.2: oculus . . . figurans] Ficino, *De sole et lumine*, 6 (*Op.*, 1.968).

3.3: Theologi . . . sole] Ficino, *De sole et lumine*, 6 (*Op.*, 1.968).

3.3: Theologi veteres, Proculo] Theologi veteres, eodem Proculo *habet* Ficino, *De sole et lumine*, 6 (*Op.*, 1.968).

3.3: dicit] ita narrat *habet* Ficino, *De sole et lumine*, 6 (*Op.*, 1.968).

3.4: Physici . . . collocarunt] Ficino, *De sole et lumine*, 6 (*Op.*, 1.968).

3.5: solem . . . testantur] Ficino, *De sole et lumine*, 9 (*Op.*, 1.970).

3.5: Jamblichus] Jamblichus et *habet* Ficino, *De sole et lumine*, 9 (*Op.*, 1.970).

3.6: ut est in Jeremia] cf. Ier. 8.1–2: "'in tempore illo,' ait Dominus, 'eicient ossa regis Iuda et ossa principum eius et ossa sacerdotum et ossa prophetarum et ossa eorum qui habitaverunt Hierusalem de sepulchris suis et pandent ea ad solem et lunam et *omnem militiam caeli*, quae dilexerunt et quibus servierunt et post quae ambulaverunt et quae quaesierunt et adoraverunt, non colligentur et non sepelientur, in sterquilinium super faciem terrae erunt. . . .'" See also

Ier. 43.13: "et conteret statuas domus solis quae sunt in terra Aegypti et delubra deorum Aegypti conburet igni."

3.6: colebant . . . retulit] cf. Act. 7.1–53 (the sermon of Stephen), esp. 7.42: "Convertit autem Deus et tradidit eos servire militiae caeli. . . ."

3.7: utpote . . . dicta] cf. Diog. Laert. 2.12 and 2.15.

3.8: Dicit . . . colere] Arist., *Eth. Nic.* 1.6.1096a14–17.

3.9: Ego . . . vita] Io. 14.6.

3.9: omnis . . . vocem] Io. 18.37.

4. *Ad finem ubi perveneris, ne velis reverti*

4.1: Omnia . . . nostram] 1 Cor. 10.11: "Haec autem in figuram contingebant illis; scripta sunt autem ad correptionem nostram, in quos fines saeculorum devenerunt."

4.1: uxore . . . dicitur] cf. Gn. 19.26: "respiciensque uxor eius post se, versa est in statuam salis;" cf. also Lc. 17.22–37, on the coming of the son of man, esp. 17.31–32: "In illa die, qui fuerit in tecto et vasa eius in domo, ne descendat tollere illa, et qui in agro, similiter non redeat retro. Memores estote uxoris Lot."

4.1: iuxta . . . domini] cf. Hier., *Ep. Ruf.* 39.57–8 (where Jerome is reporting from Porphyry, *Vita Pythagorae* 42): "'cum profectus,' inquit, 'fueris, ne redeas, id est post mortem vitam istam ne desideres.'"

4.1: ne . . . erubescant] cf. PsG. 69.4: "avertantur retrorsum et erubescant qui volunt mihi mala" and PsH.: "convertantur retrorsum et erubescant qui volunt malum mihi."

4.2: Qui . . . dominus] cf. Lc. 9.61–62: "Et ait alter: 'Sequar te, Domine, sed primum permitte mihi renuntiare his, qui domi sunt.' Ait ad illum Iesus: 'Nemo mittens manum suam in aratrum et aspiciens retro, aptus est regno Dei.'"

4.2: poenitentia . . . capitulis] *Decretum*, Pars 2, D.2 *de pen.* c.9 (Richter, 1.1193); cf. the beginning of the chapter (quoting Gregory the Great on Ezechiel): "Pennata animalia, minime revertuntur, cum incedunt, quia sancti predicatores, sic a terrenis actibus ad spiritualia transeunt, ut ad ea, que reliquerant, ulterius nullatenus reflectantur."

4.3: magnus . . . contemplaretur] cf. Hdt. 1.32 and Plutarch, *Sol.* 27.6–7.

4.4: Boetius . . . gradu] Boeth., *Cons.* 1, carm. 1, 22–23.

4.4: Omnis . . . nimis] Ps. 118.96.

4.5: perinde . . . vomitum] cf. Prv. 26.11: "sicut canis qui revertitur ad vomitum suum" and 2 Pt. 2.22: "canis reversus ad suum vomitum et sus lota in volutabri loti."

4.5: quasi . . . carnium] cf. Ex. 16.3: "dixeruntque ad eos filii Israel utinam mortui essemus per manum Domini in terra Aegypti quando sedebamus super ollas carnium et comedebamus panes in saturitate; cur eduxistis nos in desertum istud ut occideretis omnem multitudinem fame?"

4.6: Si . . . dimiseris] Eccl. 10.4.

4.6: Plangite . . . suae] Ier. 22.10 (quoniam] quia *Ier*; ultra ad terram] ultra nec videbit terram *Ier*).

4.6: egressus . . . morietur] Ier. 22.11–12: "qui egressus est de loco isto, non revertetur huc amplius, sed in loco ad quem transtuli eum ibi morietur et terram istam non videbit amplius . . ."

4.7: Ego . . . finis] Apc. 1.8 (some modern editors leave out "principium et finis").

4.7: Domine . . . dominum] Ier. 17.13 (a te] *om.* modern editors; it is attested by the Φ group of codices and adopted in the Sixto-Clementina edition of 1592, 1593, and 1598 [Rome]).

4.9: Finis . . . Methaphisicorum] cf. Arist., *Metaph.* 5.16.4 (1021b, 25–31).

4.9: dissolui . . . Christo] cf. Ph. 1.23.

5. *Amicorum omnia communia*

5.2: Terentius . . . communia] Ter., *Ad.* 1.804 (ed. R.H. Martin [Cambridge, 1976]): "communia esse amicorum inter se omnia." On this passage Donatus says, *ad loc.*: "inter Pythagoreos ortum dicitur." See also Cic., *De off.* 1.16.51: "ut in Graecorum proverbio est, amicorum esse communia omnia." Cf. A. Otto, *Die Sprichwörter und sprich-*

wörtlichen Redensarten der Römer (Leipzig, 1890, repr. Hildesheim, etc., 1988) 20; and W. Bühler, *Zenobii Athoi Proverbia*, vol. 5 (Göttingen, 1999) 619–624.

5.2: Plato . . . communes] Plato, *Resp.* 5 (457 C–D).

5.3: Lactantius . . . damnat] Lactant., *Div. inst.* 3.21–22.

5.3: divus . . . principum] Ptolemy of Lucca, *De regimine principum*, ed. J. Mathis (Turin, 1924) 4.4. A long interpretive tradition attributed this work to Aquinas, but twentieth-century scholarship has shown that Ptolemy was responsible for most of the work, if not all. At the least he is responsible for the work from the middle of Book two, Chapter four, onward. James Blythe offers a good introduction on the authorship of the work in Ptolemy of Lucca (with portions attributed to Thomas Aquinas), *On the Government of Rulers*, trans. J.M. Blythe (Philadelphia, 1997) 1–7.

5.4: et . . . gentes] Cic., *Fin.* 1.65.

6. *Amicitia est aequalitas quae gradum nescit tam in animo quam in corpore*

6.1: Ambrosius . . . nescit] cf. Ambrose, *De spiritu sancto* (*CSEL* 79) 3.16.117: "Nescit enim unitas ordinem, gradum nescit aequalitas, nec cadit in dei filium, ut per contumaciam pietatem laederet, magister ipse pietatis."

6.2: Lex . . . diligas] cf. Lv. 19.18; Mt. 5.43; Mt. 19.19; Mt. 22.39; Rm. 13.9; Gal. 5.14.

6.2: neque . . . iudicio] cf. Dt. 1.17: "nec accipietis cuiusquam personam quia Dei iudicium est."

6.2: diligite . . . terram] Sap. 1.1: "Diligite iustitiam, qui iudicatis terram; sentite de Domino in bonitate et in simplicitate cordis quaerite illum. . . ."

6.2: beati . . . tempore] Ps. 105.3.

7. *Abstine ab his qui nigram habent caudam*

7.1: Plutarchus . . . sequuntur] ps.Plut., *De lib. ed.* 12e.

7.2: in Canonibus . . . idipsum] cf. *Decretal. Greg. IX* (*Liber extra*), 5.7.13

(Richter, 2.787): "Excommunicamus itaque et anathematizamus omnem haeresim extollentem se adversus hanc sanctam, orthodoxam, et catholicam fidem quam superius exposuimus, condemnantes haereticos universos quibuscunque nominibus censeantur, facies quidem diversas habentes sed caudas ad invicem colligatas, quia de vanitate conveniunt in idipsum."

7.3: cum . . . perverteris] Ps. 17.27: "cum electo electus eris et cum perverso perverteris." In his first sermon on *Exodus*, given on 11 February 1498, Savonarola touched on this passage from the *Psalms*. The sermons on Exodus were the first sermons which he gave after having been excommunicated. In a moving, angry passage, tinged with desperation, he protested his excommunication and suggested that a line had been drawn and that there were two camps, the holy and the malicious (Savonarola, *OpNaz* 1, ed. P.G. Ricci, 25–6): "Or va', adunque, e guarda chi sono quelli che contradicono: tu vedrai che son tutti viziosi e rinvolti ne' peccati, qual tutti diavoli e qual mezzi e qual bestie. Comincia pur da Roma insino qua e vedrai che gente e' sono. Certo tu vedi che quasi tutti li uomini cattivi e infami contradicono a questa opera. Dipoi voltati, e guarda quelli che credano a questa opera: tu vedrai che vivano bene, si confessano, si comunicano spesso, vivano purificati. Se tu se' adunque bono, a quali t'accosterai tu? Certamente tu t'accosterai a boni e a quelli che vivono bene, se tu vorrai essere buono: *cum sancto sanctus eris, [si] cum perverso perverteris*. Io veggo che tu t'accosti a questi che contradicono, adunque tu debbi essere cattivo come loro. Io, per me, voglio stare con questi buoni, e se per far bene s'ha a essere scomunicato, io voglio stare con gli scommunicati." In his third sermon on *Exodus*, given 25 February 1498, he uses the phrase again, here to reinforce the notion that one might become "tepid," should one associate with the wrong people (Savonarola, *OpNaz*, 1.91): "Tu che hai il prete tepido in casa, diventerai tepido come lui. *Cum sancto sanctus eris, cum perverso perversus.*"

7.4: Pares . . . Catone] Cic., *Sen.* 7. On this proverb see Cicero, *Cato Maior, de senectute*, ed. J.G.F. Powell (Cambridge, 1988) *ad loc.*

7.5: blandi . . . colubri] cf. Prv. 23.31–32: "ne intuearis vinum quando flavescit cum splenduerit in vitro color eius, ingreditur blande sed in novissimo mordebit ut coluber et sicut regulus venena diffundet."

7.5: Ave, rabbi] Mt. 26.49; cf. Mc. 14.45.

7.6: simulator . . . scientia] Pr. 11.9.

7.6: Molliti . . . iacula] PsG. 54.22. Cf. previous verses, i.e., PsG. 54.20–2: ". . . non enim est illis commutatio et non timuerunt Deum, extendit manum suam in retribuendo, contaminaverunt testamentum eius, divisi sunt ab ira vultus eius et adpropinquavit cor illius . . ."

8. *Anulum arctum non habeto*

8.1: Divus . . . nequeas] I do not find this in Jerome, but cf. Erasmus, *Adagia*, I.1.2.v (ASD, II.1, eds. M.L. van Poll-van de Lisdonk, M. Mann Philipps, C. Robinson [Amsterdam, 1993] 94), explaining this symbol: "Arctum anulum ne gestato, hoc est interprete divo Hieronymo ne vixeris anxie et ne temet in servitutem coniicias aut in eiusmodi vitae institutum, unde non queas extricare. Siquidem quisquis anulum angustum gestat, is sibi quodammodo vincula iniicit." This was present in the first expanded edition of Erasmus's *Adagia*, entitled *Adagiorum chiliades* (Venice: Aldus Manutius, 1508).

8.2: si . . . pari] Ov., *Her.* 9.32

8.2: Quam . . . iuvenci] Ov., *Her.* 9.29.

8.3: Legi . . . duxisti] *Decretum*, Pars 2, C.17 q.2 c.2 (Richter, 1.814).

8.5: aut Mammona aut Deus est] cf. Mt. 6.24: "non potestis Deo servire et Mammonae"; and Lc. 16.9–13.

8.5: huius . . . leve] cf. Mt. 11.30: "Iugum enim meum suave et onus meum leve est." Nesi cited this biblical passage in his *Oratio de charitate*. See his *Oratio de charitate* (Florence, 1486) and the edition of the manuscript draft of the work in O. Zorzi, "Two Sermons by Giovanni Nesi and the Language of Spirituality in Late Fifteenth-Century Florence," *Bibliothèque d'Humanisme et Renaissance* 52 (1980) 641–656, at 645. This passage was also cited by Clement of Alexandria in his own interpretation of the *akousmata*; cf. Clem., *Strom.* 5.5.

8.5: eius . . . superasti] Is. 9.4. For context cf. previous verses, i.e., 9.2–6: "Populus qui ambulabat in tenebris vidit lucem magnam; habitantibus in regione umbrae mortis lux orta est eis. Multiplicasti gentem, non magificasti laetitiam; laetabuntur coram te, sicut laetantur in messe, sicut exultant quando dividunt spolia. Iugum enim oneris eius et virgam umeri eius et sceptrum exactoris eius superasti sicut in die Madian; quia omnis violenta praedatio cum tumultu et vestimentum mixtum sanguine erit in conbustionem et cibus ignis. Parvulus enim natus est nobis . . ."

8.5: ambulavimus vias difficiles] Sap. 5.7: "lassati sumus in via iniquitatis et perditionis et ambulavimus vias difficiles; viam autem Domini ignoravimus."

8.5: Non . . . dominus] Is. 48.22; cf. Is. 57.21. Is., 48 resonates with images which would be familiar to a Savanarolan crowd; it concerns what Yahweh has foretold (48.1–11; cf. 48.3: "priora ex tunc adnuntiavi et ex ore meo exierunt et audita feci ea, repente operatus sum et venerunt."); Israel's destiny (48.16–19; cf. 18: "Utinam adtendisses mandata mea! Facta fuisset sicut flumen pax tua et iustitia tua sicut gurgites maris."); and the end of the Jewish exile (48.20–22, which ends with the verse Nesi cites). Is. 57, the other place in Isaiah where there is mention of the notion that there is no peace for the wicked, is also evocative; it begins with the sentence (Is. 57.1): "Iustus perit et nemo est qui recogitet in corde suo . . ."

8.5: "quaenam summa boni, quae mens sibi conscia recti."] I have been unable to locate this quotation.

9. *Bonum cibum in matellam ne reponas*

9.1: Plutarchus . . . ingeras] ps.Plut., *De lib. ed.* 12f.

9.1: Epictetus . . . mictas] Cf. Epictetus apud Gell., *NA* 17.19.1–4: "Favorinum ego audivi dicere Epictetum philosophum dixisse plerosque istos, qui philosophari viderentur, philosophos esse huiuscemodi ἄνευ τοῦ πράττειν, μέχρι τοῦ λέγειν, id significat 'factis procul, verbis tenus.' Iam illud est vehementius quod Arrianus solitum eum dictitare in libris quos de *dissertationibus* eius composuit, scriptum reliquit. 'Nam cum,' inquit, 'animadverterat hominem pudore amisso, inportuna industria, corruptis moribus, audacem, confidentem, linguam ceteraque omnia praeterquam animum procurantem, istiusmodi,' inquit, 'hominem cum viderat studia quoque et disciplinas philosophiae contrectare et physica adire et meditari dialectica multaque id genus theoremata aucupari sciscitarique, inclamabat deum atque hominum fidem ac plerumque inter clamandum his eum verbis increpabat: Ἄνθρωπε, ποῦ βάλλεις; σκέψαι, εἰ κακάθαρται τὸ ἀγγεῖον· ἂν γὰρ εἰς τὴν οἴησιν αὐτὰ βάλλῃς, ἀπώλετο· ἢν σαπῇ, οὖρον ἢ ὄξος γένοιτο ἢ εἴ τι τούτων χεῖρον.' Nil profecto his verbis gravius, nil verius, quibus declarabat maximus philosophorum litteras atque doctrinas philosophiae, cum in hominem falsum atque degenerem tamquam in vas spurcum atque pollutum influxissent, verti, mutari, corrumpi, et, quod ipse κυνικώτερον ait, urinam fieri aut si quid est urina spurcius." (Cf. Ep. *Diss.* fr. 10, ed. Schenkl). I presume Nesi suggests that Epictetus says this "again and again" (*etiam atque etiam*) because of the use of the iterative form of the verb (*dictitare*) in the text of Gellius.

9.2: Nolite . . . porcos] Mt. 7.6.

9.2: Nam . . . Flaccus] Hor. *Epist.* 1.2.54: "Sincerum est nisi vas, quodcumque infundis acescit."

9.3: non . . . dei] Mt. 4.4; cf. Lc. 4.4 and Dt. 8.3.

9.4: De officio . . . verbo] *Decretal. Greg. IX* (*Liber extra*), 1.31.15 (Richter, 2.192): "Inter cetera quae ad salutem spectant populi Christiani, pabulum verbi Dei permaxime sibi noscitur esse necessarium, quia sicut corpus materiali, sic anima spirituali cibo nutritur, eo quod non in solo pane. . . ."

9.5: Divus . . . loquatur] cf. *Decretum*, Pars 1, D.43 c.1 (Richter, 1.154): "*Sal in vobis et pacem habete inter vos* [Mc. 9.50]. Per sal quippe verbi sapientia designatur. Qui ergo loqui sapienter nititur, magnopere metuat, ne eius eloquio audientium unitas confundetur. Hinc Paulus ait, *Non plus sapere*. . . ."

9.6: Plato . . . videatur] The author probably alludes to Plato's dissatisfaction with the learning capability and will of the younger Dionysius (cf. Plato, *Ep.* 7); perhaps also, with Plato's seventh letter in mind, he alludes to Plato's apparent dissatisfaction with the written word, also expressed in that letter (cf. 341c–e).

10. *Choenici ne insideas*

10.1: Hieronymus . . . crastinum] Cf. Hier., *Commentariorum in Hiezechielem libri XIV* in *S. Hieronymi Presbyteri opera*, (= *CCSL* 72.1.4) ed. Francesco Gloria (Turnholt, 1964) 14.45.10–12. There Jerome mentions the word "choenix," pointing out that, in the Septuagint version, Ezechiel 45.10–12 "non cohaeret et penitus intelligi non potest, dum non solum numeros mensurarum sed etiam nomina commutarunt." Among the mistranslated nouns is "choenix," which is more properly, according to Jerome, "bato." Otherwise I have been unable to find in Jerome a discussion like the one to which Nesi alludes. Oddly, in his *Epistula adversus Rufinum* 39 (the main source for Jerome's discussion of the Pythagorean *akousmata*) Jerome follows fairly closely the order of the *akousmata* in Porphyry's *Vita Pythagorae* 33–42 (and in fact does little more than present a modified translation of Porphyry there); but Jerome leaves this *akousma* out of his discussion, even though it is included in Porphyry's list (in Porphyry it appears as Μηδ' ἐπὶ χοίνικος καθέζεσθαι, οἷον μὴ ἀργὸν ζῆν). As far as the omission goes, Lardet comments (Lardet, *Comm.* 683b): "Le chénice, mesure de blé (ici ce minimum vital dont on ne devrait pas se contenter), a pu sembler obscur à Jerome, ou cet avis faire double emploi avec celui des l.63s.," which in the *Ep. Ruf.* 39.62–64, is as follows: "oneratis superponendum onus, deponentibus non communicandum, id est ad virtutem incedentibus augenda praecepta, tradentes se otio relinquendos."

11. *Cor ne edito*

11.1: Thomas . . . nostra] Ptolemy of Lucca, *De regimine principum* 4.22. See note to 5.3 for authorship.

11.3: sicut . . . nocet] Prv. 25.20; this sentence is omitted by most modern editors, but was probably in Nesi's day well-entrenched in the textual tradition of the vulgate Old Testament, as its inclusion in the Editio Sixto-Clementina of 1592 attests. (It is also present in C, the codex cavensis = Cava, Archivio della Badia 1 [14]; cf. *Biblia Sacra Vulgata, ad loc.*)

11.3: tarmes] A worm that eats wood; cf. Plaut., *Most.* 3.2.140; Isid., *Orig.* 12.5.10; and Serv., G. 1.256.

11.3: Tite . . . fixa] Cic. *Sen.* 1: "O Tite, si quid ego adiuero curamve levasso, quae nunc te coquit et versat in pectore fixa, ecquid erit praemi?" (This saying goes back to Ennius: see Ennius 10.8 [335, p. 99] in the edition of O. Skutsch [Oxford, 1985] and Skutsch's comments at pp. 510–12, though Nesi certainly knew it from Cicero.)

11.4: Cor . . . vivum] cf. PsG. 83.3.

11.4: Pax . . . scandilum] Ps. 118.165.

12. *Coronam ne carpito*

12.1: Divus . . . arguendas] cf. Hier., *Ep. Ruf.* 39.55 (quoting Porphyry, *Vita Pyth.* 42): "coronam minime carpendum, id est leges urbium conservandas."

12.1: dicit . . . rex] cf. Arist., *Pol.* 3.11.1287a20–24. Nesi's use of Aristotle here is interesting, since Aristotle reports this opinion on the primacy of law versus kingship as what others say on this point and not as his own opinion; he will soon argue that under ideal conditions it is really monarchy which is the best form of government, even if these conditions are difficult if not impossible to obtain in the world as it is. Cf. the comments of Richard Robinson, *ad loc.*, in his *Aristotle's Politics: Books III and IV*, translated with introduction and comments (Oxford, 1962).

12.2: Corsettus . . . inanimata] On Antonio Corsetto (also known as Corsetti), see the article of A. Mazzacane, in the *Dizionario biografico degli Italiani*, 29.540–2 (also for bibliography). The Sicilian-born Corsetti, 1450–1503, was a jurist and author of a number of works, the most famous and often printed of which was his *Repertorium in opera Nicolai de Tudeschis*, printed first in Venice in 1486, at the press of Andrea Torresano; the *De regia potestate* was printed first in 1499 at the press of Bernardino Stagnino (see *GW*, 7.173–80).

12.6: Non . . . resistit] Rm. 13.2.

12.7: Penituit . . . tulisset] cf. 1 Rg. 24.5–7: "Surrexit ergo David et praecidit oram chlamydis Saul silenter. Post haec cor David percussit eum, eo quod abscidisset oram chlamydis Saul, dixitque ad viros suos 'Propitius mihi sit Dominus, ne faciam hanc rem domino meo, christo Domini, ut mittam manum meam in eum, quoniam christus Domini est.'"

13. *Deponentibus ne adiicito*

13.1: Hieronymus . . . relinquendos] cf. Hier., *Ep. Ruf.* 39.62–64 (quoting Porphyry, *Vita Pyth.* 42): "deponentibus non communicandum, id est ad virtutem incedentibus augenda praecepta, tradentes se otio relinquendos."

13.3: Quintilio . . . inanem] cf. Hor., *Ars P.* 438–443: "Quintilio siquid recitares, 'corrige, sodes,/hoc,' aiebat, 'et hoc.' Melius te posse negares/bis terque expertum frustra, delere iubebat/et male tornatos incudi reddere versus./Si defendere delictum quam vertere malles,/nullum ultra verbum aut operam insumebat inanem,/quin sine rivali teque et tua solus amares."

13.4: Clama . . . eorum] Is. 58.1.

13.4: Cum . . . ceptis] I have been unable to locate this quotation.

14. *Dextram nemini cito tradas*

14.1: Solonis . . . respuendos] Solon, DK 10 β 9; cf. Diog. Laert. 1.60.

14.1: Aristoteles . . . censeamus] *Eth. Nic.* 8.3.1156b26–28.

14.2: Sed . . . Seneca] Bias: see Diog. Laert. 1.87; Seneca: Sen. *Ep.*, 95.63 and *De ira*, 3.34.2–4.

14.3: Probare . . . Apostolus] cf. 1 Jo. 4.1: "Carissimi, nolite omni spiritui credere, sed probate spiritus si ex Deo sint, quoniam multi pseudoprophetae prodierunt in mundum."

14.4: Manus imposueris] 1 Tm. 5.22.

14.4: Pravum . . . Jeremia] Ier. 17.9 (*but* hominis] omnium *consensus codicum*).

14.5: dextera . . . legimus] cf. Gn. 48.14; 48.17; 48.18; Jdc. 3.5; Ps. 72.24; 120.5; 4 Ezr. 10.30.

15. *Ex vitibus amputatis ne libaveris*

15.1: Moisi . . . tetigisset] cf. Ex. 20.25: "quod si altare lapideum feceris mihi, non aedificabis illud de sectis lapidibus."

15.1: Salomonis . . . est] cf. 3 Rg. 6.7: "domus autem cum aedificatur, lapidibus dedolatis atque perfectis aedificata est, et malleus et securis et omne ferramentum non sunt audita in domo cum aedificaretur."

15.2: misericordiam . . . sacrificium] Mt. 9.13; 12.7; cf. also 1 Rg. 15.22; Os. 6.6; Mi. 8.8; Ps. 39.7; and Prv. 21.3.

15.4: fertur . . . ledere] cf. Diog. Laert. 8.12–13, 19, 24, 33–34, 39, and 45.

15.5: si . . . tuo] Mt. 5.23–4 but cf. for the context and possible allusion to Savonarola's fate, see Mt. 5.21–24: "Audistis quia dictum est antiquis: *Non occides*; qui autem occiderit, reus erit iudicio. Ego autem dico vobis, quia omnis qui irascitur fratri suo reus erit iudicio. Qui autem dixerit fratri suo: Raca, reus erit concilio. Qui autem dixerit: Fatue, reus erit gehennae ignis. Si ergo offers munus tuum ad altare, et ibi recordatus fueris quia frater tuus habet aliquid adversum te, relinque ibi munus tuum ante altare, et vade prius reconciliari fratri tuo, et tunc veniens offeres munus tuum."

16. *Exsurgens lectu stragulas complicato: seu corporis vestigium confundito*

16.1: lavabo . . . rigabo] PsG. 6.7.

16.2: Qui . . . dormiunt] 1 Th. 5.7.

16.6: Omnis . . . affectum] cf. *Decretum*, Pars 2, C.26 q.7 c.10 (Richter, 1.1043): "Affectum illum in se recipiat poenitens quem gerebat ille, qui dixit: *Iniquitatem odio habui et abominatus sum* [PsG. 118.163]. . . ."

17. *Echon invoca flantibus ventis*

17.2: De . . . disserit] Gell., *NA* 2.22; here different names and terms related to the winds are discussed, such as *iapyx*, *favonius*, *auster*, etc.

17.3–4: In . . . interisse] Gell., *NA* 16.11, referring there to Herodotus.

17.8: Vanitas . . . vanitas] Ecl. 1.2. The remembrance of Savonarola could not be more obvious.

18. *Farinam sacrificiis apponito*

18.1: Valerius . . . moderationem] cf. V. Max. 5, "De humanitate et clementia," *passim*.

18.2: Deus . . . gratiam] 1 Petr. 5.5

18.2: inter . . . Aristoteles] cf. *Eth. Nic.* 2.7.1108a4–9 and 4.5.1125b26–1126b10.

18.4: "Agina," i.e., "tongue of a balance." For the meaning of this word see Paul. ex. Fest. (in Sexti Pompei Festi *De verborum significatu quae supersunt cum Pauli epitome*, ed. W.M. Lindsay [Stuttgart and

Leipzig, 1913, repr. 1997]) 10: "Agina est quo inseritur scapus truti-
nae, id est, in quo foramine trutina se vertit, unde aginatores dicuntur, qui parvo lucro moventur." I believe Nesi may have in mind
here Tertullian, *Adv. Hermogenem* 41.2, who is refuting there Hermogenes'
ideas on motion. The text is edited by A. Kroyman in *CCSL* 1.1
(Turnholt, 1954) 395–435; the passage printed by Kroyman at 41.2
(at p. 431) is as follows: "Si aequalis momenti, iam non turbulentus
<motus> caccabacius, sed compositus et temperatus, scilicet qui inter
bonum et malum suo arbitrio agitatus, in neutram tamen partem
pronus et praeceps, mediam, quod aiunt, aginam tenens aequilibrato
impetu ferebatur." However, for "aequilibrato" J. Waszink reads
"exinde librato." Cf. his arguments in *Vigiliae christianae* 9 (1955)
145–7. In Waszink's annotated translation of this work he renders
the passage "If this motion had a uniform momentum, then it was
not turbulent nor like the water in the pot, but well-ordered and
steady because, moving as it did between good and evil of its own
accord, yet without inclining and tending to either side, keeping the
tongue of the balance, as they say, in the center, it manifested itself
in a well-balanced course." (See Tertullian, *The Treatise Against Hermogenes*,
Ancient Christian Writers, 24, trans. and annotated by J.H. Waszink
[Westminster, Maryland and London, 1956] p. 79.) Thus both the
notion that the word "agina" could suggest a kind of mean, in keeping with the moderation of character that Nesi sees as important
here, and the possibility that "aginam tenens exinde librato" could
have brought to mind Nesi's somewhat similar sounding "agina in
dei libamine," lead me to believe that this was the *passus* he had in
mind.

18.4: quod . . . Apostolus] Col. 3.14.

19. *Gladium acutum declinato*

19.1: Democlis . . . divum] Nesi could have known the story of the
sword of Damocles from Cic., *Tusc.* 5.61–62 and Hor., *Carm.* 3.1.17.

19.2: ne loquaris . . . fluminis] cf. Sir. 4.32: "noli resistere contra
faciem potentis, nec coneris contra ictum fluvii."

19.3: Gladius . . . Apocalipsi] cf. Apc. 1.16; 2.16; 19.5.

19.3: cum . . . eius] PsG. 2.13.

19.4: Quis . . . ira] cf. Mt. 3.7: "'Progenies viperarum, quis demonstravit vobis fugere a futura ira?" (futura] ventura *Editio clementina*; cf. *Biblia sacra vulgata, ad loc.*).

20. *Gladio ignem ne fodias*

20.1: Hieronymus . . . lacessas] cf. Hier., *Ep. Ruf.* 39.54–55: "iratum videlicet et tumidum animum verbis maledicis ne lacessas."

20.2: Lucianus . . . est] cf. Lucian, *Ver. Hist.* 2.6–10. Lucian relates here three sentences pronounced by Rhadamanthus, judge of the underworld, which in a vague way can be seen to correspond with the first two of the three *admonita* listed here (I cite from the translation of A.M. Harmon, 1961, 311–13): "The first case was that of Ajax, son of Telamon, to decide whether he should be allowed to associate with the heroes or not: he was accused of having gone mad and killed himself. At last, when much had been said, Rhadamanthus gave judgment that for the present he should be given in charge of Hippocrates, the Coan physician, to take the hellebore treatment, and that later on, when he had recovered his wits, he should have a place at the table of the heroes." Ajax could thus be seen as having "poked fire with a sword." Lucian goes on: "The second case was a love affair—Theseus and Menelaus at law over Helen, to determine which of the two she should live with. Rhadamanthus pronounced that she should live with Menelaus, because he had undergone so much toil and danger on account of his marriage: then too, Theseus had other wives, the Amazon and the daughters of Minos." If one interprets "not eating lupins" here as an admonition to chastity paralleling the prohibition on eating beans, as in symbol 1, then Nesi may be reflecting Rhadamanthus' decision to have Helen live with the "more chaste" Menelaus. Finally, Lucian relates that "The third judgment was given in a matter of precedence between Alexander, son of Philip, and Hannibal of Carthage, and the decision was that Alexander outranked Hannibal, so his chair was placed next the elder Cyrus of Persia." I find no parallel here with Nesi's "tertium autem non licet homini loqui, nam bestiale est." Otherwise I find no such story regarding Rhadamanthus in Lucian. The *True Story* was translated before 1450 by Lilio Tifernati, the Umbrian humanist; see Marsh, *Lucian and the Latins*, 40, and U. Jaitner-Hahner, *Humanismus in Umbrien und Rom: Lilius Tifernas, Kanzler und Gelehrter des Quattrocento* (Baden-Baden, 1993) 268–89, cit. Marsh, 40 n.121.

20.3: Diogenes . . . exagitandam] Diog. Laert. 8.18.

20.3: Ovidius . . . habet] Ov., *Rem. am.* 119–120.

20.4: Plato . . . moliuntur] Plato, *Leg.* 6.780c.

20.5: Basilius . . . arbitratu] Basil the Great, Ὁμιλία πρὸς τοὺς νέους ὅπως ἂν ἐξ ἑλληνικῶν ὠφέλοιντο λόγων, ed. N.G. Wilson (London, 1975) ch. 7. (For Basil's treatise to the young on the value of Greek literature I have also availed myself of the Loeb volume, tr. R.J. Deferrari and M. Maguire [Cambridge, Mass. and London, 1934]; the treatise is contained at 363–435). There is no quotation matching Nesi's reference in Basil's work, but this section does discuss examples of ancients who did not let their anger get the best of them. On Basil's treatise in the Renaissance see L. Schucan, *Das Nachleben von Basilius Magnus "Ad adolescentes"*, Travaux d'Humanisme et Renaissance, 133 (Geneva, 1973); for the Savonarolan environment see 94–96.

20.5: cribro haurire aquam] cf. Erasmus, *Adag.*, 1.4.60.

21. *Figuram et aram in primis honorato*

21.1: Imprimis . . . Cereri] Verg., *G.* 1.338–339.

21.1: Si . . . colendus] *Disticha Catonis*, 1.1 (cf. ed. Boas, 34–5 for commentary). Cf. Walther, *M*: 28,436.

21.2: Marsilius . . . religione] Here Nesi alludes to the title of the first chapter of Ficino's *De christiana religione*, i.e., (*Op.* 1.2), "Religio maxime homini propria est et veridica." For Ficino religion truly separated humankind from animals (ibid., "Nullum bruta prae se ferunt religionis indicium. . . ."); its existence among humans constituted for Ficino a chief element of his thought on the dignity of humankind. Cf. Kristeller, *Pensiero*; and for the dating of the work *idem, Suppl.*, 1.LXXVII–LXXVIX.

21.3: Lactantius . . . homine] cf. Lactant., *De ira dei* 7 (Migne, *PL*, 7.94–5): "Risus quoque est homini proprius; et tamen videamus in aliis animalibus quaedam signa laetitiae, cum ad lusum gestiunt, aures demulcent, rictum contrahunt, frontem serenam, oculos in lasciviam resolvunt. . . . Quod si horum quoque deprehenditur similitudo, apparet solam esse religionem, cuius in mutis nec vestigium aliquod nec ulle suspicio inveniri potest."

21.4: et Moisis . . . Deuteronomio] cf. Dt. 16.16: ". . . et in sollemnitate tabernaculorum non apparebit ante Dominum vacuus."

21.5: ut per in lege Moisi] cf. Ex. 20.4–6; Dt. 5.8–10.

21.5: Josepho . . . potuit] cf. Joseph., *BJ* 2.170–174

21.5: et . . . libro] cf. Joseph., *BJ* 1.650–655.

22. *Gallis albis parcito*

22.1–2: Proculus . . . De sacrificio] This seems to be a paraphrase of part of Ficino's translation of Proclus, *De sacrificio et magia*. See the edition of Ficino's translation in B.P. Copenhaver, "Hermes Trismegistus, Proclus, and the Question of a Philosophy of Magic in the Renaissance," in I. Merkel and A.G. Debus, eds., *Hermeticism in the Renaissance: Intellectual History and the Occult in Early Modern Europe* (Washington, D.C. and London, 1988) 79–110, at 106–9 (an improvement on Ficino, *Op.* 2.1928–9). Cf. Ficino's translation: "Deinde et animalia sunt solaria multa, velut leones et galli, numinis cuiusdam solaris pro sua natura participes, unde mirum est quantum inferiora in eodem ordine cedant superioribus quamvis magnitudine potentiaque non cedant. Hinc ferunt gallum timeri a leone quamplurimum et quasi coli, cuius rei causam a materia sensuque assignare non possumus, sed solum ab ordinis superni contemplatione. Quoniam videlicet praesentia solaris virtutis convenit gallo magis quam leoni, quod et inde apparet quia gallus quasi quibusdam hymnis applaudit surgenti soli et quasi advocat quando ex anthipodum medio coelo ad nos reflectitur. Et quandoque nonnulli solares angeli apparuerunt formis huiusmodi praediti, atque cum ipsi in se sine forma essent, nobis tamen, qui formati sumus, occurrerunt formati. Nonnunquam etiam daemones visi sunt solares leonina fronte quibus, cum gallis obiiceretur, repente disparuerunt." On the conception of the power of the white cock among ancient Pythagoreans see F. Cumont, "Le coq blanc des Mazdéens et les Pythagoriciens." *Académie des Inscriptions et Belles-Lettres: Comptes rendus* (Paris, 1942) 284–300.

22.3: Picus . . . praedicatores] cf. G. Pico della Mirandola, *De hominis dignitate. Heptaplus. De ente et uno*, ed. E. Garin (Florence, 1942) 126 (*Oratio*): "Postremo ut gallum nutriamus nos admonebit, idest ut divinam animae nostrae partem divinarum rerum cognitione quasi solido cibo et caelesti ambrosia pascamus. Hic est gallus cuius aspectum leo, idest omnis terrena potestas, formidat et reveretur. Hic ille gallus, cui datam esse intelligentiam apud Iob legimus. Hoc gallo canente aberrans homo resipiscit. Hic gallus in matutino crepuscolo, matutinis astris Deum laudantibus, quotidie commodulatur. Hunc gallum moriens Socrates, cum divinitatem animi sui divinitati maioris mundi copulaturum se speraret, Aesculapio, idest animarum medico, iam extra omne morbi discrimen positus, debere se dixit."

22.3: veritas odium parit] Ter., *And.* 68.

22.4: Philostratum ... decessit] cf. Philostr., *VA* 7 *et passim* and Gell., *NA*, 15.11. With an eye toward determining the possible collaboration of Paolo Orlandini, it is noteworthy here that Orlandini had an interest in Philostratus, *VA*, making his own epitome thereof, which is present in MS Munich, Bayerische Staatsbibliothek Clm 173, fols. 121–128v; cf. Kristeller, *Iter*, 3.613.

22.5: ales ... redit] cf. Ambrose, *Hymni*, ed. J. Fontaine (1992) 1.1.1: "praeco diei iam sonat, noctis profundae pervigilat, nocturna lux viantibus, a nocte noctem segregans;" ibid., 1.6.21: "Gallo canente, spes redit, aegris salus refunditur, mucro latronis conditur, lapsis fides revertitur." I have been unable to find "ales diei nuncius."

22.7: The allusions to Savonarola are clear enough.

23. *Hyrundinem domi non habeto*

23.1: Hieronymus ... susurronum] Hier., *Ep. Ruf.* 39.59–61, translating Porphyry, *Vita Pyth.* 42: "hirundinem in domo non suscipiendam, id est garrulos et verbosos homines sub eodem tecto non habendos." Cf. Lardet, *Comm.*, 387, who notes Clement, *Strom.* 5.27.1 et seq., and Ambrose, *In ps.* 118.11.19. Nesi suggests that Jerome follows Aristotle here since Jerome gives this precept in a group which he calls "illaque aenigmata quae diligentissime Aristoteles in suis libris persequitur." Presumably Jerome had access to the now lost *Protreptic* of Aristotle, on which Iamblichus' *Protrepticus* is partially based.

23.2: quod . . . dicitur] cf. *Auct. ad Her.* 4.61: "Id est huiusmodi: 'Ita ut hirundines aestivo tempore praesto sunt, frigore pulsae recedunt—' ex eadem similitudine nunc per translationem verba sumimus: 'item falsi amici sereno vitae tempore praesto sunt; simul atque hiemem fortunae viderunt, devolant omnes.'" Nesi uses passive instead of active—"quod in Rhetoricis ad Herennium dicitur" (he could have said, e.g., "ut dicit Tullius," etc.). Perhaps he knew, under the influence of Poliziano, that the *ad Herrenium* was anonymous? The question was discussed in the Quattrocento; in general, the *opinio communis* among humanists (like Lorenzo Valla, Poggio Bracciolini, and Angelo Decembrio) was that the work was truly of Ciceronian authorship. See, e.g., J. Monfasani, *Language and Learning in Renaissance Italy* (Hampshire, England/Brookfield, Vermont: Variorum, 1994), II, 107–118 and III, 119–138, esp. 133, N. 103.

23.3: Plutarchus . . . versentur] cf. Plut., *Quaest. conv.* 8.7.2–3.

23.4: Albertus . . . viderit] Albert tends to discuss the swallow as representative of instinct in animals, as contrasted to humans, who are possessed of individuated reason and are capable of making individual decisions. The notion "hirundo omnis similiter facit nidum" appears often in his work in this regard (I refer to the editions established by the Albertus Magnus Institut, in Köln): *De anima* (ed. C. Stroick, 1968 = 7.1) 131.36–8 and 168.88; *Super ethica commentum et quaestiones* (ed. W. Kübel, 1968 = 14.1) 152.48 and 360.73 (in this work, as one might expect, Albert also discusses Aristotle's famous "one swallow does not spring make" (*EN* 1) at 42.22 et seq., but Albert does not there indicate that he believes swallows are mild); *De natura boni* (ed. E. Filthaut, 1974 = 27) 10.32 (here he discusses the notion that more than one swallow is necessary to build a nest); and in the *Super Dionysium De divinis nominibus* (ed. P. Simon, 1972 = 37.1) at 178.9 and 280.15. There are resonances which remind one of the present *akousma* in Albert's *Postilla super Isaiam* (ed. F. Siepmann, 1952 = 19), where, at 38.14 he comments on Isaiah 38.14, on the phrase "Sicut pullus hirundinis." Albert suggests that the expression is used in two senses; first, it is used metaphorically, to signify noise: "Metaphoram ponit ad gemitum et ad clamorem." Secondly, the swallow signifies life's vicissitudes, since it comes in two different colors: "Hirundo etiam varia avis est, nigra et alba, et significat varietatem huius vitae per prospera et adversa."

24. *In templum praeter propositum minime ingreditor*

24.1–2: Valerius . . . admoveretur] V. Max. 1.1.5.

24.3–5: Item . . . animadvertisset] V. Max 3.3.ext.1–2.

24.6: Ambrosius . . . De virginibus] Ambrose, *De virginibus*, ed. E. Cazzaniga (Turin, 1948) 3.12: "Unde illud exemplum proditur Alexandro sacrificante, Macedonum rege, puerulum barbarum qui ei lumen accenderet excepisse ignem brachio atque adusto corpore mansisse immobilem nec dolorem prodidisse gemitu nec tacito poenam indicasse fletu: tanto in puero barbaro fuit disciplina reverentiae, ut naturam vinceret. Atque ille non deos, qui nulli erant, sed regem timebat."

24.8: Si . . . vestra] Cf. *Regula Benedicti* 18.1–2: "Si, cum hominibus potentibus volumus aliqua suggerere, non praesumimus nisi cum humilitate et reverentia, quanto magis Domino Deo universorum cum omni humilitate et puritatis devotione supplicandum est." Other such hortatory *dicta* dot the *Rule*. Cf. Prologue, 1–3: "Obsculta, o fili, praecepta magistri, et inclina aurem cordis tui, et admonitionem pii patris libenter excipe et efficaciter comple, ut ad eum per oboedientiae laborem redeas, a quo per inoboedientiae desidiam recesseras. Ad te ergo nunc mihi sermo dirigitur, quisquis abrenuntians propriis voluntatibus, Domino Christo vero regi militaturus, oboedientiae fortissima atque praeclara arma sumis." Cf. also Prol. 40: "Ergo praeparanda sunt corda et corpora nostra, sanctae praeceptorum oboedientiae militanda."

25. *Iuxta sacrificium ungues ne incidito*

25.1: si . . . laborat] "Si cor non orat, in vanum lingua laborat" is a medieval proverb as well as the beginning of a medieval Latin poem which appears in MS Paris BN 15133, f.54 and MS Paris BN 8247, f.124. See B. Hauréau, *Notices et extraits de quelques manuscrits latins de la Bibliothèque Nationale Paris*, 6 vols. (Paris, 1890–3) 4.286 and Walther, *Verz.*, 17,659. In addition the line is present in MS Florence BN Landau-Finali 220, f.123 (Walther reports 121, but that is the old numeration in the manuscript, which I have examined in person; in any case, theoretically Nesi could have seen this manuscript). See Walther, *FN*, 42,445. The proverb is also cited in the earlier *Symbolum lucianum* in this manuscript (i.e., Florence BN II.I.158),

at f.262. The sentiment behind the saying would have been familiar enough from scripture; see, e.g., Matthew 6.5: "Et cum oratis,
non eritis sicut hypocritae, qui amant in synagogis et in angulis
platearum stantes orare, ut videantur ab hominibus."

25.2: Populus . . . me] Is. 29.13: "et dixit Dominus: 'eo quod adpropin-
quat populus iste ore suo et labiis suis glorificat me, cor autem eius
longe est a me.'"

25.3: distinctione 41] cf. *Decretum*, Pars 1, D.41 c.8 (Richter, 1.131):
"Clericus professionem suam et probet, et ideo nec vestibus, nec cal-
ceamentis decorem quaerat."

25.4: Benedicti virga] cf. *Regula Benedicti* 2.28: "improbos autem et
duros ac superbos vel inoboedientes, verberum vel corporis castiga-
tione ipso initio peccati coherceat, sciens scriptum: 'Stultus verbis
non corrigitur [combination of Prov. 18.2 and 29.19].'"

25.7–8: Ipocritae . . . exemplum] cf. Mt. 23.1–39, esp. 23–26: "Vae
vobis scribae et pharisaei hypocritae, qui decimatis mentham et
anethum et cyminum, et reliquistis quae graviores sunt legis, iudicium et misericordiam et fidem. Haec oportuit facere et illa non
omittere. Duces caeci excolantes culicem, camelum autem glutientes.
Vae vobis scribae et pharisaei hypocritae, quia mundatis quod deforis
est calicis et paropsidis, intus autem pleni estis rapina et immunditia. Pharisaee caece, munda prius quod intus est calicis et paropsidis, ut fiat id quod deforis est mundum."

26. *In via ne scindito*

26.1: Cum . . . novitates] *Decretal. Greg. IX* (*Liber extra*), 1.4.9 (Richter,
2.41).

26.2: Aristoteles] Cf. *Eth. Nic.* 1.3–4.1094b11–1095a13. Here Aristotle
discusses the notion that ethics is not an exact science and that happiness is by common consent agreed to be the highest practical good.

26.3: non . . . tui] cf. Prv. 22.28: "ne transgrediaris terminos antiquos
quos posuerunt patres tui." More generally, Nesi must with his reference to Moses be alluding here to *Exodus* 20.1 et seq., i.e., the ten
commandments.

26.3: Salomon . . . tuae] Prv. 3.5.

26.4: ille . . . anteponit] I have been unable to find the reference in Jerome, but perh. cf. Andreas de Sancto Victore, *Expositiones histori-cae in libros Salomonis, Expositio historica in Parabolis* (= *CM* 53B) l. 681: "Ille suae innititur prudentiae, qui neque Deo neque homine consulto contra praeceptum sapientis sapiens apud semetipsum in omnibus agendis prudentiam suam, immo praesumptionem suam sequitur."

26.5: Usus . . . philosophus] perh. cf. Aristot., *Eth. Nic.* 1.3.1094b14–16 (?).

26.5: quid . . . naturae] Cic., *Sen.* 5: "Sed tamen necesse fuit esse aliquid extremum et, tamquam in arborum bacis terraeque fructibus, maturitate tempestiva quasi vietum et caducum; quod ferendum est molliter sapienti: *quid enim aliud gigantum modo bellare cum dis, nisi natu-rae repugnare?*"

27. *Iugum ne transcendito*

27.1: Chrysippus . . . sentit] Gell., *NA* 11.12.

27.2: Iugum . . . verticem] cf. Isid., *Etym.* 14.8.20: "Iuga autem mon-tium ex eo appellata sunt quod propinquitate sui iungentur."

27.3: Iugum . . . est] Mt. 11.28–30: "Venite ad me, omnes qui lab-oratis et onerati estis, et ego reficiam vos. Tollite iugum meum super vos et discite a me quia mitis sum et humilis corde; et invenietis requiem animabus vestris. Iugum enim meum suave est et onus meum leve est."

27.3: Maro . . . amabit] Verg., *Ecl.* 5.76.

27.4: Iuga . . . demonstrant] cf. Pliny, *HN* 18.9: "Iugerum vocabatur quod uno iugo boum in die exarari posset."

27.4: Quingenta . . . Job] Iob. 1.3.

27.4: iuga boum emi quinque] Lc. 14.19.

27.5: Numeris . . . iugum] cf. Num. 19.1–5: "Locutusque est Dominus ad Mosen et Aaron dicens: ista est religio victimae quam constituit Dominus: praecipe filiis Israhel ut adducant ad te vaccam rufam aetatis integrae, in qua nulla sit macula nec portaverit iugum. Tradetisque eam Eleazaro sacerdoti, qui eductam extra castra immo-labit in conspectu omnium, et tingens digitum in sanguine eius adsper-get contra fores tabernaculi septem vicibus, comburetque eam cunctis videntibus, tam pelle et carnibus eius quam sanguine et fimo flammae traditis." A few verses later (Num. 19.8–10): "Sed et ille, qui combusserit eam, lavabit vestimenta sua et corpus, et immundus erit usque ad vesperum. Colliget autem vir mundus cineres vaccae et effundet eos extra castra in loco purissimo, ut sint multitudini filiorum Israel in custodiam et in aquam adspersionis, quia pro peccato vacca combusta est. Cumque laverit qui vaccae portaverat cineres vestimenta sua, immundus erit usque ad vesperum. Habebunt hoc filii Israel et advenae, qui habitant inter eos, sanctum iure perpetuo." Calling these verses to mind with his brief quotation, Nesi seems to allude to the events surrounding Savonarola's death.

27.5: Dirumpamus ... ipsorum] PsG. 2.3. By calling to mind the second Psalm, Nesi brings up one of Savonarola's favorite themes: that people should fear God and serve him in fear. Cf. PsG. 2.11–13: "Servite Domino in timore, et exultate ei cum tremore. Apprehendite disciplinam, nequando irascatur Dominus et pereatis de via iusta, cum exarserit in brevi ira eius. Beati omnes qui confidunt in eo." In praepositos] "Against those in power." Ps. 2.1–3 alludes to a rebellion of the peoples of Israel against the new king.

27.6: Bonum ... prima] Lam. 3.27. (Trenis = Lamentationes) Recalling Jeremiah's *Lamentations* is particularly evocative on the author's part and suggestive of the notion of Florence as a deserted Jerusalem. One recalls that the Lamentations begin as follows: "Et factum est, postquam in captivitatem redactus est Israel, et Ierusalem deserta est, sedit Ieremias propheta flens et planxit lamentatione hac in Ierusalem et amaro animo suspirans et herulans dixit ..."

27.6: Quicumque ... arbitrentur] 1 Tim. 6.1.

27.6: Nolite ... infidelibus] 2 Cor. 6.14: "Nolite iugum ducere cum infidelibus; quae enim participatio iustitiae cum iniquitate? Aut quae societas luci ad tenebras?"

27.8: abnegare ... perfectio] cf. Mt. 16.24 and Lc. 9.23: "'Si quis vult post me venire, abneget semetipsum et tollat crucem suam et sequatur me. ...'" (suam] suam cotidie *Lc*); cf. perh. Origen, *Peri Archon*, 7.5 "It were better if I were dissolved to be with Christ, far better."

27.9: oboedientia ... Samuel] cf. 1 Rg. 15.22: "Et ait Samuel: Nunquid vult Dominus holocausta et victimas, et non potius oboediatur voci Domini? Melior est enim oboedientia quam victimae, et auscultare magis quam offerre adipem arietum." Cf. Os. 6.6; Ps. 39.7–9; and Ecl. 4.17; cf. also *Decretum* Pars 1, D.50 c.14, ad fin. (Richter, 1: 183): "quia potior est misericordia omnibus holocaustomatibus et sacrificiis."

27.11: Non . . . me] Ps. 130.1: "Domine, non est exaltatum cor meum, neque elati sunt oculi mei; neque ambulavi in magnis neque in mirabilibus super me."

27.12: degalogum Moisi] I.e., Ex. 20.1–18.

27.14: Canonum . . . ducatur] *Decretal. Greg. IX* (*Liber extra*), 1.2.1 (Richter, 2.7).

28. *Lira utitor canendo*

28.1–2: Basilius . . . excitatio] Basil, Ὁμιλία (as in 20.5), 8.32–43.

28.3–4: Pythagoras . . . liberavit] Basil, Ὁμιλία (as in 20.5), 9.45–60. This story also appears in *De regimine principum* 4.21.

28.4: David . . . liberavit] 1 Rg. 16.23: "Igitur, quandocumque spiritus Dei arripiebat Saul, David tollebat citharam et percutiebat manu sua; et refocillabatur Saul et levius habebat: recedebat enim ab eo spiritus malus." 1 Rg. 18.10: "Post diem autem alteram invasit spiritus Dei malus Saul, et vaticinabatur in medio domus suae; David autem psallebat manu sua sicut per singulos dies, tenebatque Saul lanceam."

28.5: Solebant . . . occupari] On the place of music in education see Plato, *Resp.* 4.398c–412c and see next note.

28.5: quod . . . improbavit] Aristotle, *Pol.* 8.3.1338a32–8.7.1342b35. Nesi is correct to say that both Plato and Aristotle approve of the pedagogical, i.e., "gymnastic" use of music, and Nesi's formulation— that Aristotle "does not disapprove of" this shows a subtle awareness of the difference between the two thinkers. Plato accepts without debate the notion that music is pedagogically important and views music as playing a part in the ethical formulation of a properly educated citizen. Aristotle on the other hand is willing to debate the idea that music is necessary in education. In so doing he concentrates on the manner in which music can enrich the lives of citizens; thus he winds up focusing less on music's ethical import and more on the manner in which music can enrich human life in a very varied manner. See Aristotle, *The Politics of Aristotle*, ed. W.L. Newman, 4 vols. (Oxford, 1887) 1.350–67 and 405.

28.7: Magnus . . . liram] I have been unable to locate an attribution of this saying to Lorenzo.

29. *Lumine carens, de lumine ne tractes*

29.1–4: Marsilius . . . Ficinus] This is drawn from Ficino, *De sole et lumine*, ch. 2 (at *Op.*, 1.966; on this work see Kristeller, *Suppl.* 1.cxi–cxiii) and is a direct quotation, except for two omissions. See following notes.

29.3: *post* asciscunt *add.* ubique rerum penetralibus praesentissimum, commertium cum rebus nullum habet *Op.*, 1.966.

29.4: *post* ferme et lumen *add.* Hoc enim nullus adhuc definit philosophorum, ut nihil lumine clarius sit alicubi, nihil rursus videatur obscurius, sicut bonum et notissimum et omnium et pariter ignotissimum. *Op.* 1.966.

29.5: Psalmistae . . . lumen] PsG. 35.10: "Quoniam apud te est fons vitae, et in lumine tuo videbimus lumen."

29.5: Signatum . . . domine] Ps. 4.7: "Leva in signum super nos lumen vultus tui, Domine!"

29.6: Deum . . . lumine] Cf. Augustine, *De trinitate* 2.1: "sunt tamen quaedam in divinis eloquiis ita posita ut ambiguum sit ad quam potius regulam referantur, utrum ad eam qua intellegimus minorem filium in assumpta creatura, an ad eam qua intellegimus non quidem minorem esse filium sed aequalem patri, tamen ab illo hunc esse *deum de deo, lumen de lumine*. Filium quippe dicimus deum de deo; patrem autem deum tantum, non 'de deo.'" Cf. also *De trinitate*, 6.1 and 6.2 and Augustine, *In Iohannis evangelium tractatus* 34.4 and 39.1 *et passim*.

29.6: Erat . . . mundum] Jo. 1.9. For a possible remembrance of Savonarola see the passage immediately following, i.e., Jo. 1.10–11: "In mundo erat, et mundus per ipsum factus est, et mundus eum non cognovit. In propria venit et sui eum non receperunt."

29.7: Plato . . . inmensum] At *Crat.* 400d–401a, Plato's interlocutors, Hermogenes and Socrates, discuss the correctness of the names of the gods. Socrates suggests that there are two kinds of correctness, the first concerning what the gods call themselves (which humans cannot know) and the second concerning the manner in which humans address the gods in prayer. Socrates prefaces the ensuing discussion by announcing to the gods that he and Hermogenes do not intend to investigate the gods but rather men and the names men have given to gods, "for in that there is no impiety" (τοῦτο γὰρ ἀνεμέσητον). Nesi, however, seems to have followed Ficino's *Epitome* to the Cratylus (*Op.* 2.1309–14), where Ficino writes: "Nempe in ipso disputationis initio timendum est, *ne forte de Deo loquamur sine Deo*, et in media disputatione rursus, ne temere metiamur immensos."

29.7: Cum autem . . . dei] The image of the *tuba Dei* has an apocalyptic resonance. Cf. 1Th. 4.16: "quoniam ipse Dominus in iussu, in voce archangeli et in tuba Dei descendet de caelo, et mortui, qui in Christo sunt, resurgent primi." In addition the *tuba* appears often in the Book of Revelation (1.10, 4.1, 8.2, etc.).

29.10: qui . . . principio] *Decretum*, Pars 1, D.46 c.1 (Richter, 1.167), [Gratian's title]: "Arrogantes nesciunt inferre humiliter quae docent." Cf. also D.46 c.6 (Richter, 1.168): "Clericum scurrilem et verbis turpibus ioculatorem ab officio retrahendum censemus."

30. *Malacen herbam seu malvuum transferas, sed minime commedas*

30. Malace] On this herb see Pliny, *HN* 20.222: "E contrario in magnis laudibus malua est utraque et sativa et silvestris. Duo genera earum amplitudine folii discernuntur. Maiorem Graeci malopen vocant in sativis, alteram ab emolliendo ventre dictam putant malacen."

30.3: Hinc . . . plurima] Book two of Augustine's *De moribus ecclesiae catholicae* is directed toward the Manichaeans and their way of life. In chapter eight, as Augustine refutes the Manichaean notion of evil as a substance, intending to show instead that evil is a kind of incompatibility, he offers the example of a woman who habituated herself to poison by taking it a little at a time; he says there that hellebore is sometimes a food, sometimes a medicine, and sometimes a poison; to drink salt water is harmful for land animals but good to bathe in, etc. The text is edited in Augustine, *De moribus ecclesiae catholicae et moribus Manichaeorum*, ed. J.B. Bauer (Vienna, 1992 = *CSEL*, 90).

31. *Nudis pedibus rem divinam facito*

31] There is a symbolic tradition attached to naked feet. Moses (Ex. 3.5) takes off his sandals on Mt. Sinai, symbolizing openness to God's revelation. Christ is often portrayed with bare feet.

31.1–4: Aristoteles . . . calidis] Aristotle, *Probl.* 4.5.877a5–16.

31.6: Fiat voluntas tua] i.e., part of the Lord's prayer; see Mt. 6.9–13 and Lc. 11.2–4.

31.8: Pythagoras . . . sunt] cf. Philostr., *VA* 1.11 (also at 4.40): ὦ θεοί, δοίητέ μοι τὰ ὀφειλόμενα. See also note to 22.4.

31.8: Plato . . . Etyfronte] I have been unable to locate a sentiment of this sort regarding the Spartans in Plato's *Euthyphro*.

31.9–11: Socrates . . . possunt] V. Max. 7.2.ext.1.

32. *Ollae vestigium in cinere deturbato*

32.1: Plutarchus . . . esse] Plut. *Quaest. Conv.* 8.7.728b. The notion reported there is that once the "boiling" of the pot (similar to anger) has ceased, every vestige thereof should be wiped away.

32.3–8: Potissimum . . . aspernabitur] Basil, Ὁμιλία (as in 20.5), 7.18–40.

32.6: percutienti . . . ulciscamur] cf. Mt. 5.39.

32.7: Id autem Periclis aut Euclidis] Basil told irenic anecdotes regarding Pericles and Euclides at Ὁμιλία (as in 20.5), 7.5–14.

32.9: Caio . . . simus] An allusion to Caesar's having dismissed unharmed all captured enemies after the Civil War.

33. *Oleo sedem ne tergito*

33.1: oleum . . . meum] Ps. 140.5.

33.4: Adulator . . . bestiam] cf. Bernard, *Sermones super Cantica canticorum* 2.163 (sermon 63, par. 4): "Pessima vulpes occultus detractor, sed non minus nequam adulator blandus. Cavebit sapiens ab his."

33.5: Aurelius . . . velimus] Augustine, *Contra Cresconium grammaticum et Donatistam libri quattuor*, 4.16.18: "oleum peccatoris nolo ungat caput meum," alluding to Ps. 140.5: "Percutiat me iustus in misericordia et increpet me; oleum autem peccatoris non impinguet caput meum, quoniam adhuc et oratio mea in malitiis eorum." In the passage in the *Contra Cresconium*, Augustine is responding to Cresconius, who had used the phrase from the Psalms. I cite from *Sancti Aureli augustini scripta contra Donatistas* ed. M. Petschenig, 3 vols. (Vienna and Leipzig, 1908–10); the passage just cited is from 3.518. Augustine also speaks of the *oleum peccatoris* in connection with flattery in his *Contra epistulam Parmeniani libri tres*, 2.4: "Hoc est illud, quod isti non intelligentes inter calumnias suas solent habere praecipuum: 'emendabit me iustus in misericordiam et arguet me; oleim autem peccatoris non impinguit caput meum.' Quia vero isti non in misericordia emendare noverunt, et Caeciliani innocentiam saevis suspicionibus insectati sunt et Optati Gildoniani potentiam oleo fallacis adulationis unxerunt." (1.104).

34. *Panem ne frangito*

34.1: Tullii . . . rescindendas] Cic., *Amic.* 76; Augustine, *Liber de amicitia* 15 (Migne *PL* 40.839).

34.2: Eadem . . . Ambrosius] The *sententia* "idem velle, atque idem nolle, ea demum firma amicitia est," appears first in Sallust, *Catil.* 20, and then is later adopted into the proverbial tradition; Ambrose cites it in his *De fide* 5.7.74. See Otto, *Die Sprichwörter*, 19.

34.2: Unum . . . nostrae] The union of believers through the Eucharist was and is a very important effect of the sacrament in the Catholic Church. The *locus classicus* is in St. Paul, 1 Cor. 10.17: "Quoniam unus panis, unum corpus multi sumus, omnes enim de uno pane participamur."

34.3: Nam . . . Aristoteles] Aristotle, *Eth. Nic.* 8.1155a5–6. Aristotle there discusses the notion that no one would choose to live without friends even if he possessed all possible worldly goods.

35. *Pedem dextrum priorem calciato, pedem sinistrum priorem lavato*

35.1: quod diximus supra] See above, Symbol 31.

35.3: in . . . omnes] Jac. 3.2.

35.4: calciemus . . . evangelio] Cf. Eph. 6.15: "et calceati pedes in praeparatione evangelii pacis."

36. *Pisces ne commedito*

36.1: Pythagoras . . . piscatoribus] cf. Plut., *Quaest. conv.* 8.8.729d–e.

36.2: Plutarchus . . . unquam] cf. Plut., *Quaest. conv.* 8.8.729e.

36.3: Homerus . . . depellendam] cf. Plut., *Quaest. conv.* 8.8.730c–d and Hom., *Od.* 12.329 et seq.

36.4: Non . . . sint] cf. Plut., *Quaest. conv.* 8.8.728e.

36.4: Alii . . . amatores] cf. Plut., *Quaest. conv.* 8.8.729b–c or perhaps 730a–b.

36.6: Another allusion to the death of Savonarola?

37. *Peregre profectus ne redito*

37.2: hospites et advenae] Eph. 2.19.

37.2: a carnalibus . . . Apostolus] cf. 1 Pt. 2.11–12: "Carissimi, obsecro vos tanquam advenas et peregrinos abstinere vos a carnalibus desideriis quae militant adversus animam; conversationem vestram inter gentes habentes bonam, ut in eo quod detractent de vobis, tanquam de malefactoribus, ex bonis operibus vos considerantes glorificent Deum in die visitationis."

37.3: hi . . . vomitum] See Symbol 4.5.

38. *Quae ceciderunt ne accipito*

38.1: qui . . . eloquia] Sir. 3.27: "Cor durum habebit male in novissimo, et qui amat periculum in illo peribit."

38.2: Quae . . . Ruth] Cf. Rt. 4.

38.2: cananea . . . instar] Mt. 15.21–8.

38.3: illa . . . cecidit] Ier. 31.21–2: "Statue tibi speculam, pone tibi amaritudines, dirige cor tuum in viam rectam in qua ambulasti; revertere, virgo Israel, revertere ad civitates tuas istas. Usquequo deliciis desolveris, filia vaga?" Ier. 18.13: "Ideo haec dicit Dominus: Interrogate gentes, quis audivit talia horribilia, quae fecit nimis virgo Israel?" Cf. the passage a few lines later, which describes the reaction to Jeremiah's prophecy (Ier. 18.18–20): "Et dixerunt: Venite, et cogitemus contra Ieremiam cogitationes; non enim peribit lex a sacerdote, neque consilium a sapiente, nec sermo a propheta. Venite, et percutiamus eum lingua et non attendamus ad universos sermones eius." Once again one senses Nesi commenting on Florentine reactions to Savonarola. Later in the same passage in Jeremiah, the prophet is speaking to the Lord: "Tu autem, Domine, scis omne consilium eorum adversum me in mortem; ne propitieris iniquitati eorum, et peccatum eorum a facie tua non deleatur, fiant corruentes in conspectu tuo, in tempore furoris tui abutere eis."

38.3: lucifer . . . oriebatur] Is. 14.12: "Quomodo cecidisti de caelo Lucifer, qui mane oriebaris? Corruisti in terram, qui vulnerabas gentes?"

39. *Rubeum aliquid ne suscipito*

39.1: Quare . . . coinquinavi] Is. 63.2–3, but for context cf. Is. 63.1–4: "Quis est iste qui venit de Edom tinctis vestibus de Bosra? Iste formosus in stola sua gradiens in multitudine fortitudinis suae. Ego qui loquor iustitiam et propugnator sum ad salvandum. Quare ergo rubrum est indumentum tuum, et vestimenta tua sicut calcantium in torculari? Torcular calcavi solus, et de gentibus non est vir mecum; calcavi eos in furore meo et conculcavi eos in ira mea, et adspersus est sanguis eorum super vestimenta mea, et omnia indumenta mea inquinavi. Dies enim ultionis in corde meo, annus redemtionis meae venit."

39.2: libera . . . meae] PsG. 50.16. In calling this psalm to mind, perhaps Nesi is suggesting collective guilt. Cf. for instance PsG. 50.4–5: "Amplius lava me ab iniquitate mea, et a peccato meo munda me; quoniam iniquitatem meam ego conosco, et peccatum meum contra me est semper." The end of the psalm is also suggestive, where it is suggested that the Lord will not look down on a contrite heart; cf. 19–21: "Sacrificium Deo spiritus contribulatus: cor contritum et humiliatum, Deus, non despicies. Benigne fac, Domine, in bona voluntate tua Sion, ut aedificentur muri Ierusalem. Tunc acceptabis sacrificium iustitiae, oblationes et holocausta; tunc imponent super altare tuum vitulos." Could Nesi's allusion to this psalm also be suggesting, then, that Florence could become, as it was in the days of Savonarola's ascendency, like Jerusalem once again?

39.3: Si ... erunt] Is. 1.18: "si fuerint peccata vestra ut coccinum quasi nix delababuntur, et si fuerint rubra quasi vermiculus velut lana erunt."

40. *Recurvis unguibus aves ne alito*

40.1: Aeschilus ... alendum] Aesch., *Ag.* 717.

40.1: affirmabat Solon] For the opposition of Solon, the lawgiver and father of Athenian democracy, to the tyranny of Peisistratus, cf. Plut., *Conv. sept. sap.*, esp. 154–156; Plut., *Sol.* 29–32; and Diog. Laert. 1.2.45–67.

40.4: Plutharchus scribit] ps.Plut., *Reg. et imp. apophth.* 174b.

40.5: Nolite ... salus] PsG. 145.3.

40.5: eos ... fore] Cf. Ier. 17.5–6: "Haec dicit Dominus: Maledictus homo qui confidit in homine et ponit carmen bracchium suum, et a Domino recedit cor eius. Erit enim quasi myricae in deserto, et non videbit cum venerit bonum; sed habitabit in siccitate in deserto, in terra salsuginis et inhabitabili."

40.6: sicut Hieron ... retributione] Cf. Xen., *Hiero* 6.12. Xenophon's *Hiero* was the first work of Xenophon to be translated into Latin by Italian humanists; it was turned into Latin by Leonardo Bruni in 1403 and enjoyed immense popularity, having more than 200 surviving manuscript editions. See David Marsh, "Xenophon," in *CTC*, 7 (Wash., DC, 1992) 75–196, at 149–158.

41. *Salem apponito*

41.2: Gregorius ... sobrietatem] *Decretum*, Pars 1, D.43 c.1 (Richter, 1.154); '. . . Salem in vobis et pacem habete inter vos.'] Mc. 9.50; 'Non plus ... ad sobrietatem'] Rm. 12.3.

41.3: Quae ... iniuncto] cf. *Decretal. Greg. IX (Liber extra)*, 5.7.12 (Richter, 2.784–7). Interestingly, this chapter of the *Decretals* is entitled: "Laici non praedicent, nec occulta conventicula faciant, nec sacerdotes reprehendant." One passage is noteworthy and captures well the general tenor of the chapter (Richter, 2.785): "Licet autem desiderium intelligendi divinas scripturas et secundum eas studium adhortandi reprehendum non sit, sed potius commendandum; in eo tamen apparent quidam laici merito arguendi, quod tales occulta conventicula sua celebrant, officium praedicatoris Christi sibi usurpant, sacerdotum simplicitatem eludunt, et eorum consortium aspernantur qui talibus non inhaerent." The chapter goes on to say that God sent His apostles into the world to preach the *evangelium*, showing "quod evangelica praedicatio non in occultis conventiculis, sicut haeretici faciunt, sed in ecclesiis iuxta morem catholicum est publice proponenda." This is interesting if one considers Nesi's fervent participation in the lay brotherhoods of his time (Polizzotto, 100–108 and esp. 122). Could Nesi (and/or Orlandini) perhaps be poking fun at Nesi's fervent participation in lay confraternities?

42. *Sanguinem saxis operito*

42.2: Nam . . . Bernardus] I have been unable to find this in Bernard, but cf. Hier., *Epist.* 14 (in *CSEL* 54, p. 46): "Sed quid ago? Rursus inprovidus obsecro? Abeant preces blandimenta discedant; *debet amor laesus irasci.*"

42.2: furor . . .Seneca] this saying is attributed to Publilius Syrus, the first century B.C. mime who performed for Caesar, by Aulus Gellius at *NA* 17.14; for an edition of Publilius see ed. W. Meyer, *Publilii Syri mimi sententiae* (Leipzig 1880); this saying is F.13. It became proverbial in the middle ages and Renaissance; see Walther, *M*: 10124 and Walther, *FN*: 37095. Gradually in late antiquity the sayings of Publilius were organized into textbooks not unlike the *Disticha Catonis.*

42.3: Valerius . . . prosternerent] V. Max. 3.3.ext.2 (partial paraphrase, partial quotation).

42.4: eiusdem . . . privaretur] V. Max. 3.3.ext.3. Standard editions of Valerius now report Nearchus, as opposed to Clearchus.

42.5: parcere . . . superbos] Verg., *Aen.* 6.853.

42.6: in minoribus] "in the lower stations" or perhaps "in minor orders"?

42.6: percussi . . . pallium] Mt. 5.39–40; Lc. 6.29.

42.6: capitulo "Paratus"] cf. *Decretum*, Pars 2, C.23 q.1 c.2 (Richter, 1.891–2).

43. *Semitam ingreditor*

43.2: Hic ... putant] cf. Hier., *Epist.* 107 (in *CSEL* 55.297): "Qui autem parvulus est et sapit ut parvulus, donec ad annos sapientiae veniat et Pythagorae litterae eum perducant ad bivium, tam mala eius quam bona parentibus inputantur." For Palamedes and his invention of certain letters, cf. Hyg., *Fab.* 277.1; on the Renaissance availability of Hyginus see Reynolds, *Texts and Transmission*, 189–90.

43.3–8: Libet ... Basilius] Basil, Ὁμιλία (as in 20.5), 5.55–6.4.

44. *Stateram ne transilias*

44.1: The saying *Stateram ne transilias* also appears in certain medieval and Renaissance collections of proverbs. See Walther, *M*, 30321a. It is also cited twice previously by Orlandini in the *Eptathicum*, in this mansucript (i.e., MS Florence BN II.I.158), in the treatise on virtue, at f.35v ("quantus iuxta Pythagoricum symbolum ipsa rationis statera non transiliatur") and in the treatise against astrologers, at f.211 ("Fugienda est itaque scrupolositas nimia et superstitio quae ad tam nefanda perducit, et tenenda semper nec transilienda statera, ut in symbolis suis Pythagoras docebat").

44.1: quae] After "quae" there is an illegible word in the manuscript.

44.1: auriga] On the image of the chariot see Plato, *Phaedr.* 246a–d. For Ficino's interpretation of Plato's *Phaedrus*, which would have been well known to Nesi, see Ficino, ed. and trans. M.J.B. Allen, *Marsilio Ficino and the Phaedran Charioteer* (Berkeley, Los Angeles, and London, 1981) and M.J.B. Allen, *The Platonism of Marsilio Ficino: A Study of His "Phaedrus" Commentary, its Sources and Genesis* (Berkeley, Los Angeles, and London, 1984).

44.1: cupiditatum ... refrenatrix] cf. Isocrates, *Ad Nic.* 2–4, perhaps mediated through Poggio Bracciolini, *De infelicitate principum*, 50, who speaks of laws as being things "quibus immoderate cupiditates hominum frenantur," and who just a bit earlier (49) mentions prudence as the "reliquarum virtutum moderatrix et veluti quidam auriga." See ed. D. Canfora (Rome, 1998).

44.2: Tusculorum libro quarto] cf. Cic., *Tusc.* 4.78.

44.2: Ambrosius Officiorum primo] Ambr. *De officiis ministrorum* 1.94.

44.3: Sed . . . fecimus] V. Max. 4.1.ext.3.

44.4: nequid nimis] The well-known *dictum* (Greek μῆδεν ἄγαν) found in a number of ancient sources.

44.5: Omnis qui iuste . . . qui] *Decretum*, Pars 1, D.45 c.10 (Richter, 1.164–5): "Omnis qui iuste iudicat, stateram in manu gestat, et in utroque penso iustitiam et misericordiam portat."

44.5: capitulo "Ponderet"] *Decretum*, Pars 1, D.50 c.14 (Richter, 1.182–3). This chapter is entitled by Gratian, "Clerici post lapsum in suis ordinibus reparari possunt." Perhaps, then, this is another one of the allusions to Savonarola which we find scattered throughout the treatise.

44.6: Iuste iudicate, filii hominum] Ps. 57.2: "recta iudicate filii hominum."

45. *Temporum duorum curam habeto*

45.1: Aristotele . . . praesens] Cf. Arist., *Mem.* 1.449b9–15; 1.450a26–8 and *passim* on time and recollection.

45.3–4: Sed . . . neccessarias] Cic., *Off.* 1.11; for "progressus" most modern editions have "praegressus." On Cicero's use of *praegressus* (unattested before him) see A.R. Dyck, *A Commentary on Cicero, De officiis* (Ann Arbor, 1996) 89–90.

45.6: Janum . . . appareret] Nesi is probably quoting from memory here; cf. Aug., *Civ. Dei* 7.4: "Sed isti in cultu deorum omnes dedecoris adpetitores, cuius vitam minus turpem invenerunt, eum simulacri monstrosa deformitate turparunt, nunc eum bifrontem, nunc etiam quadrifrontem, tamquam geminum, facientes. An forte voluerunt ut, quoniam plurimi dii selecti erubescenda perpetrando amiserant frontem, quanto iste innocentior esset, tanto frontosior appareret?"

45.7: Manasses . . . Crinitus] Piero Crinito, *De honesta disciplina*, ed. C. Angeleri (Rome, 1955) 4.10 (132). The chapter in which this appears (i.e., 4.10) is entitled "De Pythagorica philosophia, ac de Jani fronte quadruplici, ac de Manasse rege, eiusque statua cum facie quincuplici." Pietro Crinito lived from 1475–1507 and the *De honesta disciplina* was first printed in 1504 (at the press of Filippo Giunta); cf. Angelieri's introduction, at 46. One can assume that it was circulating in draft at the time Nesi carried out his original redaction of the *Symbolum nesianum* or that Orlandini, in editing the piece later, profited from Crinito's work after it was printed. Though there is nothing whatsoever to exclude the former position, the latter seems more probable from the surviving evidence. Angelieri's statement that there is no manuscript tradition for the *De honesta disciplina* seems to be borne out (see p. 52 of his introduction). I have found only one reference to it in Kristeller's *Iter* (6.153–4), and this is only a seven folio excerpt in a *miscellanea*; it is MS Rome Accademia dei Lincei, Archivio, Manoscritti academici 80, ff. 272–279. Moreover Orlandini and Crinito were friends, and there are at least two manuscripts which preserve verses of Orlandini dedicated to Crinito; cf. MS Florence BN Conv. Sopp. D.5.875 (Kristeller, *Iter* 1.158) and MS Florence BN Conv. Sopp. G.4.826 (Kristeller, *Iter* 1.160).

46. *Vulvam animalium ne edito*

46.1–2: In . . . argenteis] A paraphrase and partial quotation of 4 Rg. 6.24–5.

46.3: Quasi . . . eorum] cf. Ez. 4.12.

46.3: Ecce . . . in eo] cf. Ez. 4.15.

46.4: Haec . . . legimus] Cf. 4 Rg. 6.28: "Mulier ista dixit 'mihi da filium tuum, ut comedamus eum hodie, et filium meum comedamus cras.'" Cf. also Lv. 26.27–32.

46.5–6: Canones . . . ibi] cf. *Decretal. Greg. IX* (*Liber extra*), 5.41.4 (Richter, 2.927): "Quod non est licitum lege, necessitas facit licitum. Nam et sabbatum custodiri praeceptum est; Macchabei tamen sine culpa sua in sabbato pugnabat; sic et hodie, si quis ieiunium fregerit aegrotus, reus voti non habetur."

46.9: Benedictus . . . monachos] Benedict, *Regula* 39.11: "Carnium vero quadrupedum omnimodo ab omnibus abstineatur comestio, praeter omnino debiles aegrotos."

46.12–13: Dicit . . . Thomas] See Ptolemy of Lucca, 4.21–22 (on authorship of the *De regimine principum*, see note to 5.3); "Laudabat . . . videtur" is a quotation from 4.21.

47. *Virgam in via ne ferto*

47.1: Salvator . . . peram] Lc. 9.3; cf. Mt. 10.10 and Mc. 6.8.

47.1: Alibi . . . tantum] cf. Mc. 6.8.

47.2: Nam . . . accenderimus] *Decretum*, Pars 2, C.20 q.3 c.4 (Richter, 1.850); *post* caelestem amorem *add.* illum *Richter; pro* accenderimus *habet* accenderitis *Richter.*

47.4: Antisthene . . . virga] cf. Diog. Laert. 6.4

47.5 Homines . . . Ethicorum] In *Eth. Nic.* 7, Aristotle discusses continence and different types of pleasure. I do not find this whole sentence as a quotation but believe Nesi is referring to the beginning of book 7 (i.e., 1145a15–33), where Aristotle avers that "brutishness" (θηριότης) is a state to be avoided along with vice (κακία) and incontinence (ἀκρασία). He writes there (tr. Thomson and Tredennick, 1976), "We also use the word brutish to express reprobation of extremely vicious persons."

47.6: Dicit . . . erudit] Prv. 13.24.

47.7–8: Non . . . inimici] Cf. *Decretum*, Pars 2, C.5 q.5 c.3 (Richter, 1.550); the reference to Ambrose is to his *Sermo* 44.2; cf. also Maximus Taurensis, *Collectio sermonum antiqua*, sermo 80, l.18 (*CCSL*, 23): "Ait sanctus apostolus: quis est autem filius quem vos verberat pater? Non enim semper pater osculat filium sed et aliquando castigat. Ergo quando castigatur qui diligeteur, tunc circa eum pietas exercetur. Habet enim et amor plagas suas, quae dulciores sunt, cum amarius inferuntur. Dulcior enim est religiosa castigatio quam blanda remissio, unde ait propheta: 'dulciora sunt vulnera amici quam voluntaria oscula inimici.'"

47.9: iudicium . . . misericordiam] Jac. 2.13. For possible Savonarolan context, cf. Jac. 2.10–13: "Quicumque autem totam legem servaverit, offendat autem in uno, factus est omnium reus. Qui enim dixit: 'non moechaberis,' dixit et: 'non occides.' Quod si non moechaberis, occides autem, factus es transgressor legis. Sic loquimini et sic facite sicut per legem libertatis incipientes iudicari. Iudicium enim sine misericordia illi, qui non fecit misericordiam; superexaltat autem misericordia iudicium."

47.10: Salomon . . . potest] *Decretum*, Pars 2, C.22 q.4 c.32 (Richter, 1.914); the biblical reference is to Ecl. 7.17: "Noli esse iustus multum neque plus sapias quam necesse est, ne obstupescas."

47.10: propterea . . . sacrificium] Mt. 9.13; cf. 12.7; there are also echoes in the Old Testament: cf. Os. 6.6; 1 Rg. 15.22; Ps. 39.7; and Prv. 21.3.

48. *Viam publicam declinato*

48.1: Hieronymus . . . errores] Hier., *Ep. Ruf.* 39.58–9 (quoting Porph. *Vita Pythagorae* 42): "per viam publicam ne ambules, id est ne multorum sequaris errores."

48.2: Bias . . . boni] Cf. Diog. Laert. 1.5 *ad fin.*

48.2: Poeta . . . virtus] Verg. *Aen.* 6.130.

48.4: Monachus . . . Placuit] *Decretum*, Pars 2, C.26 q.1 c.8 (Richter, 1.763). The sentiment is toward the end of the chapter: "Sedeat itaque solitarius [i.e., monachus], et taceat, quia mundo mortuus est, Deo autem vivit. Agnoscat nomen suum, μόνος enim grece, latine unus: ἄχος grece, latine tristis. Sedeat tristis, et offitio suo vacet."

Epilogus.3: nonum . . . edideris] Cf. Horace, *Ars P.*, 386–390: ". . . si quid tamen olim/scripseris, in Maeci descendat iudicis auris/et patris et nostras nonumque prematur in annum/membranis intus positis. Delere licebit/quod non edideris; nescit vox missa reverti."

Epilogus.7: Tu . . . repones] Cf. Iuv. *Sat.* 1.1–2: "Semper ego auditor tantum? Numquamne reponam/vexatus toties rauci Theseide Cordi?"

Epilogus.7: Paule] I.e., Paolo Orlandini.

Epilogus.10: stridoneos sales] This must refer to what will become in the *Eptathicum* the *Gymnastica monachorum*, ch.25, *De apothegmatibus et salibus patris prioris Guidi*, at f.259v–261v.

Epilogus.10: interpreter] I emend here because I read this verb as deponent first person singular present subjunctive.

APPENDIX ONE

AURISPA'S PREFACE TO HIS TRANSLATION OF HIEROCLES' *COMMENTUM IN PYTHAGORAE VERSUS AUREOS*, DEDICATED TO NICHOLAS V TEXT AND TRANSLATION

Orthography is as it is in V. I have punctuated for sense.

SIGLA:

V* = MS Città del Vaticano BAV Chis. M. VII. LII, fols. 1–3v (mbr. XV) [present base text].[1]

(Early) Printed Editions:

P* = Pannartz edition, Rome, 1475.
Pa = Padua, 1484.
B* = Besicken edition, Rome, 1493.
A* = Antonius edition, Venice, 1523.
E* = Mittarelli edition, Venice, 1779. (Taken from MS Venice Bib. San. Mur. 65 now MS Venice Bib. Marc. Lat. XIV. 130)

* = seen in person.

---

[1] Other manuscripts (drawn from Kristeller, *Iter*; I have assigned tentative sigla to them): M = MS Milano Bibl. Ambr. G. 89 sup., fols. 140–140v (cart. misc. XV, 558 fols.); N = MS Napoli Bibl. Naz. VIII. G. 6, fols. unnumbered (cart. XV); T = MS Torino Bibl. Naz. J. III. 13, fols. 85–121 (entire comm.; mbr. misc. XVI in.); Ve = MS Venezia Bib. Marc. Lat. XIV. 130 (= olim S. Michele di Murano 65, ed. in Mittarelli); B = MS Berlin Deutsche Staatsbibliothek Hamilton 296, fols. 3–4v; L = MS London British Library Burney 83. Owned by Christ. de Priolis; H = MS London British Library Harl. 2678, fols. 21–35 (fragm. of comm.; mbr. misc. XV 154 fols. large size, damaged); A = MS Amsterdam Bibliotheca Philosophica Hermetica (no shelf mark; XV Hierocles' comm.); Be = MS Bern Burgerbibliothek 211, fols. 65–65v.

Text

[1] Mirabar sepe et quidnam causae fuisset, mecum ipse dubitabam quod neque in litteris, neque in edificiis haec nostra etas maioribus responderet, sed quae scribebantur aut edificabantur multo deteriora antiquis illis et essent et viderentur, idque partim hominum negligentiae, partim facultatibus, partimque humana natura forte peior facta fuisset adscribebam. [2] Verum, beatissime pater, ita haec tempora favore et virtutibus illustrasti, ut admiratio et dubitatio illa a mente mea deciderit et omnibus qui haec cogitant manifestum sit: mira illa antiquorum edificia et clara ingenia virtutem et benignitatem principum fecisse.

[3] Videmus enim tot sanctorum edes tuo iussu, tuaque impensa, aut factas aut restitutas, tot alia et publica //1v// et privata in urbe edificia ut vix, qui presentes inspeximus tot magna tam parvo tempore fieri potuisse credamus, quae tam plura, tam egregia sunt, ut si quis de omnibus scribere velit, non parvo codice opus sit de quibus singulis. [4] Si ubertati et elegantiae orationis mee confiderem, dicere policerer, etsi pro cupiditate fecero dicam omnia, cupio equidem vitam omnem tuam scribere, quod si audeam temeritatem potius meam accusatum iri cum signo benevolentiae et caritatis volam quod tam magna ausus fuerim quam securam taciturnitatem non reprehendi: sed hoc aliquis fortasse uberius et magis eloquenter explebit. [5] Nam inter tot doctos viros quibus plurimum benefecisti, aliquis certe gratus esse debebit, qui gesta et vitam omnem tuam scribat, quippe qui argumentum //2// variis, magnisque virtutibus plenum habebit. [6] Studia enim omnis generis litterarum tantum per haec tempora creverunt ut per octigentos ante annos nulla etate tam magnus numerus aut scriptorum aut transferentium fuerit. In quo non solum presentes tibi maxime obligantur, sed etiam preteriti homines et futuri; preteriti quia eorum famam mori non permisisti, futuri quia unde meliores fiant habebunt. [7] Nam preclara quedam opera incuria et negligentia eorum qui a sexcentis annis citra fuerunt iam deperdita, magno studio perquiri fecisti, quippe qui diversos nuntios per diversas mundi partes ad libros perquirendos tam graecos quam latinos tua impensa misisti. [8] Ego vero qui te semper magnifeci, amavi, et colui, quique benevolentia non mercede ductus tibi in minoribus existenti aliqua traduxi tuoque no//2v//mini adscripsi, cum Venetiis essem tuo iussu libros aliquos graecos emi, inter quos

Translation

[1] I often used to wonder and was myself in doubt what the reason was that neither in literature nor in building does our age rise to the level of our ancestors and why what was written or built both was and seemed much worse, and I used to ascribe this partly to people's negligence, partly to their capabilities, and partly because human nature had, perhaps, grown worse. [2] In truth, most blessed father, you have lit up these times with good-will and virtue to such an extent that wonder and doubt has fallen away from my mind. To anyone who thinks about these things, it is clear: the virtue and kindness of princes made those wondrous buildings and outstanding minds of the ancients.

[3] For we see so many temples either made or restored on your order, with your expense, so many other edifices in the city both public and private that we who are present and have seen them can scarcely believe that so many great buldings could have been made in such a short span of time. The buildings are so many and so surpassing, that if someone wished to write about each and every one of them, it would be the labor of no small book.

[4] If I were to trust the richness and elegance of my own speech, I would promise to speak, and even if, on account of ambition, I were to say I would do anything, I certainly do wish to write an account of your entire life. But if I were to dare, I would rather have my temerity accused under the sign of benevolence and charity that I dared such great things, than have my secure taciturnity reprehended. But perhaps someone will explain this more widely and more eloquently. [5] For among so many learned men whom you have benefited to the greatest extent, certainly there will have to be one grateful enough to write the story of your deeds and your whole life. Certainly he will have a subject full of diverse and great virtues.

[6] After all, every kind of literary study has grown so much in these days that, throughout the last eighty years, in no era has there been such a great number of writers or translators. Of this number, not only are our contemporaries greatly obliged to you, but so too are our predecessors as well as our posterity. The men of the past are obliged because you have not permitted their reputation to die, those of the future because they will have what will make them better. [7] Indeed, with great zeal you have searched for certain outstanding works which, thanks to the lack of care and negligence of

repperi Hieroclem super versibus Pythagorae aureis appellatis, in
quibus omnis Pythagoreorum philo<so>phia continetur. [9] Tantaque
in eis est doctrina tantaque legenti utilitas ut octogenarius iam nihil
ego aut graece aut latine legerim quod magis mihi profuisse intel-
ligam. Parum enim aut nihil ubi miracula non fuerunt a fide christiana differt. [10] Hoc opusculum latinum feci et nomini sanctitatis
tue dedicavi, oroque ut semel legas. Nam quamvis ita doctus, ita
omni virtutum genere preditus sis ut neque doctrine neque virtuti
tue quicquid addi possit, placebit nihilominus legere ea que sententiam tuam confirmabunt. [11] Versus vero graecos non versus latinos feci, sed verbum e verbo expressi, ut in exponendo postea verba
non varierentur, et respon//3//²derent, et in Graeco etiam syl-
labarum quantitas, ut in heroicis fieri solent, non est servata. Rem
enim Pythagorei quaesierunt et utilitatem, non verba.

---

² *Abest pagina in codice; hic sequitur lectio ex editionibus impressis.*

the men of the last six hundred years had been lost, and yes, it was you who at your own expense have sent different messengers to different parts of the world to search for both Greek and Latin books.

[8] But I—who have always thought so much of you, loved you, revered you, and who, led by benevolence and not gain have translated certain things for you even when you were in a lower station, and have ascribed them to your name—when I was in Venice I bought on your order certain Greek books. Among them I found Hierocles on the so-called *Golden Verses* of Pythagoras, in which the whole philosophy of the Pythagoreans is contained. [9] In these books there is so much learning and usefulness for the reader that even I, now an octogenarian, have read nothing either in Greek or in Latin that I understand to have benefitted me more. For other than the lack of miracles it differs from Christian faith little or not at all.

[10] I have translated this little work into Latin and have dedicated it to the name of Your Holiness, and I ask that you read it once and for all. For although you are so learned and so endowed with every genus of the virtues that nothing could be added either to your learning or to your virtue, nevertheless it will please you to read things which will confirm your opinion. [11] To be sure, I have not translated the Greek verse into Latin verse, but have expressed it word for word, so that in setting it forth the words thereafter would not vary and would correspond. Also, the quantity of the syllables in the Greek has not been preserved, as usually happens in heroic verse. After all, the Pythagoreans were after the reality and what was useful, not the words.

LELIO GREGORIO GIRALDI'S COMMENT ON THE
SYMBOL: "NUDIS PEDIBUS SACRIFICANDUM"

Text from Giraldi, Aenigmata/Symbola, *149–50*

[1] **Nudis pedibus sacrificandum**. Nudis pedibus rem divinam facito, et adorato. Et quoniam a nemine adhuc, quod sciam, hoc symbolum explanatum reperi, ideo ne inerratum tibi mitterem, nonnulla hoc in loco collegi, ut illud saltem ipse quoquo modo aperirem.

[2] Pythagoras igitur et hoc ab Hebraeis sumpsisse videri potest, apud quos morem fuisse accepimus sacra et sancta non ingredi loca, nisi nudis pedibus. Mosi certe Deus Maximus praecipit ut calciamentum solveret, quod in quo staret loco, terra sancta esset. Post Mosen quoque Iesu Naves filio idem est imperatum. [3] Scribit et Flavius Iosephus Berenicem, regis Agrippae sororem, cum Hierosolymam profecta esset voti gratia, rem sacram facturam idem fecisse, atque (ut ipse ait) ita nudi [*leg.* nudam] pedem ante Flori praesidis tribunal stetisse. [4] Hinc illa quoque Divi Leonis in quodam de ieiunio sermone exclamatio de Hebraeorum ieiunio loquentis: Habeant illi nudipedalia sua, et in tristitia vultuum ostendant ociosa ieiunia. [5] Nunc quoque Mauri et Sarraceni, eiusmodique hominum genus, templa in qui//150//bus sacra facturi sunt, non ingrediuntur, nisi calceis depositis. [6] Ergo Pythagoram monuisse puto ut inter sacrificandum, mundi, et mundanis relictis curis et a scelerum inquinamentis expiati, rei divinae operam darent. [7] Nam et lavare pedes mystice, expurgare mentem dicimus. Qua de re et Christiani nostri theologi, dum mandatum Domini de pedum lotione exponunt, et simul illud, Excutiendos pulveres de pedibus. [8] Euthymius quoque pedes pro cogitationibus in Psalmo 72 exponit: Per pedes (inquit) cogitationes intelligit, veluti quae animae nostrae religionem pedum instar regunt, ac sustinent. Licet Cassiodorus arbitrium mentis eo loco interpretur, cogitationes tamen et ipse Psalmo 120 pedes exponit.

Translation

[1] **One must sacrifice with bare feet**. Practice religion and worship with bare feet. And because, to the best of my knowledge, I have found no one who has explained this symbol, so that I don't send you something that has wandered all over, I have collected a few things here, so that I myself might at least open the symbol up, in a way. [2] Pythagoras thus can be seen to have taken this symbol as well from the Hebrews, among whom we understand it was the custom not to enter sacred and holy places save with bare feet. Certainly the Most Supreme God ordered Moses to take off his shoes, because where he stood was holy ground. After Moses, Jesus, the son of Naves, was also ordered to do the same. [3] Flavius Josephus moreover writes that Berenice, the sister of Agrippa, after she went to Jerusalem to make her vow, did the same thing when she was about to perform the sacred rite. And, as he says, she stood bare-footed before the tribunal of the governor Florus. [4] Hence also that exclamation of divine Leo, in a certain sermon on fasting, when he is speaking of the Hebrews' fasting: "they have their bare feet in sandals, and in the sadness of their countenances they offer their idle fasts." [5] Now the Moors and Saracens as well—the same sort of men—do not go into the temples in which they are to practice religion, unless they have taken off their shoes. [6] So I think Pythagoras recommended this [to his followers] so that while they were sacrificing they would be clean, and would give their attention to religion once they were purified of any remaining worldly cares and of the impurities of wicked acts. [7] Now we also say "washing the feet" in a mystical way, to mean cleansing the mind. As far as this goes even our Christian theologians [agree], when they expound that mandate of the Lord concerning washing feet. And there is also that "Excutiendos pulveres de pedibus." [8] Also, Euthymius understands "feet" to mean "thoughts" when he treats Psalm 72: "For

[9] Sed longior sim, si eiusmodi multa tibi afferre velim. Caeterum apud scriptores proditum est, Lacedaemonios iuxta Pythagorae hoc institutum nudis pedibus adorare, et rem sacram facere solitos—quod nihil mirum. [10] Nam, Iosepho teste, Lacedaemonii Hebraeos socios habuere, et ab ipsis ut alia multa, et hoc suscipere potuerunt. [11] Porro Christianis nobis ex caerimoniarum ritu, et Pontificum institutis prohibitum est, sacram Eucharistiam nudis pedibus conficere. Et Paulus monet calciatos nos pedes habere debere in praeparatio//151//nem Evangelii. [12] Idem repetit D. Cyprianus: "Ut serpens, inquit, a nobis calcatus obteratur, neve armatos pedes possit mordere." Sedenim et per pedes humanitatem significari, ii volunt qui Evangelium illud exponunt, quod est de pedum osculo meretricis, et unguenti[s] infusione. [13] D. Augustinus per pedes humanos affectus intelligit. At vero Gregorius, dum illud interpretatur, "Calciamenta habebitis in pedibus": "Calciamenta," inquit, "in pedibus habere est mortuorum vitam conspicere, et nostra vestigia a peccati vulnere custodire." Sed de his plus iam satis.

'feet,'" he says, "one understands 'thoughts,' just as if they were things which, in the place of feet, rule and sustain the religion of our soul." On the other hand, for the same passage, Cassiodorus' interpretation is that this refers to the will of the mind, even if he does suggest that "feet" mean "thoughts" in his interpretation of Psalm 120.

[9] But I would go on longer, if I wanted to bring much more of this sort of thing to your attention. Otherwise among the authorities it is suggested that the Spartans worshipped and practiced religion with bare feet, according to this precept of Pythagoras—and no wonder. [10] For Josephus testifies that the Spartans had the Jews as allies; they could have taken this practice from them, as they did many others. [11] Of course, to us Christians it is prohibited to take the holy Eucharist with bare feet, prohibited because of the ritual of the ceremony and because of the precepts of the high religious officials. Paul, too, warns that we have to have our feet shod in preparation for the Gospel. [12] Cyprian repeats the same thing: "So that the serpent," he says, "might be passed over easily when we step on him, and so that he might not bite armed feet." But there are also those who think that "feet" signify "humanity;" they are the ones who interpret that Gospel passage, the one that is about the prostitute's kissing of the feet, and the pouring on of ointment. [13] Divine Augustine thinks that "feet" mean human emotions. But Gregory, when he interprets that passage, "you will have shoes on your feet," says "Having shoes on your feet is like observing the life of the dead, and keeping our footsteps safe from the wound of sin." But I think I have said enough about this symbol.

Commentary

2: Mosi . . . esset] Ex. 3.5. Post . . . imperatum] Ios. 5.16: "solve, inquit, calciamentum de pedibus tuis. Locus enim in quo stas sanctus est; fecitque Iosue ut sibi fuerat imperatum." Giraldi refers to "Joshua" with "Iesus," the Greek version of the name "Iosue." Joshua was the son of Nun (Num. 13.6–18). **3**: Flavius . . . stetisse] Flavius Iosephus sec. transl. et retract. Hegesippi *Historiae libri V* (*CSEL* 66. ed. V. Ussani), 2.4, 144. **4**: Hinc . . . ieiunia] Leo Magnus, *Tractatus septem et nonaginta* (*CCSL* 138A, ed. A. Chavasse), 89, l.15. **8**: Euthymius . . . sustinent] cf. Euthymii monachi *Commentarii in omnes Psalmos e Graeco in Latinum conversi per Philipum Saulum Episcopum Brunatensem* (Parisiis: Apud Ioannem Foucherium, 1547), 202. On Euthymius, see *Dictionnaire de spiritualité*, 4, 1720–22. Cassiodorus . . . exponit] Cassiodorus, *Expositio psalmorum* (*CCSL* 98), 72, l.62 and l.64. **10**: Nam . . . potuerunt] Flavius Iosephus sec. transl. et retract. Hegesippi *Historiae libri V* (*CSEL* 66, ed. V. Ussani) **11**: Paulus . . . Evangelii] Eph. 6.15. **12**: Cyprianus . . . mordere] Cyprianus, *Epist.* 58 (*CCSL* IIIC, ed. G.F. Dirks), 208–10 (p. 332). Evangelium . . . infusione] Lc. 7.38. **13**: Augustinus . . . intellegit] cf. Augustinus, *In Iohannis evangelium tractatus* (*CCSL* 36, ed. R. Willems), 56.4, 58.4, 58.5; *Enarrationes in Psalmos* (*CCSL* 38, eds. E. Dekkers and J. Fraipont), 38.2.19, (*CCSL* 39, eds. E. Dekkers and J. Fraipont), 64.2.42, 94.2.31; *Contra Cresconium* (*CSEL* 52, ed. M. Petschenig), 3.23.26 (p. 432). Gregorius . . . custodire] Gregorius Magnus, *XL Homiliarum in Evangelia libri duo* (*PL* 76), 2.22.9.28.

DESCRIPTION OF MS FLORENCE BN II. I. 158

Material: Parchment and Paper.

Dating: 1518 (cf. f.312v).

Size: 352 × 234mm.

Pages: a (from the restoration), i–viii (paper), I–VIII (parchment), 1–320 (Parchment). 42 lines per page.

Quires: (only of the part of the codex composed of parchment): 1 × 18 (I–VIII, 1–10v); 28 × 10 (11–290v); 1 × 12 (291–302v); 1 × 18 (303–320v).

Scribe: "Presbiter Joannes Columna alias Gattula" as he himself writes on f.312v.

Contents:

I. Table of contents (ff.I–VIIIv).

II. Eptathicum Pauli Orlandini (ff.1–312v), a work in seven parts
   A. Opus I: *De virtute* in five books (1–68).
      Present also in MS Munich, Bayerische Staatsbibliothek Clm 172; cf. Kristeller, *Iter*, 3.613.
   B. Opus II: *De triplici theologia* in five books (68v–122v).
   C. Opus III: *De scolastica scripturarum sanctarum interpretatione contra prophetas vanos, quae alio nomine dicitur Expugnatio Miletana* (122v–147v).
   D. Opus IV: *De agone sprituali*, divided into in 24 *lectiones* (147v–186).
      Present also in MS Munich, Bayerische Staatsbibliothek Clm 172; cf. Kristeller, *Iter*, 3.613.
   E. Opus V: *Decalogus (de animae rationalis essentia vel natura)* in ten parts (186–200).

Present also in MS Munich, Bayerische Staatsbibliothek Clm 173; cf. Kristeller, *Iter*, 3.613.

F. Opus VI: *Liber satyricus contra astrologos* (200–236).

G. Opus VII: *Gymnastica monachorum* (236–312v).

III. Miscellanea.

A. *De sancto Apollinari*, letter from Orlandini to Paulus de Laude abbas Classensis (313–315).

B. *De insomnibus quibusdam arguentibus immortalitatem animorum*, letter from Orlandini to Paolo Giustiniani (315v–317).

C. *De fuga prelationum*, letter from Orlandini to Petrus Delfinus (317v–319).

D. *Apologia pro monasterio Angelorum* of Orlandini (319–320).

Literature on this manuscript:
Garin, *La cultura*, 213–23; Kristeller, *Iter*, 1.112–113; Swogger, 88–93; Vasoli, "Pitagora in monastero;" Weinstein, *Savonarola and Florence*, 202.

BIBLIOGRAPHY

Manuscripts

Florence

Bibl. Laurenziana 54.10
Bibl. Laurenziana 77.24 (Nesi's *De moribus*)
Bibl. Laurenziana 86.6

Bibl. Nazionale Centrale, II. I. 158
Bibl. Nazionale Centrale, Conv. Sopp. C. 8. 277
Bibl. Nazionale Centrale, Conv. Sopp. D. 5. 875
Bibl. Nazionale Centrale, Conv. Sopp. D. 9. 278
Bibl. Nazionale Centrale, Conv. Sopp. G. 4. 826
Bibl. Riccardiana, 383 and 384

Munich

Bayerische Staatsbibliothek, Clm 172 and 173

Naples

BN VIII F 9

Rome

Accademia dei Lincei, Archivio, Manoscritti academici 80

Vatican City

Biblioteca Apostolica Vaticana, Vat. Lat. 5953

Printed Primary Sources

This bibliography of primary sources includes only those sources cited in the introductory study or appendices. For those alluded to in the *Symbolum nesianum*, see the
Indices locorum.

Alberti, Leon Batista, *Intercenali inediti*, ed. E. Garin (Florence, 1965).
—— *Dinner Pieces: A Translation of the "Intercenales"* tr. D. Marsh (Binghamton, NY,
    1987).
Ambrose, *Epistola* 81, in Migne, *PL* 16.
Aristotle, ed. W.D. Ross, *Aristotelis fragmenta selecta* (Oxford, 1955).
—— ed. V. Rose, *Aristotelis fragmenta* (Leipzig, 1886).
Augustinus, *In Iohannis evangelium tractatus* (*CCSL* 36, ed. R. Willems).
—— *Enarrationes in Psalmos* (*CCSL* 38 and 39, eds. E. Dekkers and J. Fraipont).
—— *Contra Cresconium* (*CSEL* 52, ed. M. Petschenig).

Benivieni, Domenico, *Dialogo della verità della doctrina predicata da Frate Hieronymo da Ferrara nella ciptà di Firenze* (Florence, 1497); also ed. G. Garfagnini in his "'Lumen propheticum' e 'lumen fidei' nel *Dialogo* de Domenico Benivieni," in eds. A. Fontes, J.-L. Fournel, and M. Plaisance, *Savonarole: Enjeux, débats, questions* (Paris, 1997) 149–71, at 157–71.

Beroaldo, Filippo, *Annotationes centum*, ed. L.A. Ciapponi (Binghamton, N.Y., 1995).

—— *Varia Philippi Beroaldi opuscula* (Basel: Gregorius Bartholomeus, 1509).

—— *Symbola pythagorica moraliter explicata* (Bologna: Benedictus Hectoris, 1503).

—— *Commentarii in Propertium* (Bologna: Benedictus Hectoris and Plato de Benedictis, 1487).

Bianchini, Bartolomeo, "Philippi Beroaldi vita," in *Commentationes conditae a Philippo Beroaldo in Suetonium Tranquillum* (Bologna, 1506).

Biblia sacra iuxta vulgatam versionem, eds. Robert Weber, Roger Gryson, et al. (Stuttgart: Deutsche Bibelgesellschaft, 4th ed., 1994).

Bisticci, Vespasiano da, *Le vite*, 2 vols., ed. A. Greco (Florence, 1970).

Bracciolini, Poggio, *Opera Omnia*, 4 vols., ed. R. Fubini (Turin, 1963–69).

ps.-Burlamacchi, *La vita del Beato Ieronimo Savonarola scritta da un anonimo del sec XVI e già attribuita a Fra Pacifico Burlamacchi, pubblicata secondo il codice ginoriano*, ed. P. Ginori Conti (Florence, 1937).

Cassiodorus, *Expositio psalmorum* (*CCSL* 98).

Clement, *Stromata*, in *Die griechischen christlichen Schriftsteller der ersten drei Jahrhunderte*, 2, ed. O. Stählin (Leipzig, 1906).

Corpus iuris canonici, ed. E.L. Richter, with revisions by E. Friedberg (Leipzig, 1879; repr. Graz, 1959).

Cyprianus, *Epistulae* 58 (*CCSL* IIIC, ed. G.F. Dirks).

Erasmus, *Adagiorum chilia prima, pars prior*, eds. M.L. van Poll-van de Lisdonk et al. (*ASD*, 2.1.5–19).

Euthymius, *Euthymii monachi Commentarii in omnes Psalmos e Graeco in Latinum conversi per Philipum Saulum Episcopum Brunatensem* (Parisiis: Apud Ioannem Foucherium, 1547).

Ficino, Marsilio, *De triplici vita*, ed. and trans. C. Kaske and J. Clark (Binghamton, NY, 1989).

Giraldi, Lilio Gregorio, *De poetis nostrorum temporum*, ed. K. Wotke, in Lateinische Litteraturdenkmäler, 10 (Berlin, 1894), reprinted in *La storiografia umanistica*, eds. A. Di Stefano et al., 2 vols. in 3 parts (Messina, 1992).

—— *Lelii Gregorii Gyraldi ferrariensis libelli duo, in quorum altero aenigmata pleraque antiquorum, in altero Pythagorae symbola, non paulo quam hactenus ab aliis, clarius faciliusque sunt explicata, nunquam antea in lucem editi. Accesserunt eiusdem Lilii, et alii duo libelli, Adversus ingratos, et Quomodo quis ingrati nomen et crimen effugere possit.* (Basel: Johannes Oporinus, 1551).

Gregorius Magnus, *XL Homiliarum in Evangelia libri duo* (*PL* 76).

Hermias, *In Platonis Phaedrum Scholia*, ed. P. Couvreur (Paris, 1901; repr. with additions by C. Zintzen, Hildesheim, 1971).

Hierocles, *In Aureum Pythagoreorum carmen commentarius*, ed. F. Köhler (Stuttgart, 1974).

Iamblichus, *Protrepticus*, ed. H. Pistelli (Stuttgart, 1888).

—— *De communi mathematica scientia*, ed. N. Festa (Stuttgart, 1891).

—— *In Nicomachi Arithmeticam introductionem*, ed. H. Pistelli (Stuttgart, 1894).

—— *De vita pythagorica*, ed. L. Deubner (Stuttgart, 1937).

—— *On the Pythagorean Life*, tr. G. Clark (Liverpool, 1989).

Jerome, "Epistola adversus Rufinum," in *S. Hieronymi Presbyteri opera*, 3.1, ed. P. Lardet, *CCSL* 79 (Turnholt, 1982) 73–116.

Josephus, Flavius, sec. transl. et retract. Hegesippi *Historiae libri V* (*CSEL* 66. ed. V. Ussani).

Laertius, Diogenes, *Lives of Eminent Philosophers*, 2 vols., ed. and trans. R.D. Hicks (Cambridge, Mass., and London, 1938).
—— *La vie de Pythagore de Diogène Laërce*, ed. A. DeLatte, (Brussels, 1932).
Leo Magnus, *Tractatus septem et nonaginta* (*CCSL* 138A, ed. A. Chavasse).
Nesi, Giovanni, *Oraculum de novo saeculo* (Florence, 1497).
Oliviero da Siena, *Tractatus rationalis scientiae* (Siena, 1491).
Origen, *Contra Haereses*, in Migne, *PG* 16.3, coll. 3023–3232.
The Picatrix: The Latin Version of the Ghāyat Al-Hakīm, ed. D. Pingree, Studies of the Warburg Institute, 39 (London, 1986).
"Picatrix": Das Ziel des Weisen von Pseudo-Magrītī, trans. H. Ritter and M. Plessner, Studies of the Warburg Institute, 27 (London, 1962)
Pico della Mirandola, Gianfrancesco, *Examen vanitatis doctrinae gentium et veritatis Christianae disciplinae, distinctum in libris sex* (Mirandola: Ioannes Mazochius, 1520).
Pico della Mirandola, Giovanni, *De hominis dignitate, Heptaplus, De ente et uno, e scritti vari*, ed. E. Garin (Florence, 1942).
Pins, Jean de, "Vita Philippi Beroaldi Bononiensis," in ed. J.G. Meuschen, *Vitae summorum dignitate et eruditione virorum ex rarissimis monumentis literato orbi restitutae* (Coburg: J.G. Steinmark, 1735) 1: 123–51.
—— *Divae Catherinae Senensis simul et clarissimi viri Philippi Beroaldi Bononiensis vita* (Bologna, 1505).
Poliziano, Angelo, *Opera Omnia* (Venice: Aldus Manutius, 1498).
—— *Lamia: Praelectio in priora Aristotelis analytica*, Studies in Medieval and Reformation Thought, 38, ed. A. Wesseling (Leiden, 1986).
Porphyry, *Vita Pythagorae*, in *Opuscula selecta*, ed. A. Nauck (Leipzig, 2nd ed., 1886) 17–52.
Proclus, *In Platonis Timaeum commentaria*, ed. E. Diehl (Leipzig, 1903–6).
Reuchlin, Johannes, *Briefwechsel*, Band I, 1477–1505, Unter Mitwirkung von Stefan Rhein, bearbeitet von Matthias Dall'Asta und Gerald Dörner (Stuttgart-Bad Cannstatt: Frommann-Holzboog, 1999).
—— idem, *Schriften zum Bücherstreit, 1. Teil Reuchlins Schriften*, eds. W.-W. Ehlers, L. Mundt, H.-G. Roloff, and P. Schäfer, in Johannes Reuchlin, Sämtliche Werke, 4 (Stuttgart-Bad Cannstadt: Fromann-Holzboog, 1999).
Simplicius, *In Aristotelis de caelo commentaria*, *CAG* 7, ed. J.L. Heiberg (Berlin, 1894).
—— *In Aristotelis Physica commentaria*, *CAG* 9 and 10, ed. H. Diels (Berlin, 1882–95).
Suda, in *Lexicographi graeci*, 1.1, ed. A. Adler (Stuttgart 1928 and repr. 1971).
Themistius, *In Aristotelis Physica paraphrasis*, *CAG* 5.2, ed. H. Schenkel (Berlin, 1900).

Secondary Sources

Allen, M.J.B., *Marsilio Ficino and the Phaedran Charioteer* (Berkeley, Los Angeles, and London, 1981).
—— *The Platonism of Marsilio Ficino: A Study of His "Phaedrus" Commentary, its Sources and Genesis* (Berkeley, Los Angeles, and London, 1984).
—— *Icastes: Marsilio Ficino's Interpretation of Plato's Sophist* (Berkeley, Los Angeles, and London, 1989).
—— *Nuptial Arithmetic: Marsilio Ficino's Commentary on the Fatal Number in Book VIII of Plato's* Republic (Berkeley, Los Angeles, and London, 1994).
—— *Plato's Third Eye: Studies in Marsilio Ficino's Metaphysics and its Sources.* (Hampshire and Brookfield, Vermont, 1995).
—— "The Second Ficino-Pico Controversy: Parmenidean Poetry, Eristic and the One," in ed. Gian Carlo Garfagnini, *Marsilio Ficino e il ritorno di Platone: Studi e documenti*, 2 vols. (Florence, 1986) 2: 417–455, now in Allen, *Plato's Third Eye*, X.

—— "Summoning Plotinus: Ficino, Smoke, and the Strangled Chickens," in M.A. DiCesare, ed., *Reconsidering the Renaissance* (Binghamton, NY, 1992) 63–88, now in Allen, *Plato's Third Eye*, XIV.

—— *Synoptic Art: Marsilio Ficino on the History of Platonic Interpretation* (Florence, 1998).

Augustijn, C., *Erasmus: His Life, Works, and Influence*, tr. J.C. Grayson (Toronto, 1991).

Bacchelli, F., "Science, Cosmology, and Religion in Ferrara, 1520–1550," in Ciammitti, Ostrow, and Settis, *Dosso's Fate*, 333–354.

Bigi, E., "Aurispa, Giovanni," *DBI* 4 (1962) 593–5.

Billanovich, G., "La tradizione del 'Liber de dictis philosophorum antiquorum' e la cultura di Dante del Petrarca e del Bocaccio," *Studi Petrarcheschi* 1 (1948) 111–123.

Barotti, G., *Memorie istoriche di letterati Ferraresi*, second edition, 2 vols. (Ferrara, 1792).

Black, R., "Humanism," in ed. C. Allmand, *The New Cambridge Medieval History* (Cambridge, 1998) 243–277 and 906–915.

Blaisdell, C.J., "Politics and Heresy in Ferrara," *Sixteenth Century Journal* 6 (1975) 67–93.

Blumenthal H.J., and E.G. Clark, eds., *The Divine Iamblichus: Philosopher and Man of Gods* (London, 1993).

Boehm, F., *De symbolis Pythagoreis* (Berlin, 1905).

Bonfanti, R., "Su un dialogo filosofico del tardo '400: Il *De moribus* del fiorentino Giovanni Nesi (1456–1522?)," *Rinascimento*, 2nd ser., 11 (1971) 203–221.

Bostick, C.V., *The Antichrist and the Lollards: Apocalypticism in Late Medieval and Reformation England*, Studies in Medieval and Reformation Thought, LXX (Leiden, Boston, Cologne, 1998).

Bowersock, G., *Hellenism in Late Antiquity* (Ann Arbor, 1990).

Branca, V., *Poliziano e l'umanesimo della parola* (Turin, 1983).

Brundage, J., *Medieval Canon Law* (London and New York, 1995).

Buck, A. and O. Herding, eds., *Der Kommentar in der Renaissance*, Kommission für Humanismusforschung, Mitteilung I (Bonn, 1975).

Burkert, W., *Lore and Science in Ancient Pythagoreanism*, trans. E. Minar, Jr. Cambridge, Mass., 1972 (a revised and translated version of Burkert's *Weisheit und Wissenschaft: Studien zu Pythagoras, Philolaos und Platon.* Nürnberg, 1962).

Cammelli, G., *I dotti bizantini e le origini dell'umanesimo. I: Manuele Crisolora; II: Giovanni Argiropulo; III: Demetrio Calcondila* (Florence, 1941–54).

Camporeale, S., "Humanism and the Religious Crisis of the Late Quattrocento: Giovanni Caroli, O.P., and the *Liber dierum lucensium*," in eds. T. Verdon and J. Henderson, *Christianity and the Renaissance: Image and Religious Imagination in the Quattrocento* (Syracuse, 1990) 445–466.

—— "*Repastinatio, liber primus*: retorica e linguaggio," in O. Besomi and M. Regoliosi, eds., *Lorenzo Valla e l'umanesimo italiano: Atti del convegno internazionale di studi umanistici (Parma, 18–19 ottobre 1984)* (Padua, 1986) 217–239.

—— "Giovanni Caroli: Dal 'Liber dierum' alle 'Vitae fratrum,'" *Memorie dominicane*, n.s., 16 (1985) 199–233.

—— "Giovanni Caroli e le 'Vitae fratrum S.M. Novellae.' Umanesimo e crisi religiosa (1460–1480)," *Memorie dominicane*, n.s., 12 (1981) 141–267.

Cao, G.M., "L'eredità pichiana: Gianfrancesco Pico tra Sesto Empirico e Savonarola," in ed. P. Viti, *Pico, Poliziano e l'Umaniesimo di fine Quattrocento* (Florence, 1994) 231–45.

Casella, M.T., "Il metodo degli umanisti esemplato sul Beroaldo," *Studi Medievali*, 3rd. ser. 16 (1975) 627–701.

Castelli, P., *I geroglifici e il mito dell'Egitto nel Rinascimento* (Florence, 1979).

Cavini, W., "Appunti sulla prima diffusione in Occidente delle opere di Sesto Empirico," *Medioevo* 3 (1977) 1–20.

Celenza, C.S., *Renaissance Humanism and the Papal Curia: Lapo da Castiglionchio the Younger's* De curiae commodis (Ann Arbor, 1999).

—— "Late Antiquity and Florentine Platonism: The 'Post-Plotinian' Ficino," forthcoming in M.J.B. Allen and V.R. Rees, eds., *Marsilio Ficino: His Sources, His Circle, His Legacy* (Brill, 2001).

—— "Temi neopitagorici nel pensiero di Marsilio Ficino," in ed. S. Toussaint, *Actes du XLIIe Colloque International d'Etudes Humanistes "Marsile Ficin 1499–1999,"* Cahiers de l'Humanisme, Les Belles Lettres, forthcoming (Paris, 2001)

—— "Antiquité tardive et platonisme florentin," in Fosca Mariani Zini, ed., *Penser entre les lignes: philosophie et philologie au Quattrocento* (Lille: Presses Universitaires du Septentrion, 2001) 197–226.

—— "The Search for Ancient Wisdom in Early Modern Europe: Reuchlin and the Late Ancient Esoteric Paradigm," *Journal of Religious History* (2001).

—— "Pythagoras in the Renaissance: The Case of Marsilio Ficino," *Renaissance Quarterly* 52 (1999) 667–711.

—— "Renaissance Humanism and the New Testament: Lorenzo Valla's Annotations to the Vulgate," *The Journal of Medieval and Renaissance Studies* 21 (1994) 33–52.

Ciammitti, L., Ostrow, S.F., and Settis, S., eds., *Dosso's Fate: Painting and Court Culture in Renaissance Italy* (Los Angeles, 1998).

Ciapponi, L.A., "Introduction," Beroaldo, Filippo, *Annotationes centum*, 1–52.

Clark, S., *Thinking with Demons: The Idea of Witchcraft in Early Modern Europe* (Oxford, 1997).

Copenhaver, B.P., "Scholastic Philosophy and Renaissance Magic in the *De vita* of Marsilio Ficino," *Renaissance Quarterly* 37 (1984) 523–554.

—— "Iamblichus, Synesius, and the Chaldaean Oracles in Marsilio Ficino's *De vita libri tres*: Hermetic Magic or Neoplatonic Magic?" in eds. J. Hankins, J. Monfasani, and F. Purnell, *Supplementum Festivum: Studies in Honor of Paul Oskar Kristeller* (Binghamton, 1987) 441–455.

—— "Hermes Trismegistus, Proclus, and the Question of a Philosophy of Magic in the Renaissance," in I. Merkel and A.G. Debus, eds., *Hermeticism in the Renaissance: Intellectual History and the Occult in Early Modern Europe* (Washington, D.C. and London, 1988) 79–110.

—— "Renaissance Magic and Neoplatonic Philosophy: 'Ennead' 4.3–5 in Ficino's 'De vita coelitus comparanda," in Garfagnini, ed., *Marsilio Ficino e il ritorno di Platone*, 2: 351–69.

Coppini, D., "Filologi del Quattrocento al lavoro su due passi di Properzio," *Rinascimento* 2nd ser. 16 (1976) 219–229.

Cumont, F., "Le coq blanc des Mazdéens et les Pythagoriciens." *Académie des Inscriptions et Belles-Lettres: Comptes rendus* (Paris, 1942) 284–300.

Dallari, U., *I rotuli dei lettori legisti e artisti dello Studio bolognese dal 1384 al 1799*, vol. 1 (Bologna, 1888).

Daniel, E.R., "The Spread of Apocalypticism, 1100–1500. Why Calvin Could Not Reject It," *Calvin Studies* 5 (1990) 61–71.

D'Ascia, L., "Humanistic Culture and Literary Invention in Ferrara at the Time of the Dossi," in Ciammitti, Ostrow, and Settis, *Dosso's Fate*, 309–332.

Davies, J., *Florence and its University during the Early Renaissance*, Education and Society in the Middle Ages and Renaissance, 8 (Leiden, Boston, Cologne, 1998).

Della Torre, A., *Storia dell' Accademia platonica di Firenze* (Florence, 1902).

Diels, H. and W. Kranz, *Die Fragmente der Vorsokratiker*, 6th ed. (Berlin 1951–52).

Dillon, J., "Iamblichus of Chalcis (c. 240–325 A.D.)" in *ANRW* 36.2 (Berlin and New York, 1988) 862–909.

Dionisotti, C., "Calderini, Poliziano ed altri," *Italia medievale e umanistica* 11 (1968) 151–85.

Eisenbichler, K., *The Boys of the Archangel Raphael: A Youth Confraternity in Florence, 1411–1785* (Toronto, Buffalo and London, 1998).

Farulli, G., *Istoria cronologica del nobile ed antico monastero degli Angioli di Firenze del sacro Ordine Camaldolese dal principio della sua fondazione al presente giorno* (Lucca, 1710).

Fera, V., "Tra Poliziano e Beroaldo: l'ultimo scritto filologico di Giorgio Merula," *Studi umanistici* 2 (1991) 7–88.

Field, A., *The Origins of the Platonic Academy of Florence* (Princeton, 1988).

Findlen, P., *Possessing Nature: Museums, Collecting, and Scientific Culture in Early Modern Italy* (Berkeley, Los Angeles, and London, 1994).

Fowden, G., *The Egyptian Hermes: A Historical Approach to the Late Ancient Pagan Mind* (Cambridge, 1986; reissued with new preface, Princeton, 1993).

—— "The Pagan Holy Man in Late Antique Society," *The Journal of Hellenic Studies* 102 (1982) 33–59.

Franceschini, A., *Giovanni Aurispa e la sua biblioteca: Notizie e documenti* (Padua, 1976).

Frati, L., "I due Beroaldi," *Studi e memorie per la storia dell'Università di Bologna* 2 (1911) 209–228.

Fubini, R., "Ficino e i Medici all'avvento di Lorenzo il Magnifico," *Rinascimento*, 2nd series, 24 (1984) 3–52.

—— "Ancora su Ficino e i Medici," *Rinascimento*, 2nd series, 27 (1987) 275–91.

—— *Quattrocento fiorentino: Politica diplomazia cultura* (Pisa, 1996).

Garfagnini, G., ed., *Marsilio Ficino e il ritorno di Platone: Studi e documenti*, 2 vols. (Florence, 1986).

—— "Savonarola e la profezia: tra mito e storia," *Studi Medievali*, 3rd series, 29 (1988) 173–201.

—— "La polemica antiastrologica del Savonarola ed i suoi precedenti tomistici," in eds. G. Federici Vescovini and F. Barocelli, *Filosofia scienza astrologia nel Trecento* (Padua, 1992) 155–179.

Garin, E., *Giovanni Pico della Mirandola: Vita e dottrina* (Florence, 1937).

—— *La cultura filosofica del Rinascimento italiano* (Florence, 1961).

—— *Ritratti di umanisti* (Florence, 1967).

—— *L'età nuova* (Naples, 1969).

—— "Venticinque intercenali inedite e sconosciute di Leon Batista Alberti," *Belfagor* 19 (1964) 377–96.

—— "Note in margine all'opera di Filippo Beroaldo il Vecchio," in eds. G. Bernardoni Trezzini et al., *Tra latino e volgare. Per Carlo Dionisotti*, Medioevo e umanesimo, 18 (Padua, 1974) 2: 437–60.

Gentile, S., "Sulle prime traduzioni dal greco di Marsilio Ficino," *Rinascimento*, 2nd series, 30 (1990) 57–104.

Gerl, H.-B., *Rhetorik als Philosophie: Lorenzo Valla* (Munich, 1974).

Gianini, M.A., "The Manuscripts of Giovanni Aurispa (1376–1459)," Unpublished doctoral dissertation, University of North Carolina at Chapel Hill, 1974.

Gilmore, M., "Beroaldo, Filippo, senior," in *Dizionario Biografico degli Italiani* 9 (Rome, 1967) 382–384.

Godman, P., *From Poliziano to Machiavelli: Florentine Humanism in the High Renaissance* (Princeton, 1998).

Grafton, A., *Leon Battista Alberti: Master Builder of the Italian Renaissance* (New York, 2000).

—— *Commerce with the Classics: Ancient Books and Renaissance Readers*, Thomas Spencer Jerome Lectures, 20 (Ann Arbor, 1997).

—— *Joseph Scaliger: A Study in the History of Classical Scholarship*, 2 vols. (Oxford, 1983–93).

—— "Renaissance Readers and Ancient Texts: Comments on Some Commentaries," *Renaissance Quarterly* 38 (1985) 615–649.

Halm, C., G. Laubmann, et al., eds., *Catalogus codicum latinorum Bibliothecae Regiae Monacensis*, 2 vols. in 7 parts (Munich, 1868–81); 1.1–2 published in a second edition (1892–4).

Hankins, J., *Plato in the Italian Renaissance*, 2 vols. (Leiden, New York, etc., 1990).

—— "Cosimo de' Medici and the 'Platonic Academy.'" *Journal of the Warburg and Courtauld Institutes* 53 (1990) 144–162.

—— "The Myth of the Platonic Academy of Florence." *Renaissance Quarterly* 44 (1991) 429–75.

—— "Lorenzo de' Medici as a Patron of Philosophy," *Rinascimento*, 2nd series, 34 (1994) 15–53.

Heninger, S.K., *Touches of Sweet Harmony: Pythagorean Cosmology and Renaissance Poetics* (San Marino, California, 1974).

Hölk, C., *De acusmatis sive symbolis pythagoricis*, Doctoral dissertaion, Kiel, 1894.

Huffman, C.A., *Philolaus of Croton: Pythagorean and Presocratic* (Cambridge, 1993).

Jaitner-Hahner, U., *Humanismus in Umbrien und Rom: Lilius Tifernas, Kanzler und Gelehrter des Quattrocento* (Baden-Baden, 1993).

Jardine, L., *Erasmus, Man of Letters: The Construction of Charisma in Print* (Princeton, 1993).

Katinis, T., "Bibliografia Ficiniana," *Accademia* 2 (2000) 101–36.

Kingsley, P., *Ancient Philosophy, Mystery, and Magic: Empedocles and the Pythagorean Tradition* (Oxford, 1995).

Kirk, G.S., J.E. Raven, and M. Schofield, *The Presocratic Philosophers*, second edition (Cambridge, 1983).

Koltay-Kastner, E., "L'umanesimo italiano in Ungheria," *La rinascita* 2 (1939).

Krautter, K., *Philologische Methode und Humanistische Existenz: Filippo Beroaldo und sein Kommentar zum Goldenen Esel des Apuleius* (Munich, 1971).

—— "Angelo Poliziano als Kritiker von Filippo Beroaldo," *Res publica litterarum* 4 (1981) 315–330.

—— "Der Grammaticus Poliziano in der Auseinandersetzung mit Zeitgenössischen Humanisten," in eds. A. Buck and K. Heitmann, *Die Antike-Rezeption in den Wissenschaften während der Renaissance*, Mitteilungen der Kommission für Humanismusforschung, 10 (Weinheim, 1983) 103–16.

Kraye, J., "Moral Philosophy," in C.B. Schmitt and Q. Skinner, eds., *The Cambridge History of Renaissance Philosophy* (Cambridge, New York, etc., 1988) 303–386.

Kristeller, P.O., *Supplementum ficinianum*, 2 vols. (Florence, 1937).

—— *Studies in Renaissance Thought and Letters* (Rome, 1956).

—— *Iter Italicum: A Finding List of Uncatalogued or Incompletely Catalogued Humanistic Manuscripts of the Renaissance in Italian and Other Libraries*, 6 vols. (Leiden and London, 1963–1995).

—— *Marsilio Ficino and his Work After Five Hundred Years*, Quaderni di Rinascimento, no. 7 (Florence, 1987), reprinted from Garfagnini, 1986.

—— "The University of Bologna and the Renaissance," *Studi e memorie per la storia dell'Università di Bologna* n.s. 1 (1956) 313–23.

—— "Humanism and Moral Philosophy," in Rabil, ed., *Renaissance Humanism*, 3: 271–309.

Lardet, P., *L'Apologie de Jérôme contre Rufin: Un commentaire*, Supplements to Vigiliae Christianae, 15 (Leiden, 1993).

Lauster, J., *Die Erlösungslehre Marsilio Ficinos*, Arbeiten zur Kirchengeschichte, 69 (Berlin and New York, 1998).

Lines, D.A., "'Faciliter Edoceri': Niccolò Tignosi and the Audience of Aristotle's 'Ethics' in Fifteenth-Century Florence," *Studi medievali*, 3rd series, 40 (1999) 139–68.

Lubac, H. de, *Exégése médiévale: Les quatres sens de l'Ecriture*, 4 vols. in 2 parts (Paris, 1959–1964).

Ludwig, W., "Literatur und Geschichte – Ortwin Gratius, die Dunkelmännerbriefe und 'Das Testament des Philipp Melanchthon' von Walter Jens," *Mittellateinisches Jahrbuch* 34 (1999) 125–67.

MacMullen, R., *Paganism in the Roman Empire* (New Haven, 1981).

Maier, I., *Ange Politien: La formation d'un poète humaniste (1469–1480)* (Geneva, 1966).

Mansfield, B., *Phoenix of his Age: Interpretations of Erasmus, c. 1550–1750* (Toronto, 1979).

—— *Interpretations of Erasmus, c. 1750–1920: Man on his Own* (Toronto, 1992).

Mariotti, I., "Lezioni di Beroaldo il Vecchio sulla *Thebaide*," in eds. R. Cardini,

E. Garin, et al., *Tradizione classica e letteratura umanistica. Per Alessandro Perosa* (Rome, 1985) 2: 577–93.

Marsh, D., *Lucian and the Latins: Humor and Humanism in the Early Renaissance* (Ann Arbor, 1998).

Minnich, N.H., "The Autobiography of Antonio degli Agli (ca. 1400–77), Humanist and Prelate," in eds. A. Morrough et al., *Renaissance Studies in Honor of Craig Hugh Smyth*, 2 vols., Villa I Tatti Studies, 7 (Florence, 1985) 1.177–91.

Mittarelli, G.B. and A. Costadoni, *Annales Camaldulenses Ordinis Sancti Benedicti*, vii–ix (Venice, 1762–73).

Monfasani, J., "Was Lorenzo Valla an Ordinary Language Philosopher?" in *Journal of the History of Ideas* 50 (1989) 309–323.

Moss, A., *Printed Commonplace-Books and the Structuring of Renaissance Thought* (Oxford, 1996).

Oberman, H.A., *The Dawn of the Reformation* (Grand Rapids, Michigan, 1986).

O'Meara, J., *Pythagoras Revived: Mathematics and Philosophy in Late Antiquity* (Oxford, 1989).

—— "New Fragments from Iamblichus' *Collection of Pythagorean Doctrines*," *American Journal of Philology* (1981) 26–40.

Orlandi, S., *Necrologio di Santa Maria Novella: 1235–1504. Testo e commenti biografici*, 2 vols. (Florence, 1955).

Otto, A., *Die Sprichwörter und sprichwörtlichen Redensarten der Römer* (Leipzig, 1890, repr. Hildesheim, etc., 1988).

Perrone Compagni, V., "La magia cerimoniale del 'Picatrix' nel Rinascimento," *Atti dell'Accademia di Scienze Morali e Politiche (Napoli)* 88 (1977) 279–330.

Pettinelli, R.A., *Tra antico e moderno: Roma nel primo Rinascimento* (Rome, 1991).

Pezzarossa, F., "'Vita mihi ducitur inter paginas': la biblioteca di Filippo Beroaldo il Vecchio," *Schede umanistiche*, N.s. 1 (1997), 109–130.

Phillips, M.M., *The 'Adages' of Erasmus: A Study with Translations* (Cambridge, 1964).

Piaia, G., *'Vestigia philosophorum' e la storiografia* (Rimini, 1983).

Polizzotto, L., *The Elect Nation: The Savonarolan Movement in Florence, 1494–1545* (Oxford, 1994).

Prelog, J., "Die Handschriften und Drucke von W. Burley's *Liber de vita et moribus philosophorum*," *Codices manuscripti* 9 (1983) 1–18.

Rabil, A., ed., *Renaissance Humanism: Foundations, Forms, and Legacy*, 3 vols. (Philadelphia, 1988).

Raimondi, E., *Politica e commedia: Dal Beroaldo al Machiavelli* (Bologna, 1972).

—— *Codro e l'umanesimo a Bologna* (Bologna, 1950).

Renaudet, A., *Préreforme et humanisme à Paris pendant les guerre d'Italie, 1494–1517* (Paris, 1916, repr. 1953).

Ridolfi, R., *Vita di Girolamo Savonarola*, 2 vols. (Rome, 1952).

Rizzi, F., "Un maestro d'umanità: Filippo Beroaldo," *Archiginnasio* 48 (1953) 77–111.

Rizzo, S., *Il lessico filologico degli umanisti* (Rome, 1973).

Sabbadini, R., *Storia del Ciceronianismo e di altre questioni letterarie nell'età della Rinascenza* (Turin, 1885).

—— *Biografia documentata di Giovanni Aurispa* (Noto, 1890).

—— ed., *Il carteggio di Giovanni Aurispa* (Rome, 1931).

Saffrey, H.D., "Allusions antichrétiennes chez Proclus le diadoque platonicien," *Revue des sciences philosophique et théologique* 59 (1975) 553–63.

Schmitt, C.B., *Gianfrancesco Pico della Mirandola (1469–1533) and his Critique of Aristotle* (The Hague, 1967).

Schnitzer, J., *Savonarola*, 2 vols. (Milan, 1931).

Schucan, L., *Das Nachleben von Basilius Magnus "Ad adolescentes"*, Travaux d'Humanisme et Renaissance, 133 (Geneva, 1973).

Stigall, J.O., "The Manuscript Tradition of the *De vita et moribus* of Walter Burley," *Medievalia et humanistica* 11 (1957) 44–57.

Struever, N., *The Language of History in the Renaissance: Rhetorical and Historical Consciousness in Florentine Humanism* (Princeton, 1970).

Swogger, J.H., "Antonio degli Agli's 'Explanatio symbolorum Pythagorae:' An Edition and a Study of its Place in the Circle of Marsilio Ficino," Ph.D. diss., University of London, 1975.

Thom, J.C., *The Pythagorean* Golden Verses *with Introduction and Commentary* (Leiden, New York, Cologne, 1995).

Toscani, B., ed., *Lorenzo de' Medici: New Perspectives*, Studies in Italian Culture, 13 (New York, etc., 1993).

Toussaint, S., "Un cas de 'Theologie Poetique': Le portrait mythologique de Jean Pic de la Mirandole e l'*Heptaplus*," in *Momus, studi umanistici* (Lucca, 1994) 75–89.

—— ed., *L'esprit du Quattrocento: De l'être et de l'un et Réponses à Antonio Cittadini* (Paris, 1995).

Tracy, J., *Erasmus of the Low Countries* (Berkeley, Los Angeles, and London, 1996).

Ullman, B.L. and P. Stadter, *The Public Library of Renaissance Florence* (Padua, 1972).

Valcke, L. and R. Galibois, *Le périple intellectuel de Jean Pic de la Mirandole* (Sainte–Foy: Les Presses de l'Université Laval, 1994).

Vasoli, C., "L'attesa della nuova era in ambienti e gruppi fiorentini del Quattrocento" in *L'attesa dell'età nuova nella spiritualità della fine del medioevo*, Convegni del centro di studi sulla spiritualità medievale, 3 (Todi, 1962) 370–432.

—— "Giovanni Nesi tra Donato Acciauoli e Girolamo Savonarola: testi editi e inediti," *Memorie Dominicane* n.s. 4 (1973) 103–179.

—— *Profezia e ragione: Studi sulla cultura del Cinquecento e del Seicento* (Naples, 1974).

—— "Pitagora in monastero," *Interpres* 1 (1978) 256–272.

—— *Filosofia e religione nella cultura del Rinascimento* (Naples, 1988).

—— *Tra 'Maestri' umanisti e teologi: studi quattrocenteschi* (Florence, 1991).

Verde, A., *Lo studio fiorentino, 1473–1503: Ricerche e documenti* (Florence, 1973–).

Wadsworth, J.B., "Filippo Beroaldo the Elder and the Early Renaissance in Lyon," *Medievalia et Humanistica* 11 (1957) 78–89.

Walker, D.P., *The Ancient Theology* (London, 1972).

Walser, E., *Poggius florentinus: Leben und Werke* (Leipzig and Berlin 1914; repr. Hildesheim and New York, 1974).

Waswo, R., *Language and Meaning in the Renaissance* (Princeton, 1987).

Weber, M., *Economy and Society: An Outline of Interpretive Sociology*, 2 vols, ed. and trans. G. Roth C. Wittich, et al. (Berkeley, Los Angeles, and London, 1978).

Weinstein, D., *Savonarola and Florence: Prophecy and Patriotism in the Renaissance* (Princeton, 1970).

Wilson, N.G., *From Byzantium to Italy* (Baltimore, 1992).

Witt, R.G., *Hercules and the Crossroads: The Life, Works, and Thought of Coluccio Salutati* (Durham, North Carolina, 1983).

—— "Medieval Italian Culture and the Origins of Humanism as a Stylistic Ideal," in Rabil, ed., *Renaissance Humanism*, 1: 29–70.

Wittkower, R., "Hieroglyphics in the Renaissance," in idem, *Allegory and the Migration of Symbols* (London, 1977) 113–28.

Yates, F., *Giordano Bruno and the Hermetic Tradition* (London, 1964).

Zimmermann, T.C. Price, *Paolo Giovio: The Historian and the Crisis of Sixteenth-century Italy* (Princeton, 1995).

INDEX LOCORUM SYMBOLI NESIANI

Index Locorum Veteris Testamenti

[Numbers in square brackets in this and the remaining indices locorum refer to the *Symbolum nesianum*]

Genesis
19.26 [4.1]
48.14; 48.17; 48.18 [14.5]

Exodus
16.3 [4.5]
20.4–6 [21.5]
20.1–18 [27.12]
20.25 [15.1]

Leviticus
19.18 [6.2]
26.27–32 [46.4]

Numeri
19.1–5 [27.5]

Deuteronominium
1.17 [6.2]
5.8–10 [21.5]
16.16 [21.4]

Iudices
3.5 [14.5]

Ruth
4 (*passim*) [38.2]

1 Regum
15.22 [27.9]
16.23; 18.10 [28.4]
24.5–7 [12.7]

3 Regum
6.7 [15.1]

4 Regum
6.24–5 [46.1–2]
6.28 [46.4]

Iob
1.3 [27.4]

Psalmi*
*If neither "PsG" nor "PsH" appear before the given citation, it signifies that PsG. and PsH. are in agreement
PsG. 2.3 [27.5]
PsG. 2.13 [19.3]
4.7 [29.5]
PsG. 6.7 [16.1]
17.27 [7.3]
PsG. 35.10 [29.5]
PsG. 50.16 [39.2]
PsG. 54.22 [7.6]
57.2 [44.6]
PsG. 69.4 [4.1]
72.24 [14.5]
PsG. 83.3 [11.4]
105.3 [6.2]
118.96 [4.4]
118.165 [11.4]
120.5 [14.5]
130.1 [27.11]
140.5 [33.1]
PsG. 145.3 [40.5]

Proverbia
3.5 [26.3]
11.9 [7.6]
13.24 [47.6]
22.28 [26.3]
23.31–32 [7.5]
25.20 [11.3]
26.11 [4.5]

Ecclesiastes
1.2 [17.8]
7.17 [47.10]
10.4 [4.6]

Sapientia
1.1 [6.2]
5.7 [8.5]

Index Locorum Novi Testamenti

Ad Ephesios
  2.19 [37.2]
  6.15 [35.4]

Ad Phillipenses
  1.23 [4.9]

Ad Colossenses
  3.14 [18.4]

1 ad Thessalonicenses
  5.7 [16.2]

1 ad Timotheum
  5.22 [14.4]
  6.1 [27.6]

2 ad Timotheum
  2.4 [1.1]

Epistula Iacobi
  2.13 [47.9]
  3.2 [35.3]

1 Petri
  2.11–12 [37.2]
  5.5 [18.2]

2 Petri
  2.22 [4.5]

1 Iohannis
  4.1 [14.3]

Apocalypsis
  1.8 [4.7]
  1.16 (?) [19.3]
  2.16 (?) [19.3]
  19.5 (?) [19.3]

IV Ezrah
  10.30 [14.5]

Index Locorum Antiquorum Gentilium

Aeschylus
  Ag.
    717 [40.1]

Aristotle
  Eth. Nic.
    1.3.1094b14–16 (?) [26.5]
    1.3–4.1094b11–1095a13 [26.2]
    1.6.1096a14–17 [3.8]
    2.7.1108a4–9 [18.2]
    4.5.1125b26–1126b10 [18.2]
    7.1145a15–33 [47.5]
    8.1155a5–6 [34.3]
    8.3.1156b26–28 [14.1]

  Mem.
    1.449b9–15 [45.1]
    1.450a26–8 (?) [45.1]

  Metaph.
    5.16.4.1021b25–31 [4.9]

  Pol.
    8.3.1338a32–8.7.1342b35 [28.5]
    3.11.1287a20–24 [12.1]

  Probl.
    4.5.877a5–16 [31.1–4]

Bias Pireneus
  apud Diog. Laert. 1.87 [14.2]
  apud Diog. Laert. 1.87 (= DK 10ς1)
    [48.2]

Boethius
  Cons.
    1, carm. 1, 22–23 [4.4]

Cicero
  Amic.
    76 [34.1]

  Div.
    1.62 *apud* Gell., *NA* 4.11 [1.4]

  Fin.
    1.65 [5.4]

  Off.
    1.11 [45.3–4]

Index Locorum Patrum

De civitate dei
7.4 [45.6]

Contra Cresconium grammaticum et Donatistam libri quattuor
4.16.18 [33.5]

De moribus ecclesiae catholicae
2 [30.3]

De trinitate
2.1 [29.6]

Basilius Magnus
'Ομιλία
5.55–6.4 [43.3–8]
7 (?) [20.5]
7.5–14 [32.7]
7.18–40 [32.3–8]
8.32–43 [28.1–2]
9.45–60 [28.3–4]

Hieronymus
Ep. Ruf.
39–40 [Introductio.9]
39.54–55 [20.1]
39.55 [12.1]

39.57–8 [4.1]
39.58–9 [48.1]
39.59–61 [23.1]
39.62–64 [13.1]

Epist.
14 [42.2]
107 [43.2]

Comm. in Hiezech.
14.45.10–12 (?) [10.1]

locus incertus
[2.2]
[8.1]

Lactantius
Div. inst.
3.21–22 [5.3]

De ira dei
7 [21.3]

Tertullianus
Adv. Hermogenem
41.2 (?) [18.4]

Index Locorum Aetatis Mediae Scriptorum

Albertus Magnus
locus incertus
[23.4]

Andreas de Sancto Victore
Expositiones historicae in libros Salomonis, Expositio historica in Parabolis
l. 681 (?) [26.4]

Anonymus
"Si cor non orat, in vanum lingua laborat"
[25.1]

Benedictus
Regula
2.28 [25.4]
18.1–2 [24.8]
39.11 [46.9]

Bernardus Clarevallensis
Sermones super Cantica canticorum
2.163 [33.4]

locus incertus [42.2]

Isidorus
Etym.
14.8.20 (?) [27.2]

Ptolomeus Luccae
De regimine principum
4.4 [5.3]
4.21–22 [46.12–13]
4.22 [11.1]

Thomas Aquinas
vide Ptolomeum Luccae

Index Locorum Corporis Iuris Canonici

Decretum Gratiani
  Pars 1
    D.41 c.8 [25.3]
    D.43 c.1 [9.5 et 41.2]
    D.45 c.10 [44.5]
    D.46 c.1 [29.10]
    D.50 c.14 [44.5]

  Pars 2
    C.5 q.5 c.3 [44.5]
    C.17 q.2 c.2 [8.3]
    C.20 q.3 c.4 [44.5]
    C.22 q.4 c.32 [47.10]

C.23 q.1 c.2 [42.6]
C.26 q.1 c.8 [48.4]
C.26 q.7 c.10 [16.6]
D.2 de pen. c.9 [4.2]

Liber Extra
  1.2.1 [27.14]
  1.4.9 [26.1]
  1.31.15 [9.4]
  5.7.12 [41.3]
  5.7.13 [7.2]
  5.41.4 [46.5–6]

Index Locorum Aetatis Renatae Scriptorum

Antonius Corsettus
De regia potestate [12.2]

Petrus Crinitus
De honesta disciplina [45.7]
  4.10 (132)

Marsilius Ficinus
De christiana religione
  1 (*Op.* 1.2) [21.2]

Comm. in Epist. Pauli
  (*Op.* 1.443) [Introductio.2]

Epitome in Cratylum
  (*Op.* 2.1309–14) [29.7]

De sole et lumine
  passim (*Op.*, 1.965–975) [3.1]
  2 (*Op.*, 1.966) [29.1–4]

6 (*Op.*, 1.968) [3.2–4]
9 (*Op.*, 1.970) [3.5]

Laurentius Medices
locus incertus (dictum Laurentii) [28.7]

Iohannes Nesius
Oraculum de novo saeculo
  a^{ix-x} [Introductio.10]

Iohannes Picus Mirandulanus
Oratio
  126 [22.3]

Angelus Politianus
Praefatio in Epicteti enchiridion
  [Introductio.7]

Lamia
  4 [Introductio.9]

INDICES TO THE INTRODUCTORY STUDY

These indices refer to the introductory study. For the *Symbolum Nesianum*, see the Index Locorum Symboli Nesiani.

Index of Names

Index of Subjects

Index of Place Names

Studies in the History
of Christian Thought

EDITED BY ROBERT J. BAST

51. O'MALLEY, J. W., IZBICKI, T. M. and CHRISTIANSON, G. (eds.). *Humanity and Divinity in Renaissance and Reformation.* Essays in Honor of Charles Trinkaus. 1993
52. REEVE, A. (ed.) and SCREECH, M. A. (introd.). *Erasmus' Annotations on the New Testament.* Galatians to the Apocalypse. 1993
53. STUMP, Ph. H. *The Reforms of the Council of Constance (1414-1418).* 1994
54. GIAKALIS, A. *Images of the Divine.* The Theology of Icons at the Seventh Ecumenical Council. With a Foreword by Henry Chadwick. 1994
55. NELLEN, H. J. M. and RABBIE, E. (eds.). *Hugo Grotius – Theologian.* Essays in Honour of G. H. M. Posthumus Meyjes. 1994
56. TRIGG, J. D. *Baptism in the Theology of Martin Luther.* 1994
57. JANSE, W. *Albert Hardenberg als Theologe.* Profil eines Bucer-Schülers. 1994
59. SCHOOR, R.J.M. VAN DE. *The Irenical Theology of Théophile Brachet de La Milletière (1588-1665).* 1995
60. STREHLE, S. *The Catholic Roots of the Protestant Gospel.* Encounter between the Middle Ages and the Reformation. 1995
61. BROWN, M.L. *Donne and the Politics of Conscience in Early Modern England.* 1995
62. SCREECH, M.A. (ed.). *Richard Mocket, Warden of All Souls College, Oxford, Doctrina et Politia Ecclesiae Anglicanae.* An Anglican Summa. Facsimile with Variants of the Text of 1617. Edited with an Introduction. 1995
63. SNOEK, G.J.C. *Medieval Piety from Relics to the Eucharist.* A Process of Mutual Inter-action. 1995
64. PIXTON, P.B. *The German Episcopacy and the Implementation of the Decrees of the Fourth Lateran Council, 1216-1245.* Watchmen on the Tower. 1995
65. DOLNIKOWSKI, E.W. *Thomas Bradwardine: A View of Time and a Vision of Eternity in Fourteenth-Century Thought.* 1995
66. RABBIE, E. (ed.). *Hugo Grotius, Ordinum Hollandiae ac Westfrisiae Pietas (1613).* Critical Edition with Translation and Commentary. 1995
67. HIRSH, J.C. *The Boundaries of Faith.* The Development and Transmission of Medieval Spirituality. 1996
68. BURNETT, S.G. *From Christian Hebraism to Jewish Studies.* Johannes Buxtorf (1564-1629) and Hebrew Learning in the Seventeenth Century. 1996
69. BOLAND O.P., V. *Ideas in God according to Saint Thomas Aquinas.* Sources and Synthesis. 1996
70. LANGE, M.E. *Telling Tears in the English Renaissance.* 1996
71. CHRISTIANSON, G. and T.M. IZBICKI (eds.). *Nicholas of Cusa on Christ and the Church.* Essays in Memory of Chandler McCuskey Brooks for the American Cusanus Society. 1996
72. MALI, A. *Mystic in the New World.* Marie de l'Incarnation (1599-1672). 1996
73. VISSER, D. *Apocalypse as Utopian Expectation (800-1500).* The Apocalypse Commentary of Berengaudus of Ferrières and the Relationship between Exegesis, Liturgy and Iconography. 1996
74. O'ROURKE BOYLE, M. *Divine Domesticity.* Augustine of Thagaste to Teresa of Avila. 1997
75. PFIZENMAIER, T.C. *The Trinitarian Theology of Dr. Samuel Clarke (1675-1729).* Context, Sources, and Controversy. 1997
76. BERKVENS-STEVELINCK, C., J. ISRAEL and G.H.M. POSTHUMUS MEYJES (eds.). *The Emergence of Tolerance in the Dutch Republic.* 1997
77. HAYKIN, M.A.G. (ed.). *The Life and Thought of John Gill (1697-1771).* A Tercentennial Appreciation. 1997
78. KAISER, C.B. *Creational Theology and the History of Physical Science.* The Creationist Tradition from Basil to Bohr. 1997
79. LEES, J.T. *Anselm of Havelberg.* Deeds into Words in the Twelfth Century. 1997
80. WINTER, J.M. VAN. *Sources Concerning the Hospitallers of St John in the Netherlands, 14th-18th Centuries.* 1998
81. TIERNEY, B. *Foundations of the Conciliar Theory.* The Contribution of the Medieval Canonists from Gratian to the Great Schism. Enlarged New Edition. 1998
82. MIERNOWSKI, J. *Le Dieu Néant.* Théologies négatives à l'aube des temps modernes. 1998
83. HALVERSON, J.L. *Peter Aureol on Predestination.* A Challenge to Late Medieval Thought. 1998.
84. HOULISTON, V. (ed.). *Robert Persons, S.J.: The Christian Directory (1582).* The First Booke of the Christian Exercise, appertayning to Resolution. 1998
85. GRELL, O.P. (ed.). *Paracelsus.* The Man and His Reputation, His Ideas and Their Transformation. 1998
86. MAZZOLA, E. *The Pathology of the English Renaissance.* Sacred Remains and Holy Ghosts. 1998.
87. 88. MARSILIUS VON INGHEN. *Quaestiones super quattuor libros sententiarum.* Super Primum. Bearbeitet von M. Santos Noya. 2 Bände. I. Quaestiones 1-7. II. Quaestiones 8-21. 2000
89. FAUPEL-DREVS, K. *Vom rechten Gebrauch der Bilder im liturgischen Raum.* Mittelalterliche Funktionsbestimmungen bildender Kunst im *Rationale divinorum officiorum* des Durandus von Mende (1230/1-1296). 1999

90. KREY, P.D.W. and SMITH, L. (eds.). *Nicholas of Lyra*. the Senses of Scripture. 2000
92. OAKLEY, F. *Politics and Eternity*. Studies in the History of Medieval and Early-Modern Political Thought. 1999
93. PRYDS, D. *The Politics of Preaching*. Robert of Naples (1309-1343) and his Sermons. 2000
94. POSTHUMUS MEYJES, G.H.M. *Jean Gerson – Apostle of Unity*. His Church Politics and Ecclesiology. Translated by J.C. Grayson. 1999
95. BERG, J. VAN DEN. *Religious Currents and Cross-Currents*. Essays on Early Modern Protestantism and the Protestant Enlightenment. Edited by J. de Bruijn, P. Holtrop, and E. van der Wall. 1999
96. IZBICKI, T.M. and BELLITTO, C.M. (eds.). *Reform and Renewal in the Middle Ages and the Renaissance*. Studies in Honor of Louis Pascoe, S.J. 2000
97. KELLY, D. *The Conspiracy of Allusion*. Description, Rewriting, and Authorship from Macrobius to Medieval Romance. 1999
98. MARRONE, S.P. *The Light of Thy Countenance*. Science and Knowledge of God in the Thirteenth Century. 2 volumes. 1. A Doctrine of Divine Illumination. 2. God at the Core of Cognition. 2001
99. HOWSON B.H. *Erroneous and Schismatical Opinions*. The Question of Orthodoxy regarding the Theology of Hanserd Knollys (c. 1599-1691). 2001
100 ASSELT, W.J. VAN. *The Federal Theology of Johannes Cocceius (1603-1669)*. 2001
101 CELENZA, C.S. *Piety and Pythagoras in Renaissance Florence the* Symbolum Nesianum. 2001

Prospectus available on request

BRILL — P.O.B. 9000 — 2300 PA LEIDEN — THE NETHERLANDS